Directory of Parishes & Institutions in North America 1998

MILLENNIUM EDITION

Orthodox Christian Communications Network

Copyright 1998
Orthodox Christian Communications Network
Directory Offices:
P.O. Box 1128
Torrance, California 90505-0128
(310) 378-9245

Dedicated to the Celebration of the
Millennium of Christ's
Nativity

Published by: Oakwood Publications for
OCCNET
George Bedrin/Philip Tamoush, Coordinators
2 Lakeshore Blvd., Box 35
Grand Isle VT 05458

ISBN 1-891295-10-1

Editor/Publisher: Philip Tamoush
Computer Input: Reader Michael Bishop
Advertisers' Layout: James Tamoush
Directory Layout: Copyrite Printing

Table of Contents

Introduction	1
Jurisdictions included in Directory	3
Parishes and Missions in the United States	17
Parishes in Canada	91
Parishes in Mexico and Central America	104
Monastic Communities in North America	106
Education	113
Orthodox Publications and Publishers	117
Social Services/Pan-Orthodox Groups	126
Campus Fellowship	130
Youth Camps and Shrines	132
Icons and Iconographers	135
Military Chaplains	138
Hospital Chaplains	140
Prison Ministries/Addendum	143
Appendix (Other Directories)	144
Advertisers/Supporters Listing	145
Advertisements/Supporters	147

Introduction

Today, given the state in which (Eastern) Orthodox Christianity finds itself organizationally in North America, it is difficult to maintain an accurate and current Directory of jurisdictions, parishes and individual organizations and institutions. This is especially the fact with regard to jurisdictional affiliations of many individual entities. New bishoprics are being established within jurisdictions, new titles are being given to some hierarchs, and additional jurisdictions, which identify themselves as traditional Orthodox Christian bodies, are being 'discovered'. We include all those groups since it is the function of this Directory to identify all those who are Orthodox, at least nominally, and who appear to profess the Seven Great Councils of the 'One Holy Catholic Apostolic Church'. We could not identify any commonly accepted definitions or standards that would permit the exclusion of any group included here. Thus, our objective has been to be inclusive rather than exclusive.

The goal of this Directory is to provide the user with helpful identifying information for over 3000 listings. The information in this Millennium Edition is taken from the latest source material provided to us by the various Orthodox jurisdictions. As well, survey forms were distributed to all 2800 entries in the 1994 edition of the Directory. In several cases, jurisdictions or organizations provided no current information. To be complete, therefore, we have included what information we had on file from 1994, if we were relatively certain that the organization still existed. Telephone area codes change so routinely now, that it is impossible to remain current. Responsibility for the actual computer input is ours. New categories, such as Iconographers, Publishers, Hospital Chaplains, etc. have been added in this Edition. Still missing due to lack of time and information are accurate listings of Orthodox Supply Houses, Architects and Convalescent/Retirement Homes that cater to Orthodox Christians. Contact the larger individual jurisdictions for such information.

We acknowledge and thank all those individuals and organizations which provided the actual data. Thanks to the advertisers who financed the first printing, thus permitting us to offer the Directory at the lowest possible price. Please support their good works and offerings. The proceeds from the sale of the Directory will help our new organization, OCCNET, which provides valuable resources to the Orthodox communities in North America. This Directory is available on CD-Rom (compact disk), and 3.5 inch floppy disk. Adhesive labels are available for the whole Directory or by state or jurisdiction. The listings herein are formatted so that they can be copied and used as labels.

The Editor

Jurisdictions Included in This Directory

Albanian Orthodox Diocese of America ADA G
5300 S. El Camino Road
Las Vegas, NV 89118 USA
Phone: 702-221-8245
Fr. Ilia Katre

American Carpatho-Russian Orthodox Greek Catholic Diocese of the U.S.A CRC G/J
312 Garfield Street
Johnstown, PA 15906 USA
Phone: 814-539-9143
BISHOP NICHOLAS

Antiochian Orthodox Archdiocese of North America ANT G
358 Mountain Road
Englewood, NJ 07631 USA
Phone: 201-871-1355
METROPOLITAN PHILIP

BISHOPS:

ANTOUN - Bishop of Selevkias, Auxiliary
358 Mountain Road
Englewood, NJ 07631 USA
Phone: 201-871-1355

BASIL - Bishop of Enfeh, Auxiliary
1559 Woodlawn
Wichita, Kansas 67208
Phone: 316-687-3169
FAX: 316-687-3327

DIMITRI - Bishop of Dsamble, Auxiliary
2652 Pemberton Drive
Toledo, Ohio
Phone: 419-535-1390

JOSEPH - Bishop of Katana, Auxiliary
454 S. Lorraine Blvd.
Los Angeles, CA 90020
Phone: 213-934-3131
FAX: 213-934-1389

Antiochian Orthodox Patriarchal Vicariate of Mexico and the Carribean Islands AMC G
Dr. Barrigan 568, Narvate
Mexico City, 12 Mexico
Phone: 535-652-7772
METROPOLITAN ANTONIO

Apostolic Orthodox Catholic Church AOC G
Box 1834
Glendora CA 91740
Phone: 818-563-5426

Bulgarian Eastern Orthodox Church BEC G
550 A West 50th Street
New York City, NY 10019 USA
Phone: 212-581-3756

Byelorussian Autocephalic Orthodox Church BAI J
401 Atlantic Avenue
Brooklyn, NY 11217-1702 USA
Phone: 908-560-0058
BISHOP IZIASLAV

Byelorussian Authocephalic Orthodox Church BAM J
524 St. Clarens Avenue
Toronto, ON M6H 3W7 Canada
ARCHBISHOP MIKALAY

Byleorussian Council of Orthodox Churches in North America BYC J
P. O. Box 36
South River, NJ 08882 USA
Phone 908-254-6267
FR. SVIATOSLAW KOUS

Chasnoverian Union of Old Orthodox CHU J

Eastern Orthodox Christian Church of America & Dependencies ECC J
1311 Veterans Memorial Hwy
Mableton GA 30126-3040
Phone: 770-309-5123
METROPOLITAN IGNATIUS

Eastern Orthodox Diocese of Houston and All Texas HUS J
3011 Roe Drive
Houston, TX 77087-2409 USA
Phone: 713-645-0843
BISHOP MAKARIOS

Free Orthodox Church International FOCI
Box 188742
Sacramento CA 95818-8742
Phone: 916-455-9853

Greek Orthodox Archdiocese of America GOA G/J
8-10 East 79th Street
New York City, NY 10021 USA
Phone 212-570-3500
FAX: 202-861-2183
ARCHBISHOP SPYRIDON

BISHOPS:

PHILOTHEOS of Meloa
8-10 East 79th Street
New York City, NY 10021 USA
Phone 212-570-3500
FAX: 202-861-2183

ANTHIMOS of Olympos
8-10 East 79th Street
New York City, NY 10021 USA
Phone: 212-570-3506

JOHN of Amorion
41 St. George Street
P. O. Box 1960
St. Augustine, FL 32095
Phone: 904-829-8205

ALEXIOS of Troas, Locum Tenes of Atlanta
2480 Clairmont Rd. N.E.
Atlanta, GA 30329
Phone:

METHODIOS of Boston
162 Goddard Avenue
Brookline, MA 02146
Phone: 617-277-4742
FAX: 617-739-9229

IAKOVOS of Chicago
40 East Burton Place
Chicago, IL 60610
Phone: 312-337-4130
FAX: 312-337-9391

ISIAH of Denver
4610 East Alameda Avenue
Denver, CO 80222
Phone: 303-333-7794
FAX: 303 333-7796

MAXIMOS of Pittsburgh Locum Tenens
19405 Renfrew
Detroit, MI 48221
Phone: 313-864-5433
FAX: 313-864-5543

MAXIMOS of Pittsburgh
5201 Ellsworth Avenue
Pittsburgh, PA 15232
Phone: 412-621-5529
FAX 412-621-1522

ANTHONY of San Francisco
Santa Clara Avenue
San Francisco, CA 94127

DIMITRIOS of Xanthos
Orthodox Christian Mission Center
Box 4319
St. Augustine, FL 32085-4319
Phone. 904-829-5132
FAX. 904-829-1635

GEORGE of Komanon
(Archdiocese Headquarters)

Greek Orthodox Church of Panama, Mexico, Central America & the Carribean ECP G
Metropolitan ATHENAGORAS (including Mexico, Central America and the Carribean)
Agua Caliente Esq Saratoga
Col. Lomas – Hipodromo
Mexico City, CP 11000, MEXICO

Greek Orthodox Old Calendar (Synod of Souris) GSS J
Phone: 602-957-0869
BISHOP GREGORY

Greek Orthodox Metropolis of Canada GOC J
1474 Jarry Street
Chamedy, PQ H2E 1A7 Canada
METROPOLITAN AKAKIOS

Greek Orthodox Metropolis of North & South America ECU J
(reunited with GOA in 1997)
36-07 23rd Avenue
Astoria, NY 11105 USA
METROPOLITAN PAISIOS

Hellenic Orthodox Traditionalist Church of America CHR J
22-68 26th Street
Astoria, NY 11105 USA
Phone: 718-932-1592
FAX: 218-274-2879
BISHOP PETROS
METROPOLITAN PAUL

Holy Orthodox Archdiocese of Vasiloupolis and Missionary Eparchy of America VAS G/J
44-02 48th Avenue
Woodside, NY 11377-6344 USA
Phone: 718-786-4495
FAX: 718-786-7887
METHROPOLITAN PANGRATIOS

Holy Orthodox Church in North America (Metropolitan Auxentios) AUX J
850 South Street
Roslindale, MA 02130 USA
BISHOP EPHRAIM

Holy Orthodox Church, American Jurisdiction HOC G
355 Tusculum Road
Nashville, TN 37211 USA
Phone: 615-834-1938
FAX: 615-833-9564
METROPOLITAN FRANCIS

Holy Orthodox Synod for Diaspora & Hellas, (also Mar Thoma Church Outside of India) Greek Orthodox Eparchy of Lincoln DHE J
740 S. 11th St., P. O. Box 22237
Lincoln, NE 68543-2237 USA
Phone: 402-475-6492
BISHOP MELCHIZEDEK

Italo-Greek Orthodox Church IGO G
1101 Howard Ave
Utica NY 13501
Phone: 315-798-4457
Archimandrite Stephen, Administrator

Macedonian Orthodox Church of North America MCI J
Ft. Wayne, IN USA
BISHOP STEFAN

Macedonian Orthodox Church in North America MOC J
c/o Box 171
Blacklick OH 43004

Metropolia of Western Europe & the Americas WEA G
1905 S Third St
Austin TX 78704-4122
Phone: 512-442-2289
FAX: 512-416-6556
BISHOP HILARION

Old Ritualist Metropolia of Moscow & All Russia MAR J
Moscow, Russia
METROPOLITAN ALIMPY

Orthodox Church in America OCA G/J
P. O. Box 675
Syosset, NY 11791 USA
Phone: 516-922-0550
FAX: 516-922-0924
METROPOLITAN THEODOSIUS

BISHOPS:

KYRILL
Archbishop of Pittsburgh and Western Pennsylvania and the Bulgarian Diocese
P. O. Box 1769
Cranberry TWNP., PA 16066-1769
Phone: 724-776-5555

FAX 724-776-5549

PETER
Archbishop of New York and New Jersey
33 Hewitt Avenue
Bronxville, NY 10708
Phone: 914-337-6222
FAX: 914-793-3947

DIMITRI
Archbishop of Dallas and the South
Exarch of Mexico
P. O. Box 191109
Dallas, TX 75219-1109
Phone: 214-559-4425
FAX: 214-526-7170

HERMAN
Archbishop of Philadelphia and
Eastern Pennsylvania
P. O. Box 130
South Canaan, PA 18459
Phone: 717-927-4686
FAX 717-937-4939

NATHANIEL
Bishop of Detroit and the Romanian
Episcopate
P. O. Box 309
Grass Lake, MI 49240-0309
Phone: 517-522-4800
FAX: 517-522-5907

JOB
Bishop of Chicago and the Midwest
605 Iowa Street
Oak Park, IL 60302
Phone: 708-524-5750
FAX: 708-524-5754

TIKHON
Bishop of San Francisco and the West
649 Robinson Street
Los Angeles, CA 90026
Phone: 213-913-3615
FAX: 213-913-0316

SERAPHIM
Bishop of Ottawa and Canada
P. O. Box 179
Spencerville, ON KOE 1XO
Phone: 613-925-5226
FAX: 613-925-1521

INNOCENT
Bishop of Anchorage
513 E. 24th Street, Ste. #3
Anchorage, AK 99503
Phone: 907-279-0025
FAX: 907-279-9748

MARK
Bishop of Bethesda
9511 Sun Pointe Drive
Boynton Beach, FL 33437
Phone 407-369-0247

Orthodox Church in the Carribean (under AMC) ECP G
LYNX Air, P. O. Box 407139
Ft. Lauderdale, FL 33340
USA
Phone: 509-57-48-05
FAX: 509-57-06-72

Orthodox Fellowship of St. Germanus of Paris
(St. Germaine) SGP G
P. O. Box 704
Baraboo, WI 53913-0704 USA
Phone: 608-356-2808

Orthodox Old Ritualists of the Metropolis of Romina (Metropolitan Timofel) MOR J
    ARCHBISHOP IOSIF

Patriarchal Parishes of the Russian Orthodox Church in Canada PCN J
    10812 108th Street
    Edmonton, AF T5H 3A6 Canada
    BISHOP GEORGE

Patriarchal Parishes of the Russian Orthodox Church in the United States PER J/G
    15 East 97th Street
    New York City, NY 10029 USA
    Phone: 212-289-1915 or 212-831-6294
    FAX 212-427-5003

Romanian Orthodox Archdiocese in America RMA G
    19959 Riopelle Street
    Detroit, MI 48203 USA
    Phone: 718-784-4453
    FAX: 313-893-8390
    ARCHBISHOP VICTORIN

Romano Byzantine Orthodox Catholic Church RBS G
    2123 W 5th St #2
    Duluth MN 55806
    Phone:
    METROPOLITAN STEPHEN

Russian Orthodox Church (Moscow Patriarchate) PRC J
    15 E. 97th St.
    New York NY 10029
  Phone: 212-289-1915
  FAX: 212-427-5003
    BISHOP PAUL

Russian Orthodox Church Outside of Russia ROR J
75 East 93rd Street
New York City, NY 10028 USA
Phone: 212-410-4258
FAX: 212-426-1086
METROPOLITAN VITALY

BISHOPS;

ALIPHY
Diocese of Chicago, Detroit and Midwest America
1800 Lee Street
Des Plaines, IL 609018-2024
Phone: 847-824-6531
FAX: 759-9836

ANTHONY
Diocese of San Francisco & Western America
473 26th Avenue
San Francisco, CA 94121-1905
Phone: 415-387-8757
FAX: 415-387-5955

GABRIEL
75 East 93rd Street
New York City, NY 10028 USA
Phone: 212-410-4258
FAX: 212-426-1086

KYRILL
473 26th Avenue
San Francisco, CA 94121-1905
Phone: 415-387-8757
FAX: 415-387-5955

LAURUS
75 East 93rd Street
New York City, NY 10028 USA
Phone: 212-410-4258
FAX: 212-426-1086

MICHAEL
Diocese of Montreal and Canada
8011 Champagneur Avenue
Montreal Quebec H3N 2K4
Phone: 415-387-3757
FAX 415-387-5955

Serbian Orthodox Church in the United States and Canada SOC J
P. O. Box 519
Libertyville, IL 60048 USA
Phone: 312-362-2440
METROPOLITAN CHRISTOPHER

BISHOPS:

JOVAN (Los Angeles) (Western USA)
1621 West Garvey Avenue
Alhabra, CA 91803
Phone: 626-284-9100
FAX: 626-281-5045

MITROFAN (Eastern USA)
Box 386
Way Hollow Road
Edgeworth PA 15143
Phone: 412-741-5686
FAX: 412-741-9235

Serbian Orthodox New Gracanica Metropolitanate Diocese of America and Canada NGM J
P. O. Box 371
Grayslake, IL 60030-0371 USA
Phone: 708-223-4300
FAX 708-223-4312
METROPOLITAN IRENEY
-There has been a restoration of Communion between the New Gracanica Metropolitanate and the SOC

True (Old Calendar) Orthodox Church of Greece MAT J
    60 Mott Street
    New Bedford, MA 02744 USA
    ARCHBISHOP ANDREAS

True (Old Calendar) Orthodox Church of Greece CYP J (Metropolitan Cyprian)
    P. O. Box 398
    Etna, CA 96027-0398
    BISHOP CHRYSOSTOMOS

Ukrainian Autocephalous Orthodox Church: Holy Synod of the West UAO
    1671 Golden Gate #2
    San Francisco, CA 94115
    Phone: 415-563-8514
    Bishop JONAH, Locum Tenens

Ukrainian Autocephalous Orthodox Church in the USA UIU J/G
    3107 Bailey Avenue
    Bronx, NY 10463 USA
    METROPOLITAN ALEXIS

Ukrainian Autocephalous Orthodox Church of the USA UOD J
    5130 Prescott Street
    Detroit, MI 48212 USA
    ARCHBISHOP ISIASLAV

Ukrainian Orthodox Church of America and Canada UOA G/J
    (merged with UCU)
    90-34 139th St.
    Jamaica, NY 11435 USA
    Phone: 718-297-2407
    BISHOP VSEVOLOD

Ukrainian Orthodox Church of Canada UOC J
    5 St. John's Avenue
    Winnipeg, MB R2W IG8 Canada
    METROPOLITAN VASILY

Ukrainian Orthodox Church of the USA UCU J
P. O. Box 495
South Bound Brook, NJ 08880 USA
Phone: 908-356-0090
FAX: 908-356-5556
METROPOLITAN CONSTANTINE

Ukrainian Orthodox Patriarchate of Kiev UOP J
(Archdiocese of Canada)
37323 Hawkins Rd
Dewdney BC V0M 1H0
Phone: 604-482-6936
FAX: 604-820-9758
ARCHBISHOP LAZAR

STANDING CONFERENCE OF (CANONICAL) ORTHODOX BISHOPS OF THE AMERICAS (SCOBA)
Archbishop Spyridon, Chairman
8-10 E. 79th St.
New York, NY 10021
(Note: Since 1960, SCOBA has been in existence as a confederation of the following canonical Orthodox jurisdictions in America: ADA, CRC, ANT, BEC, GOA, OCA, RMA, SOC (including NGM), UOA (including UCU))

J – Julian Calendar(sometimes referred to as the 'Old' Calendar)
G – Revised Julian (sometimes referred to as the 'New' Calendar or Gregorian Calendar)

Parishes and Missions
in the United States

ALASKA

St Innocent Chapel OCA
Adak AK

St Alexander Nevsky
OCA
PO Box 14
Akutan AK 99553
Phone:

Holy Resurrection OCA
PO Box 98
Aleknagik AK 99555
Phone:

Holy Transfiguration GOA
2800 O'Malley Rd.
Anchorage AK 99516
Phone: 907-344-0190
FAX: 907-344-9909

Holy Trinity Chapel/Patriarch Tikhon
513 E 24th St #6 OCA
Anchorage AK 99503-2235
Phone: 907-272-6468

St Innocent Cathedral
OCA
6724 E 4 Ave
Anchorage AK 99504
Phone: 907-333-9723
FAX: 907-338-3910

St John the Baptist OCA
PO Box 94
Angoon AK 99820
Phone: 907-463-3472
FAX: 907-463-2038

Protection of the Theotokos

PO Box 201 OCA
Aniak AK 99557-0201
Phone:

St Nicholas OCA
PO Box 47006
Atka AK 99502
Phone:

St Herman of Alaska
OCA
General Delivery
Atmartluaq AK 99557
Phone:

Holy Resurrection OCA
General Delivery
Belkofsky AK 99612
Phone:

St Sophia OCA
PO Box 1972
Bethel AK 99557
Phone:

Chignik Lagoon Mission
OCA
PO Box KCQ
Chignik AK 99548
Phone: 907-845-2222

St Agaphia OCA
Port Heiden AK 99549
PO Box KCQ
Chignik AK 99548
Phone: 907-845-2222

St Nicholas OCA
Box KXQ
Chignik Lake AK 99558
Phone:

St Sergius OCA
Choathbaluk via Aniak AK 99557
Phone:

St Nicholas OCA
PO Box 671035
Chugiak AK 99567-1035
Phone: 907-522-2397

Orthodox Community
OCA
General Delivery
Clarks Point AK 99569-9999
Phone:

St Michael the Archangel
OCA
PO Box 1694
Cordova AK 99574
Phone: 907-424-7304

St Seraphim of Sarov
OCA
PO Box 553
Dillingham AK 99576
Phone:

St John Cathedral ANT
18936 Monastery Dr -
PO BOX 771108
Eagle River AK 99577-9248
Phone: 907-696-2002
FAX: 907-696-5555

St Nicholas OCA
Ekuk AK 99576
Phone:

St John OCA
General Delivery
Ekwok AK 99580-9999
Phone:

Ss Sergius/Herman of Valaam
PO Box 8005 OCA
English Bay, Nanwalek AK 99559
Phone: 907-281-2235

St Herman OCA
2108 Goldstream Rd
PO BOX 80971
Fairbanks AK 99708
Phone:

St Nicholas OCA
PO Box 35
False Pass AK 99583
Phone: 907-548-2256

Gustavus Orthodox Community
1 Mile Wilson Rd OCA
PO Box 218
Gustavus AK 99826
Phone: 907-697-2272

St Nicholas OCA
PO Box 453
Hoonah AK 99829-0453
Phone:

Protection of the Virgin Mary
Lovelock AK 99625 OCA
PO Box 4044
Igiugig AK 99613
Phone:

St Nicholas   OCA
General Delivery
Igiugig AK 99613
Phone:

Ss Constantine and Helen OCA
LIme Village AK 99668
PO Box 042
Iliamna AK 99606-0042
Phone: 907-563-1236

St Nicholas   OCA
326Nn 5th St
PO Box 20130
Juneau AK 99801-1109
Phone: 907-586-1023

Ascension of Our Lord OCA
General Delivery
Karluk AK 99608-9999
Phone:

Holy Trinity   OCA
PO Box 44
Kasigluk AK 99609-9999
Phone: 907-477-6528

St Gabriel OCA
Kongiganak AK 99559
PO Box 03
Kasigluk AK 99609
Phone:

Holy Assumption OCA
1106 Mission Ave
PO BOX 1227
Kenai AK 99611-8017
Phone:

Ketchikan Orthodox Community
P.O. Box 7015 OCA
Ketchikan AK 99901
Phone: 907-225-6802
FAX: 907-225-8850

St Herman   OCA
PO Box 169
King Cove AK 99612-9999
Phone:

Ss Peter and Paul   OCA
PO Boxc 1001
Kockhonak AK 99606
Phone: 907-533-3208

Holy Resurrection   OCA
410 Mission Road
Kodiak AK 99615-6329
Phone: 907-486-5532

Ss Sergius and Herman of Valaam
PO Box 3576 OCA
Kodiak AK 99615
Phone:

St Michael the Archangel OCA
Box 5057
Koliganek AK 99576-5051
Phone:

St Nicholas   OCA
PO Box 92
Kwethluk AK 99621-0092
Phone:

St Michael   OCA
PO Box 03
Kwigillingok AK 99609
Phone:

St Herman   OCA
General Delivery
Larsen Bay AK 99624-9999
Phone:

St Seraphim   OCA
General Delivery
Lower Kalskag AK 99626-9999
Phone:

St Michael   OCA
General Delivery
Marshall AK 99585-9999
Phone: 907-549-3827

St Peter the Aleut OCA
PO Box 139
Mountain Village AK 99632
Phone:

St Jacob OCA
General Delivery
Napaskiak AK 99559
Phone:

St Michael the Archangel OCA
Eel AK 99559
PO Box 6048
Napaskiak AK 99559
Phone: 907-737-7815

Transfiguration of Our Lord

PO Box 225 OCA
New Halen AK 99806
Phone:

St Sergius   OCA
General Delivery
New Stuyahok AK 99636-9999
Phone: 907-693-3161

St Nicholas   OCA
General Delivery
Nikolski AK 99638
Phone: 907-576-2206

Transfiguration of Our Lord
General Delivery OCA
Ninilchik AK 99369
Phone:

St Nicholas   OCA
PO Box 11
Nondalton AK 99640
Phone: 907-294-2232

General Delivery OCA
Nunapitchuk AK 99641-0057
Phone:

Protection of the Theotokos
Akhiok AK 99615 OCA
PO Box 3
Old Harbor AK 99643-0003
Phone: 907-286-2257

Three Saints   OCA
Box 149
Old Harbor AK 99643-0149
Phone: 907-286-2294

Nativity of Our Lord OCA
PO Box 62
Ouzinkie AK 99644-0062
Phone: 907-486-5800

St John the Baptist OCA
Naknek AK 99633-0285
PO Box 464
Pilot Pt AK 99649
Phone: 907-797-2289

St Nicholas OCA
General Delivery
Pedro Bay AK 99647-9999
Phone:

St John the Theologian
OCA
PO Box 98
Perryville AK 99648-0098
Phone: 907-845-2222

St Nicholas OCA
PO Box 476
Pilot Point AK 99649
Phone:

Transfiguration of Our Lord
Egegik AK 99579 OCA
PO Box 464
Pilot Pt AK 99649
Phone: 907-797-2289

Nativity of the Theotokos
OCA
Port Lions AK 99550
PO Box 5058
Pilot Station AK 99650
Phone: 907-549-3647

Orthodox Community
OCA
St Michael AK
PO Box 10
Pilot Station AK 99650
Phone: 907-549-3827

Transfiguration of Our Lord
PO Box 10 OCA
Pilot Station AK 99650
Phone: 907-549-3827

Ss Peter and Paul OCA
PO Box 188
Pitkas Pt AK 99658
Phone: 907-549-3827

St Herman of Alaska

PO Box 5505
Port Graham AK 99603
Phone: 907-284-2237

St Basil OCA
General Delivery
Portage Creek AK 99576
Phone:

Elevation of the Holy Cross

PO Box 70105 OCA
S Naknek AK 99670
Phone: 907-797-2289

Ss. Peter & Paul OCA
PO Box 46
Saint Paul Island AK 99660-0046
Phone:

St Nicholas OCA
PO Box 149
Sand Point AK 99661-0149
Phone: 907-845-2222

St Nicholas OCA
General Delivery
Seldovia AK 99663-9999
Phone:

Annunciation to the Theotokos
PO Box 697 OCA
Sitka AK 99835
Phone:

St Michael Cathedral
OCA
503 Lincoln St
PO Box 697
Sitka AK 99835-0697
Phone: 907-747-8120

Ss. Peter & Paul OCA
General Delivery
Sleetmute AK 99668-9999
Phone:

St Herman OCA
PO Box 74
Sleetmute AK 99668
Phone: 907-449-4264

St Nicholas OCA
Crooked Creek AK 99575
PO Box 74
Sleetmute AK 99668
Phone: 907-449-4264

St George OCA
PO Box 961
St George Island AK 99591
Phone: 907-859-2235

St Nicholas OCA
PO Box 125
Tatitlek AK 99677
Phone:

St Basil OCA
General Delivery
Telida AK 99691
Phone:

St Agaphia OCA
General Delivery
Tuntutuliak AK 99680
Phone:

St Nicholas OCA
PO Box 82052
Tyonek AK 99682
Phone:

Holy Ascension Cathedral

PO Box 96 OCA
Unalaska AK 99685-0145
Phone: 907-581-1667

St Nicholas Community

General Delivery OCA
Valdez AK 99686-9999
Phone:

St Lazarus OCA
HC 32 PO Box 6667
Wasilla AK 99654
Phone: 907-274-4252

ALABAMA - ARKANSAS - ARIZONA

Elevation of the Holy Cross

Russian Mission AK OCA
Yukon River AK 99657
Phone: 907-584-5113

St Innocent Chapel OCA
PSC 486-Adak Box 2103,
Intra-AK Z 1
FPO AP 96506
Phone:

ALABAMA

St Nicholas   MPA
5301 Bellwood Dr
Adamsville AL 35005
Phone: 205-674-1325

All Saints ROR
3537 27th St N
Birmingham AL 35207-2811
Phone:

Holy Trinity-Holy Cross
Cathedral
307 19th St S   GOA
Birmingham AL 35233
Phone: 205-716-3080
FAX: 205-716-3085

St Symeon the New
Theologian
3101 Clairmont Ave S OCA
Birmingham AL 35205-1114
Phone: 205-930-9681

Sts Rita and Jude   FOCI
4249 Warren Rd
Birmingham AL 35213
Phone:

St Nicholas   PER
5301 Bellwood Dr
Brookside AL 30536
Phone: 205-674-1325

Orthodox Christian Mission
Daleville AL 36322 ANT
Phone:

Presentation of the Virgin
Mary
PO Box 639   GOA
Daphne AL 36526-8568
Phone:

St Michael
ANT
218 Hodgesville Rd
Dothan AL 36301
Phone: 334-792-4912

Holy Cross-Ss Constantine &
Helen 3021 University Dr
NW   GOA
Huntsville AL 35816-3133
Phone: 205-534-4221
FAX: 205-534-4206

Annunciation   GOA
50 S Ann St
Mobile AL 36604-2131
Phone: 334-438-9888
FAX: 334-438-9889

St John of Shanghai/San
Francisco
2000 Rivrside Dr   ROR
Mobile AL 36615
Phone: 334-471-1454

St Gregory the Theologian
1014 Hackberry Ln OCA
Tuscaloosa AL 35401
Phone: 205-674-8644

ARKANSAS

All Saints of America Mission
193 Brooks Rd   ROR
De Queen AR 71832-9704
Phone: 501-642-3973

St George   GOA
220 N 7th St
Fort Smith AR 72901-2112
Phone:

Ss George and Alexandra
OCA
Phoenix Village Mall
2732 Brooken Hill Dr
Ft Smith AR 72908
Phone: 501-648-3449
FAX: 501-64602513

Zoodochos Peghe   GOA
502 Morrison Ave
Hot Aprings AR 72211
Phone: 501-623-4646

St Archangel Michael
NGM
PO Box 1523
Hot Springs Natl Park AR
71902-1523
Phone: 501-525-8847

St George   SOC
108 Donnie Ct
Hot Springs Natl Park AR
71913-4731
Phone: 501-525-4285

Annunciation   GOA
1100 Napa Valley Dr
Little Rock AR 72211-2312
Phone: 501-225-6726
FAX: 501-225-6749

ARIZONA

St Stephen Nemanja
SOC
PO Box 3666
Bisbee AZ 85603
Phone: 602-997-0232

St Katherine   GOA
2716 N Dobson Rd
Chandler AZ 85224-1806
Phone: 602-899-3330

St Demetrius   ANT
3000 N 4th St Ste 29
5250 E Cortland Blvd, Apt 100
Flagstaff AZ 86004
Phone: 520-714-9810

ARIZONA - CALIFORNIA

Prison Ministry   ANT
PO Box 629
Florence AZ 85232-0629
Phone: 602-868-4011

Holy Trinity   ROR
3208 W Glendale Ave Ste 1
5814 W. Shangri-La Rd.
Glendale AZ 85304-3818
Phone: 602-979-5537

St John the Baptist OCA
3749 W Behrend Dr
Glendale AZ 85308-2252
Phone: 602-582-3156

St Peter the Aleut Mission
OCA
Po Box 2248
Lake Havasu City AZ 86405-2248
Phone: 818-996-7013

St Haralambos   GOA
10320 N 84 Ave
Peoria AZ 85345
Phone: 602-486-8665
FAX: 602-486-5290

Holy Trinity Cathedral
GOA
1973 E Maryland Ave
Phoenix AZ 85016
Phone: 602-264-7863
FAX: 602-230-9099

Ss. Peter & Paul   OCA
1614 E Monte Vista Rd
Phoenix AZ 85006
Phone: 602-253-9515

St George   ANT
4530 E Gold Dust Ave
Phoenix AZ 85028
Phone: 602-953-1921
FAX: 602-953-2460

St Gregory   FOCI
2526 N 32nd St B-27
Phoenix AZ 85008
Phone:

St Gregory   PER
PO Box 25233
Phoenix AZ 85002
Phone: 602-420-9415

St Mary Protectress UCU
1102 N 10th St
Phoenix AZ 85006
Phone: 602-254-3752

St Nectarios   CHR
3044 N 27th St
Phoenix AZ 85016
Phone: 602-957-3054

St Nikola NGM
P.O. Box 9935
Phoenix AZ 85020
Phone: 602-943-3459

St Parascheva   OCA
8822 N 7th St
PO Box 42311
Phoenix AZ 85080-2331
Phone: 602-582-3150

St Sava SOC
4436 E McKinley St
Phoenix AZ 85008
Phone: 602-275-7360

Assumption   GOA
8202 E Cactus Rd
Scottsdale AZ 85260-5211
Phone: 602-991-3009
FAX: 602-991-3717

Holy Resurrection   ANT
715 W Vanover Rd
Tucson AZ 85705-2265
Phone: 520-622-2265

St Demetrios   GOA
1145 E Fort Lowell Rd
Tucson AZ 85719
Phone: 520-888-0505
FAX: 520-888-3089

St Germain of Alaska
ROR
501 W Columbia St
Tucson AZ 85714-2525
Phone: 602-979-5537

St Stephen Nemanja
SOC
216 Park Ave
Warren AZ
Phone: 602-997-0232

CALIFORNIA

St Steven's Cathedral
SOC
1621 Garvey Ave
Alhambra CA 91803-4222
Phone: 818-284-9100

St Basil of Ostrog   SOC
PO Box 673
Altaville CA 95221-0673
Phone: 209-736-2340

Falling Asleep of the Virgin Mary
555 S Walnut St   OCa
Anaheim CA 92802-1450
Phone: 714-776-1972

St John the Baptist GOA
405 N Dale St
Anaheim CA 92801-4818
Phone: 714-827-0181
FAX: 714-827-8143

St Basil of Ostrog   SOC
930 N Main St
Angels Camp CA 95222
Phone: 209-736-2340

St Demetrios   GOA
13677 Lakota Rd - PO Box 332
Apple Valley CA 92307
Phone: 619-247-2701

Christ the Savior   NGM
1424 S Baldwin Ave
Arcadia CA 91007-7923
Phone:

Holy Virgin Mary   OCA
2998 S. Buhach Rd.
Atwater CA 95301
Phone:

St George　　　GOA
401 Truxtun Ave
Bakersfield CA 93301-5315
Phone: 805-325-8602
FAX: 805-325-8694

Holy Cross　　　GOA
900 Alameda de las Pulgas
Belmont CA 94002
Phone: 415-591-4447
FAX: 415-508-9848

Ss Peter & Paul Orthodox Church
9980 Highway 9　ANT
PO Box 458
Ben Lomond CA 95005
Phone: 408-336-2228
FAX: 408-336-5118

Ss. Kyrill & Methodius
OCA
P.O. Box 11672
Berkeley CA 94712-2672
Phone: 510-215-0301
FAX: 510-531-3711

St John the Baptist OCA
1900 Essex St
Berkeley CA 94703-2511
Phone: 510-540-0617

Holy Myrrhbearing Women

833 Water St.　　OCA
Broderick CA 95605-1741
Phone: 916-371-1041

Holy Apostles　　FOCI
933 E Valencia Ave
Burbank CA 91501
Phone:

All Saints of Russia ROR
744 El Camino Real
Burlingame CA 94010-5005
Phone: 415-343-7935

St Simeon Verkhotursky
ROR
1421 Cedar St
Calistoga CA 94515-1609
Phone: 707-942-6697

St Demetrios　　GOA
400 Skyway Dr
Camarillo CA 93010-8577
Phone: 805-482-1273

Ss. Constantine & Helen
GOA
3459 Manchester Ave #32
Cardiff By The Sea CA 92007-1525
Phone: 619-942-0920

Our Lady of Guadalupe
UAC
PO Box 221364
Carmel CA 93922-1364
Phone: 408-899-1098

Resurrection　　GOA
20104 Center St.
Castro Valley CA 94546-4712
Phone: 510-581-8950

Holy Archangels Michael and Gabriel
47535 Highway 74　OCA
32200 Cathedral Canyon Dr
Cathedral City CA 92234-4033
Phone:

San Luis Obispo Parish
GOA
10820 Santa Rita Rd
Cayucos CA 93430-1566
Phone: 805-434-2813

St Sergius & Herman of Valaam
252 E 4th St　　VAS
Chico CA 95928-5414
Phone: 916-343-2859

St Anne OCA
Artesia St & Park Ave
966 W Maryhurst Dr
Claremont CA 91711-3319
Phone: 714-779-2681

St George　　　BAM
830 W Bonita Ave
Claremont CA 91711-4113
Phone: 909-981-2882
FAX: 909-798-5545

St John the Evangelist
OCA
Claremont College Campus
966 W Maryhurst Dr
Claremont CA 91711-3319
Phone:
FAX: 909-621-8463

St John Chrysostomos
CYP
1801 Hillside Blvd
Colma CA 94014-2871
Phone:

St John Chrysostom Mission

1418 Miller Dr　　AOC
Colton CA 92324
Phone: 909-424-0141.

St Demetrios　　GOA
1955 Kirker Pass Rd
Concord CA 94521-1627
Phone: 510-676-6967
FAX: 510-676-3910

St Michael the Archangel
OCA
2425 Olivera Rd
Concord CA 94520-1628
Phone: 510-676-4940

Ss Kiril and Methodi OCA
Methodist Church, Richmond CA
4185 Huckleberry Dr
Concorde CA 94502
Phone:

Holy Virgin of Kazan
Monastic Chapel
　　　　　　PER
4400 Green River Rd

Corona CA 91720
Phone: 909-736-7595
FAX: 714-774-9358

St Nectarios　　GOA
20340 E Covina Blvd
Covina CA 91724-1608
Phone: 818-967-5524

St Sava SOC
7811 Orion Ln
Cupertino CA 95014-5011
Phone: 408-257-6652

St George GOA
12147 Lakewood Blvd
Downey CA 90242-2636
Phone: 310-862-6461

St Nicholas GOA
38526 Dunlap Rd
PO Box 400
Dunlap CA 93621-0400
Phone: 209-338-2103

St Gregory of Nyssa
GOA
311 Highland Ave
El Cajon CA 92020
Phone: 619-593-0707
FAX: 619-593-0894

St Elias Mission ROR
5490 Merchant Circle
PO Box 1146
El Dorado CA 95623
Phone: 530-622-2765

St Katherine GOA
9165 Peets St
Elk Grove CA 95624-9474
Phone: 916-683-3443

Orthodox Community of Etna

PO Box 677 CYP
Etna CA 96027-0677
Phone:

St Innocent OCA
936 F St
Eureka CA 95501
Phone: 707-443-2099

St Timothy
4593 Central Way
Fairfield CA 94585
Phone: 707 864-6236

Apostolic Mission AOC
8728 Bluff Ln
Fair Oaks CA 95628
Phone: 916-966-1361

Holy Assumption SOC
7777 Sunset Ave.
Fair Oaks CA 95628-4848
Phone: 916-966-5438

St Innocent OCA
PO Box 41615
Fremont CA 95439
Phone:

St George GOA
2219 N Orchard Ave
Fresno CA 93703-2323
Phone: 209-233-0397
FAX: 209-233-0564

St Peter SOC
3502 N 1st St
Fresno CA 93726-6807
Phone: 209-227-5565

St Peter the Alleut ROR
1001 N Palm Ave
Fresno CA 93728-3144
Phone: 209-486-6334

St Athanasios CYP
PO Box 2833
Garden Grove CA 92642-2833
Phone:

St Luke ANT
13261 Dunklee Ave
Garden Grove CA 92640-6158
Phone: 714-971-2244
FAX: 714-971-2252

Chapel of the Theotokos
AOC
PO Box 1834
Glendora CA 91740
Phone: 818-335-7369
FAX: 818-857-7642

St Athanasius ANT
777 Camino Pascadeero
Goleta CA 93117-4817
Phone: 805-968-4014
FAX: 805-968-3767

Holy Virgin of Kazan
ROR
17370 Neeley Rd.
Guerneville CA 95446-9120
Phone: 707-869-2637

Holy Resurrection OCA
26051 Calaroga Ave
PO Box 55695
Hayward CA 94545-0695
Phone: 510-264-0805

Holy Innocents AOC
Hemet CA 92544
Phone: 909-927-8747

St George the Great Martyr

17323 Main St OCA
PO Box 400504
Hesperia CA 92345-0504
Phone:

St Gregory CRC
6634 Orange Wood Rd
Highland CA 92346
Phone: 714-792-6977

St Barnabas ANT
8011 Taylor Dr.
Huntington Beach CA 92646-1548
Phone: 714-842-6282

Paraclete Mission AOC
PO Box 3600
Idyllwild CA 92549
Phone: 909-659-4445

St Mark
ANT
17840 Skypark Cir
Irvine CA 92714-6401
Phone: 714-851-8933
FAX: 714-851-2076

St Paul
GOA
4949 Alton Pkwy
Irvine CA 92604-8606
Phone: 714-733-2366
FAX: 714-733-0962

St Sava   SOC
724 N Main St - PO BOX 1243
Jackson CA 95642-9536
Phone: 209-223-4320

St George   ANT
PO Box 7157
La Verne CA 91750-7157
Phone: 818-852-0377

Ss. Constantine & Helen   GOA
4304 30th St W
PO Box 4404
Lancaster CA 93539-4404
Phone: 818-345-4724

St Timothy   ANT
403 N J St
PO Box 795
Lompoc CA 93438
Phone: 805-736-6220
FAX: 805-737-3990

Assumption of Blessed Virgin Mary
5761 E Colorado St GOA
Long Beach CA 90814-1900
Phone: 310-493-8929
FAX: 310-985-1379

Orthodox Church of the Redeemer
380 Magdalena Ave ANT
Los Altos Hills CA 94024
Phone: 650-941-1570
FAX: 650-948-6045

Fellowship of the Apostle Silas
PO Box 1949   ANT
Los Angeles CA 90078-1949
Phone: 818-896-0177

Holy Transfiguration Cathedral
5432 Fernwood Ave ROR
Los Angeles CA 90027-5603
Phone: 213-469-0366

Holy Trinity   OCA
3315 Verdugo Rd
Los Angeles CA 90065
Phone: 213-255-8583
FAX: 818-365-4274

Holy Virgin Mary Cathedral
650 Micheltorena St OCA
Los Angeles CA 90026
Phone: 213-666-4077

Parroquia de San Judas Tadeo
812 N Alvarado St   IND
Los Angeles CA 90026
Phone: 213-483-6952
FAX: 213-483-2561

Protection of the Holy Virgin Church
2045 Argyle Ave   ROCOR
Los Angeles CA 90068
Phone: 213-466-4845
FAX: 213-466-3557

St Andrew   UCU
1456 Sutherland St
Los Angeles CA 90026-3455
Phone: 213-250-4285

St George   BEC
150 S Alexandria Ave
Los Angeles CA 90004
Phone: 213-480-8555

St John the Baptist   OCA
6301 W Olympic Blvd
Los Angeles CA 90048-5411
Phone: 213-874-9980

St Klement Ohridsky   OCA
5861 Virginia Ave
Los Angeles CA 90038-2005
Phone: 213-467-2711

St Nicholas Cathedral   ANT
Angeles 2300 W 3rd St
Los CA 90057-1906
Phone: 213-382-6269
FAX: 213-382-0175

St Sava   SOC
4355 E 2nd St
Los Angeles CA 90022-1540
Phone: 818-288-1977

St Sophia Cathedral GOA
1324 S Normandie Ave
Los Angeles CA 90006-4310
Phone: 213-737-2424
FAX: 213-737-7029

St Vladimir   UCU
4025 Melrose Ave
Los Angeles CA 90029-3607
Phone: 213-665-7604

Nativity of the Holy Virgin
1220 Crane St OCA
Menlo Park CA 94025-4213
Phone: 415-326-5622

Holy Virgin Mary   OCA
79 Emerald Dr
PO Box 3704
Merced CA 95344-3704
Phone:

St Mary Magdalene Mission
79 Emerald Dr   OCA
Merced CA 95340
Phone: 209-384-0673

Annunciation   GOA
313 Tokay Ave
PO BOX 707
Modesto CA 95350-3532
Phone: 209-522-7694
FAX: 209-522-3926

St Seraphim of Sarov   ROR
PO Box 5813
Monterey CA 93944-0813
Phone: 408-394-1611

Holy Trinity   SOC
1700 School St.
Moraga CA 94556-1121
Phone: 510-376-5982

St Nicholas   GOA
9501 Balboa Blvd
Northridge CA 91325
Phone: 818-886-4040
FAX: 818-886-3933

Nativity of Christ   GOA
1110 Dickson Dr
Novato CA 94947
Phone: 415-883-1998
FAX: 415-883-1998

Ascension Cathedral   GOA
4700 Lincoln Ave.
Oakland CA 94602-2535
Phone: 510-531-3400
FAX: 510-533-3711

St George   NGM
94-9th St
Oakland CA 94607
Phone: 510-836-0591

St John the Evangelist   ANT
501 Moraga Way
Orinda CA 94563-4219
Phone: 510-939-4255

Holy Trinity   ROR
2784 Alvarado St.
Oxnard CA 93030-1735
Phone: 805-278-2085

St Herman   OCA
142 W Wooley Rd
Oxnard CA 93030-7443
Phone: 805-486-5793

Holy Cross   ANT
38201-D 6th St E
Palm Dale CA 93550
Phone: 805-245-3571
FAX: 805-245-0710

St George   GOA
74-109 Larrea
PO Box 4755
Palm Desert CA 92260-4770
Phone: 619-568-9901

Holy Cross Mission ANT
38201 6th St E - Ste D
Palmdale CA 93550
Phone: 805-245-3571
FAX: 805-245-0710

Protection of the Holy Virgin
3475 Ross Rd.   ROR
Palo Alto CA 94303-4412
Phone: 415-494-6397

San Tomas   UAC
PO Box 1804
Paradise CA 95969
Phone: 916-877-4193

St Anthony   GOA
778 S Rosemead Blvd
Pasadena CA 91107-5613
Phone: 818-449-6943
FAX: 818-449-6974

Holy Cross   ANT
344 Egret Pl.
Pittsburg CA 94565-2078
Phone: 510-437-8150

St Dionysios   GOA
1105 Harbor St
Pittsburg CA 94565-2613
Phone: 510-432-3336

Holy Cross   ANT
2110 Hoover Ct
Pleasant Hill CA 94523-4646
Phone:

St Sergius of Radonezh
OCA
135 Balboa Rd
PO BOX 563
Point Reyes Station CA 94956-9714
Phone: 415-663-1705

St Anne   OCA
Artesia & Park Sts
Pomona CA
(Mail: 966 Maryhurst Dr
Claremont CA 91711
Phone: 909-625-5540

St Demetrios   AUX
1495 S Reservoir St
Pomona CA 91766-3875
Phone: 909-623-9563

St Mark   VAS
1425 Main St Ste 144
Ramona CA 92065-2128
Phone:

Chapel   GOA
1959 Eureka Way
PO BOX 492584
Redding CA 96001-0452
Phone: 916-241-1575

Theotokos Icon - Surety of Sinners   ROR
1972 Jewell Ln
531 Chancellor Blvd
Redding CA 96003-9029
Phone: 916-241-1732

St Katherine   GOA
722 Knob Hill Ave
Redondo Beach CA 90277-4345
Phone: 310-540-2434
FAX: 310-316-4655

St Andrew   ANT
10120 Indiana Ave.
Riverside CA 92503
Phone: 909-352-9678

All Saints ANT
5930 Commerce Blvd
Rohnert Park CA 94928-3510
Phone: 707-795-8093

St George   JER
4687 Snyder Ln
Rohnert Park CA 94928-1872
Phone: 415-334-2234

St Paul Mission   AOC
PO Box 2401
Running Springs CA 92382
Phone: 909-867-2659

Annunciation   GOA
3022 F St
Sacramento CA 95816-3806
Phone: 916-443-2033
FAX: 916-443-2743

Ascension of Christ ROR
714 13th St.
Sacramento CA 95814-1903
Phone: 916-443-2271
FAX: 916-443-2271

Elevation of Holy Cross OCA
9000 Jackson Ave
2443 Fair Oaks Blvd
Sacramento CA 95825-7684
Phone: 916-857-0806

Holy Theotokos FOCI
PO Box 188 742
Sacramento CA 95818
Phone:

Our Lady of Prayer UIU
4748 Greenholme Dr
Sacramento CA 95842-3221
Phone:

Sacramento Mission VAS
3181 High St.
Sacramento CA 95815-1337
Phone: 916-929-4898

Ss Michael and Gabriel OCA
4633 Raley Blvd
Sacramento CA 95832-2422
Phone: 916-723-4421

St Athanasius ANT
7921 Cottonwood Ln.
Sacramento CA 95828-5403
Phone: 916-689-9074

St John the Baptist GOA
326 Park St
Salinas CA 93901-2033
Phone: 408-424-4434

St Nicholas OCA
102 Ross Ave
San Anselmo CA 94960-2941
Phone: 415-454-0982

Prophet Elias GOA
1035 Inland Center Dr
PO Box 296
San Bernardino CA 92402
Phone: 909-885-6213

Our Lady of Kazan
3703 Central Ave
San Diego CA 92105
Phone: 619-589-8182

St George SOC
3025 Denver St
San Diego CA 92117-6140
Phone: 619-275-4476

St George ANT
4175 Poplar St
San Diego CA 92105-4558
Phone: 619-282-2417

St John of Damascus OCA
PO Box 28291
San Diego CA 92064-1535
Phone: 619-674-1931
FAX: 619-674-1831

St John of Kronstadt ROR
5131 Rex Ave
PO Box 5611
San Diego CA 92165-5611
Phone: 619-282-3304
FAX: 619-286-5844

St Mary Protectress UCU
9558 Campo Rd
San Diego CA 92077
Phone: 619-464-1830

St Nicholas OCA
3873 Cherokee Ave
San Diego CA 92104-3109
Phone: 619-284-9476

St Spyridon GOA
3655 Park Blvd
San Diego CA 92103-4546
Phone: 619-297-4165
FAX: 619-297-4181

Venerable Mother Angelina
4808 Trojan Ave NGM
San Diego CA 92115-4951
Phone: 619-286-4438

Annunciation Cathedral GOA
245 Valencia St
San Francisco CA 94103-2320
Phone: 415-861-0057
FAX: 415-431-5860

Christ the Savior OCA
490 12th Ave
2040 Anza St
San Francisco CA 94118-2904
Phone: 415-386-9815

Christ the Savior VAS
720 Duboce Ave
San Francisco CA 94117-3215
Phone:

Holy Archangels Michael, Gabriel, & Raphael VAS
1065 Sutter St.
San Francisco CA 94109-5817
Phone: 415-474-4621

Holy Ascension UAC
1671 Golden Gate AVe #2
San Francisco CA 94115
Phone: 415-563-8514

Holy Spirit Community UIU
47 W Portal Ave
San Francisco CA 94127-1338
Phone:

Holy Theotokos VAS
20 Steiner St
San Francisco CA 94117-3325
Phone:

Holy Trinity GOA
999 Brotherhood Way
San Francisco CA 94132-2904
Phone: 415-584-4747
FAX: 415-584-3340

Holy Trinity Cathedral OCA
1520 Green St @ Van Ness Ave
1520 Green St
San Francisco CA 94123-5102
Phone: 415-673-8565
FAX: 415-673-8565

Holy Virgin Cathedral
ROR
6210 Geary Blvd.
San Francisco CA 94121-1822
Phone: 415-221-3255

Mother of God of Kazan
ROR
5717 California St.
San Francisco CA 94121-2210
Phone: 415-824-3475

OCHAG ROR
451 27th Ave.
San Francisco CA 94121-1813
Phone: 415-751-4623

Old Holy Virgin Cathedral
864 Fulton St. ROR
San Francisco CA 94117-1752
Phone: 415-752-4162

Resurrection of Christ
ROR
109 6th Ave.
San Francisco CA 94118-1325
Phone: 415-386-0452
FAX: 415-386-1472

Russkiy Pastyr ROR
738 27th Ave
San Francisco CA 94121-3618
Phone:

Ss Dominic and Francis
UAC
130 11th Ave
San Francisco CA 94118-1107
Phone: 415-751-8701

St George JER
399 San Fernando Way @ Ocean Ave
San Francisco CA 94127
Phone: 415-334-2234

St John the Baptist NGM
900 Baker St
San Francisco CA 94115-3811
Phone: 415-567-5869

St Michael UCU
345 7th St
San Francisco CA 94103-4029
Phone: 415-861-4066

St Nicholas ANT
5200 Diamond Hts Blvd
San Francisco CA 94131-2118
Phone: 415-648-5200
FAX: 415-647-0610

St Nicholas Cathedral
PER
2005 15th St.
San Francisco CA 94114-1306
Phone: 415-621-1849

St Sergius of Radonezh
ROR
1346 12th Ave
San Francisco CA 94122-2214
Phone: 415-664-8442

St Tikhon of Zadonsk
ROR
598 15th Ave
San Francisco CA 94118-3531
Phone: 415-221-0234

Sts Dominic and Francis
UAC
130-11th Ave
San Francisco CA 94118-1107
Phone: 415-751-8701

St Sava SOC
1700 S San Gabriel Blvd
San Gabriel CA 91776-3928
Phone: 818-288-8811

St Barbara OCA
Agnews Cntr Catholic Chap
3500 Zanker Rd
San Jose CA 95134-2299
Phone: 510-226-0688

St Basil GOA
6430 Bose Ln
San Jose CA 95120-2816
Phone: 408-268-3214
FAX: 408-268-0646

St Nicholas GOA
1260 Davis St
San Jose CA 95126-1404
Phone: 408-246-2770

St Nicholas OCA
155 Manton Ave
San Jose CA 95126
Phone: 408-867-0628

St Stephen ANT
1570 Branham Ln
San Jose CA 95118-2241
Phone: 408-266-6477

St. John the Theologian
Mission Station ANT
31495 El Camino Real
San Juan Capistrano CA
Phone: 714-459-2299

St Petka SOC
1854 Knob Hill Rd
San Marcos CA 92069-3302
Phone: 619-743-2178

Holy Resurrection ROR
411 W. Victoria St.
Santa Barbara CA 93101-3619
Phone: 805-966-4063

St Barbara GOA
1205 San Antonio Creek Rd
Santa Barbara CA 93111
Phone: 805-683-4492
FAX: 805-964-2774

St Luke ANT
331 W Cota St
Santa Barbara CA 93101-3368
Phone: 805-899-3007

Prophet Elias   GOA
223 Church St
Santa Cruz CA 95060-3809
Phone: 408-429-6500

Annunciation   OCA
124 S College Dr
PO Box 5032
Santa Maria CA 93454-5325
Phone: 805-928-7386
FAX: 805-934-1917

Dormition of the Mother of God   VAS
1468 Gloria Dr
Santa Rosa CA 95407-7256
Phone:

Protection of the Holy Virgin OCA
90 Mountain View Ave
Santa Rosa CA 95405
Phone: 707-584-9491
FAX: 707-585-9445

Ss. Peter & Paul   ROR
850 St Olga St
PO Box 8277
Santa Rosa CA 95407-1277
Phone: 707-584-4092
FAX: 707-588-0502

St Michael the Archangel NGM
18870 Allendale Ave
Saratoga CA 95070
Phone: 408-867-4876
FAX: 408-867-7794

St Nicholas   OCA
14220 Elva Ave
Saratoga CA 95070-3629
Phone: 408-867-0628
FAX: 408-867-0628

St Seraphim of Sarov ROR
1159 Canyon Del Ray & Francis
PO Box 5813
Seaside CA 93944-0813
Phone: 408-394-1611

St Peter of Cetinje   NGM
1064 Stanford Dr
Simi Valley CA 93065-4953
Phone: 805-527-4561
FAX: 805-522-3161

St Demetrios the Physician VAS
22666 Broadway
Sonoma CA 95476-8217
Phone:

St Mary Protectress UCU
9558 Campo Rd
Spring Valley CA 92020
Phone: 619-464-1830

Apostlic Miss.   AOC
11572 Santa Maria St
Stanton CA 90680
Phone: 410-892-0726

St Basil   GOA
920 March Ln
Stockton CA 95207
Phone: 209-478-7564
FAX: 209-478-1814

St Herman of Alaska ROR
161 N Murphy St
Sunnyvale CA 94086-5061
Phone: 408-733-9475

St Peter of Cetinje   NGM
13211 Hubbard St
Sylmar CA 91342-3329
Phone: 805-527-4561
FAX: 805-522-3161

St Innocent   OCA
5657 Lindley Ave
Tarzana CA 91356-2507
Phone: 818-881-1123
FAX: 818-609-7527

St Vladimir   OCA
1328 Castillo St
5657 Lindley Ave
Tarzana CA 91356-2507
Phone: 818-996-7013
FAX: 818-609-7527

St Nicholas Mission GOA
37645 Via de Los Arboles
Temecula CA 92592-8961
Phone: 909-676-6067

St
OCA
833 W. Torrance Blvd.
Torrance CA
Phone: 310-644-9802

Ss Archangels   RMA
4102 Hickman Dr
Torrance CA 90503
Phone:

St Matthew   ANT
2368 Sonoma St..
Torrance CA 90501
Phone: 310-782-9468
FAX: 310-782-0317

Falling Asleep of the Virgin Mary   OCA
1221 Wass St.
Tustin CA 92680-2897
Phone: 714-730-6674

Greatmartyr St George BAM
906 N Euclid Ave
Upland CA 91186
Phone: 909-981-2882

St Spyridon   GOA
1391 Chaffee St
Upland CA 91786-5552
Phone: 909-985-4411

St Timothy   ANT
Vacaville CA

Ss. Constantine & Helen GOA
1224 Alabama St.
Vallejo CA 94590-4648
Phone: 707-642-6916

St Michael   ANT
16643 Vanowen St
Van Nuys CA 91406-4622
Phone: 818-994-2313

COLORADO

St Innocent VAS
2505 Walnut Ave
Venice CA 90291
Phone: 310-821-8121

Holy Myrrhbearing Women OCA
833 Water St
W Sacramento CA 95605
Phone: 916-371-1041

Virgin Mary ANT
3060 Jefferson Blvd.
W Sacramento CA 95691-5320
Phone: 916-372-7776

St John the Evangelist ANT
1878 Olympic Blvd
Walnut Creek CA 94596-5013
Phone: 510-939-4255

St Mary MIC
10550 E Whittier Blvd
Whittier CA
Phone:

St Michael ANT
3333 Workman Mill Rd
Whittier CA 90601-1615
Phone: 213-692-6121

St Peter AOC
35020 Orange St
PO Box 1477
Wildomar CA 92595-1477
Phone: 909-674-1377

St John the Almsgiver ROR
24200 N Highway 101
PO Box 302
Willits CA 95490
Phone: 707-459-5424

COLORADO

St Elias ANT
14336 E Temple Pl Unit A
Aurora CO 80015-1177
Phone: 303-690-6045

Ss. Peter & Paul GOA
3101 Jay Rd
Boulder CO 80301-1693
Phone: 303-443-0501

St Columba ANT
536 Countughn
Boulder CO 80303
Phone: 303-499-0476

St Luke ANT
8212 Kincross Dr
Boulder CO 80301-4229
Phone: 303-530-5680

Ss Constantine and Helen OCA
2770 N Chestnut St
Colarado Springs CO 80907
Phone: 719-473-9238
FAX: 719-473-9238

Rocky Mt. Mission VAS
16755 Southwood Dr
Colorado Springs CO 80908-1611
Phone: 303-495-0005

Ss. Constantine & Helen OCA
2770 N Chestnut St
Colorado Springs CO 80907-5916
Phone: 719-473-9238
FAX: 719-473-9238

St John the Baptist GOA
691 Green St
PO Box 848
Craig CO 81625-3029
Phone: 303-824-6664

St Andrew the First Called

298 Bert St OCA
Delta CO 81416
Phone: 970-874-5225

All Russian Saints ROR
3274 E Iliff Ave
Denver CO 80210-5510
Phone: 303-757-3533

Assumption Cathedral GOA
4610 E Alameda Ave
Denver CO 80222-1301
Phone: 303-388-9314
FAX: 303-329-6337

St Augustine ANT
55 W 3rd Ave-PO Box 9913
Denver CO 80223-1307
Phone: 303-698-2433

St Elias ANT
Denver CO
Phone: 303-690-6045

St Mark ANT
1405 S Vine St
Denver CO 80210-2336
Phone: 303-722-0707

St Mary Protectress UCU
1136 Ogden St
Denver CO 80218-2810
Phone: 303-831-0497

Transfiguration of Christ Cathedral 349 E 47th Ave OCA
Denver CO 80216-2702
Phone: 303-294-0938
FAX: 303-294-0938

St Nicholas GOA
3585 N 12th St
PO Box 1122
Grand Junction CO 81506-5405
Phone: 303-242-9590

St Catherine GOA
5555 S Yosemite St
Greenwood Village CO 80111-3319
Phone: 303-773-3411
FAX: 303-773-0343

Prophet Elias GOA
County Line Rd
Hot Sulphur Springs CO
Phone:

St Luke ANT
7200 Stonehenge Dr
Lafayette CO 80026
Phone: 303-665-4013

CONNECTICUT

St Herman OCA
991 W Prentice Ave
Littleton CO 80120-1455
Phone: 303-798-7306

St Columba ANT
10656 Parkridge Ave
Longmont CO
Phone: 303-499-0476

St John the Baptist GOA
1010 Spruce St
PO Box 3011
Pueblo CO 81004
Phone: 719-544-8554

St Michael OCA
801 W Summit Ave
Pueblo CO 81004-2574
Phone: 719-544-8423

CONNECTICUT

Holy Trinity GOA
Hubbell Ave
P.O. Box 145
Ansonia CT 06401-0145
Phone: 203-735-1919

St Nicholas OCA
Stratford CT
26 Howard Ave
Ansonia CT 06401
Phone:

Three Saints OCA
26 Howard Ave
Ansonia CT 06401-2208
Phone: 203-735-0317
FAX: 203-735-3406

Ss Peter and Paul Mission OCA
93 Dodgingtown Rd
PO Box 84
Bethel CT 06801
Phone: 203-791-9994

Holy Ghost OCA
1540 E Main St
PO Box 55339
Bridgeport CT 06610
Phone: 203-732-5057
FAX: 203-732-5057

Holy Trinity UCU
99 York St
Bridgeport CT 06610-1931
Phone: 203-729-1887

Holy Trinity GOA
4070 Park Ave
Bridgeport CT 06604-1047
Phone: 203-374-5561
FAX: 203-374-5770

St Dimitrie OCA
579 Clinton Ave
Bridgeport CT 06605
Phone: 203-334-5649

St John the Baptist CRC
384 Mill Hill Ave
Bridgeport CT 06610-2863
Phone: 203-335-6170

St Mary's Protection UOA
10 Oakwood St
Bridgeport CT 06606-4829
Phone: 203-372-4883

St Nicholas ANT
5458 Park Ave
Bridgeport CT 06604-1021
Phone: 203-372-9767

St Demetrios GOA
31 Brightwood Rd
Bristol CT 06010-4936
Phone: 203-583-3476

St Alexis of Wilkes-Barre Mission
10 Bluff Ave #1-1-1 OCA
Clinton CT 06413
Phone: 203-664-9434

St Barbara GMA
27 Brickyard Rd
Clinton CT 06413-1438
Phone:

Assumption GOA
30 Clapboard Ridge Rd
Danbury CT 06811-4542
Phone: 203-748-2992

Holy Trinity CRC
Eighth and Roberts Ave
Danbury CT 06810-6862
Phone: 203-748-0671

St George ANT
125 Kohanza St
Danbury CT 06811-4423
Phone: 203-798-1771

St Peter & St. Paul VAS
12 Alan Ave
Danbury CT 06811-4737
Phone:

Holy Trinity GOA
80 Water St
PO BOX 236
Danielson CT 06239-3522
Phone: 203-774-6245

St Nicholas GOA
Church and Chapel Sts
PO Box 1155
Enfield CT 06083-1155
Phone: 203-745-3880

All Saints OCA
205 Scarborough St
Hartford CT 06105
Phone: 860-233-9234
FAX: 860-233-6055

St George Cathedral GOA
433 Fairfield Ave
Hartford CT 06114-2718
Phone: 860-936-7586
FAX: 860-956-8466

St Panteleimon ROR
19 Becket St
Hartford CT 06114-2402
Phone: 860-956-0561

St Volodymyr UCU
110 Russ St
Hartford CT 06106-1432
Phone: 203-246-0248

Ss. Peter & Paul OCA
54 Park Ave
PO Box 334
Meriden CT 06450
Phone: 203-634-9584

St Cyril of Turov
204 Point Beach Dr
Milford CT 06460
Phone: 203-877-0896

Holy Trinity　　　OCA
305 Washington St
PO Box 2876
New Britain CT 06051-4404
Phone: 860-223-1976
FAX: 860-620-0739

St George　　　GOA
301 W Main St
301 W Main St - PO BOX 1753
New Britain CT 06052-1331
Phone: 203-229-0055

St Mary　UCU
54 Winter St
New Britain CT 06051-1908
Phone: 860-229-3833

Holy Transfiguration OCA
285 Alden Ave
25 Kohary Dr
New Haven CT 06515-2418
Phone: 203-387-3882
FAX: 203-387-3043

St Basil the Great　GOA
1 Tower Ln　PO Box 9956
New Haven CT 06533
Phone: 203-777-8294

St Mary Protectress UCU
50 Fowler St
New Haven CT 06515-1420
Phone: 203-387-4305

St Sophia GOA
200 Hempstead St
New London CT 06320-6205
Phone: 860-442-2377
FAX: 860-442-1020

St George　　　GOA
238 W Rocks Rd
Norwalk CT 06851-1133
Phone: 203-849-0611
FAX: 203-750-0138

Holy Trinity　　　GOA
247 Washington St
Norwich CT 06360-3517
Phone: 860-887-1458
FAX: 860-887-1458

St Nicholas　　　OCA
35 Convent Ave
Norwich CT 06360-4716
Phone: 860-889-4699

St Barbara　　　GOA
480 Racebrook Rd
Orange CT 06477-2514
Phone: 203-795-1347
FAX: 203-795-1348

Holy Epiphany　　VAS
43 Liberty St
Pawcatuck CT 06379
Phone:

All Saints of America OCA
313 Twin Lakes Rd
PO Box 45
Salisbury CT 06068-1407
Phone: 860-824-1340

Christ the Savior　OCA
1369 Southford Rd. (Rt. 68)
Southbury CT 06488
Phone: 203-732-5057

St Sergius　　　ROR
PO Box 29
Southbury CT 06488-0029
Phone: 203-264-8808

Annunciation　　GOA
1230 Newfield Ave
Stamford CT 06905-1411
Phone: 203-322-2093
FAX: 203-322-2093

Archangels　　　GOA
1327 Bedford St
Stamford CT 06905-5201
Phone: 203-348-4216
FAX: 203-353-0371

Holy Assumption　OCA
141 Den Rd
Stamford CT 06903-4308
Phone: 203-329-9933

Presentation of Christ in the Temple
5 Wheeler Ter　ROR
Stratford CT 06497-4931
Phone: 203-375-8342

St John the Baptist　CRC
1240 Broadridge Ave
Stratford CT 06497
Phone: 203-375-2564

St Nicholas　　　ROR
1 Honeyspot Rd
Stratford CT 06497-6402
Phone: 203-375-2786

Ss. Cyril & Methodius OCA
34 Fairview Ave
Terryville CT 06786-1519
Phone: 860-582-3631
FAX: 860-583-1515

St George　　　OCA
5490 Main St
Trumbull CT 06611-2932
Phone: 203-268-1968

Holy Trinity　　　GOA
937 Chase Pky
Waterbury CT 06708-2903
Phone: 203-754-5189

Holy Virgin　　　OCA
3125 N Main St
PO Box 4519
Waterbury CT 06704-4519
Phone: 203-753-4866

St Mary Protection　UOD
74 Fairview Ave
Waterbury CT 06716
Phone:

Holy Trinity　　　OCA
414 Valley St
Willimantic CT 06226-2008
Phone: 203-423-3531

Christ the Savior Mission OCA
706 Main St S　Bldg #8
Woodbury CT 06798
Phone: 203-263-0809

DISTRICT OF COLUMBIA - DELAWARE - FLORIDA

Holy Mother of God The Life-Giving Fount   CRC
1484 Star Route 171
Woodstock Valley CT 06282
Phone: 203-974-2133

DISTRICT OF COLUMBIA
Ss. Constantine & Helen GOA
4115 16th St NW
Washington DC 20011-7003
Phone: 202-829-2910

St George   ANT
4335 16th St NW
Washington DC 20011-7001
Phone: 202-723-5335
FAX: 202-723-7924

St Isidore of Seville Mission AOM
1425 Rhode Island Ave NW
Washington DC 20005
Phone: 202-265-3436

St John Rilski   BEC
1629 Van Buren St NW
Washington DC 20012
Phone:

St John the Baptist Cathedral
4001 17th St NW
ROR
Washington DC 20011-5302
Phone: 202-726-3000
FAX: 202-723-5981

St Luke   NGM
PO Box 6468 Fr Sta
Washington DC 20011
Phone: 718-279-4010

St Luke   SOC
5917 16th St NW
Washington DC 20011-2816
Phone: 202-829-4274

St Moses the Black   SGP
1223 Girard St NE
Washington DC 20017-2324
Phone: 202-832-6750

St Nicholas Cathedral OCA
3500 Massachusetts Ave NW
Washington DC 20007-1447
Phone: 202-333-5060
FAX: 202-965-3788

St Sophia Cathedral GOA
36th St & Massachusetts Ave NW
Washington DC 20007
Phone: 202-333-4730

DELAWARE
St Athanasius   ANT
22 Stature Dr
Newark DE 19713-3561
Phone: 302-737-9770

Holy Transfiguration GMA
802 Orange St
Wilmington DE 19801-1710
Phone: 302-836-3959

Holy Trinity   GOA
808 N Broom St
Wilmington DE 19806-4625
Phone: 302-654-4446
FAX: 302-654-4204

Holy Trinity   GOA
808 N Broom St
Wilmington DE 19806
Phone: 302-654-4446
FAX: 302-654-4204

Ss. Peter & Paul   UCU
1406 Philadelphia Pike
Wilmington DE 19809-1824
Phone: 302-798-4588

St Michael the Archangel OCA
2300 W Huntington Dr
Wilmington DE 19808-4952
Phone: 302-998-1747

FLORIDA
St Mark   GOA
2100 Yamato Rd
Boca Raton FL 33431-4323
Phone: 561-994-4822
FAX: 561-998-7875

St Mark   OCA
3415 9th St E
Bradenton FL 34208-4513
Phone: 941-747-5989

Holy Cross   OCA
2365 S Olga Dr SE, Ft Myers FL
3704 SE 12th Ct
Cape Coral FL 33904-4762
Phone: 941-549-0523

Holy Dormition of the Theotokos
1910 Douglas Ave   CHR
Clearwater FL 34615-1411
Phone: 813-443-3999
FAX: 813-446-0290

Holy Trinity   GOA
409 S Old Coachman Rd
Clearwater FL 34625-4410
Phone: 813-799-4605
FAX: 813-998-9173

St George   NGM
15250 58th St N
Clearwater FL 34620-2109
Phone: 813-531-0052

St Nectarios   ROCOR
1845 Asbury Dr
Clearwater FL 33765
Phone: 813-724-9140
FAX: 813-724-9236

St Nicholas   UCU
5031 SW 100th Ave
Cooper City FL 33328-4124
Phone: 305-434-2461

St George Cathedral ANT
320 Palermo Ave
Coral Gables FL 33134
Phone: 305-444-6541
FAX: 305-445-6530

St Phillip   ANT
4870 Griffin Rd
Davie FL 33314-4636
Phone: 305-584-4030

St Demetrios GOA
129 N Halifax Ave
Daytona Beach FL 32118-4250
Phone: 904-252-6012
FAX: 904-253-7613

Orthodox Mission OCA
St Peters Church, DeLand FL
10 MOnroe Ave
DeBary FL 32713
Phone: 407-668-6020

St Stephen OCA
1985 Lake Emma Rd, Longwood FL
10 Monroe Ave
DeBary FL 32713
Phone: 407-668-6020

St John GOA
PO Box 277
Destin FL 32540-0277
Phone:

Protection of Theotokos Orthodox Church UCU
3820 Moores Lake Rd
Dover FL 33527
Phone: 813-659-0123
FAX: 813-659-0123

St Demetrios VAS
10606 N Citrus Springs Blvd
Dunnellon FL 34434-2616
Phone: 901-489-2147

St Andrew the Apostle ANT
2815 S Bay St
Eustis FL 32726
Phone: 352-357-1549

Maison Orthodoxe (Central Office)
PO Box 407103 Maf – Pa OCC
Ft Lauderdale FL 33340-7103
Phone: 509-57-48-05
FAX: 509-57-06-72

St Demetrios GOA
815 NE 15th Ave
Ft Lauderdale FL 33304
Phone: 954-467-1515
FAX: 954-467-0212

St Nicholas OCA
2001 N Andrews Ave
Ft Lauderdale FL 33311-3918
Phone: 954-566-6358
FAX: 561-998-0132

Annunciation GOA
8210 Cypress Lake Dr
Ft Myers FL 33919-5116
Phone: 941-481-2099
FAX: 941-481-2099

Holy Cross OCA
2365 S Olga Dr
Ft Myers FL 33905-7114
Phone: 813-549-0523

St Nicholas GOA
2525 S 25th St
Ft Pierce FL 34981-5644
Phone: 561-464-7194
FAX: 561-464-2712

Ss Markella and Demetrios
PO Box 2135 GOA
Ft Walton Beach FL 32549
Phone: 850-244-0822
FAX: 850-243-7995

St Elizabeth GOA
5129 NW 53rd Ave
Gainsville FL 32653
Phone: 352-371-7258

St Mary's Protection UOA
6102 9th Ave S
Gulfport FL 33707-3155
Phone: 813-381-1619

Presentation of Our Lord CRC
5801 Grant St
Hollywood FL 33201
Phone: 305-987-8058

St Dimitrija MOC
Box 22-2467
Hollywood FL 33022-2467
Phone: 305-922-2755

St George GOA
425 N 58th Ave
Hollywood FL 33021-6213
Phone: 954-966-1898
FAX: 954-966-1906

Three Saints OCA
5801 Grant St
Hollywood FL 33021-5160
Phone:

St Michael the Archangel GOA
4705 W Gulf-to-Lake Hwy, Lecan
PO Box 241
Inverness FL 34451-0241
Phone: 352-527-0766

St Anne's Mission OCA
4518 Clinton Ave
Jacksonville FL 32207-6859
Phone:

St Augustine of Canterbury
1411 Belvedere Ave AOM
Jacksonville FL 32205
Phone:

St George ANT
1600 Ashland St
Jacksonville FL 32207-5435
Phone: 904-398-1855

St John the Divine GOA
3850 Atlantic Blvd
Jacksonville FL 32207-2033
Phone: 904-396-5383
FAX: 904-399-1547

St Justin Martyr OCA
8535-61 Bay Meadows Rd
Jacksonville FL 32256
Phone: 904-367-0570
FAX: 904-367-0570

St Herman of Alaska
OCA
7099 S Military Tr
Lake Worth FL 33463-7507
Phone: 561-968-5343

Ss. Cyril & Methodius
BEC
3829 Kewanee Rd
Lantana FL 33462-2213
Phone:

St Nicholas Mission ROR
6200 N University Dr
4206 Inverrary Blvd #79B
Lauderhill FL 33319-4139
Phone: 305-486-6320

Holy Trinity Mission OCA
St Petka Serbian Church
1900 Lake Emma Rd
Longwood FL 32750
Phone:

St Petka SOC
1990 Lake Emma Rd
Longwood FL 32750-7127
Phone: 407-831-SERB

Holy Trinity GOA
1217 Trinity Woods Lan
Maitland FL 32751
Phone: 407-331-4687
FAX: 407-331-4898

St Gerasimos VAS
2223 Dordon Dr
Melbourne FL 32935-3204
Phone:

St Katherine GOA
5965 N Wickham Rd
Melbourne FL 32940-2003
Phone: 407-254-1045
FAX: 407-254-1045

Christ the Savior Cathedral

16601 NW 77th Ct OCA
Miami FL 33015
Phone: 905-822-0437

Our Lady of Regla ANT
1920 SW 6th St
Miami FL 33135-3208
Phone: 305-642-7878

Ss. Peter & Paul OCA
1411 SW 11th St
Miami FL 33135-5301
Phone: 305-858-2924

St Andrew GOA
7901 N Kendall Dr
Miami FL 33156-7456
Phone: 305-595-1343
FAX: 305-595-1369

St Jude GOA
4269 SW 6th St
Miami FL 33134-1905
Phone: 305-445-0915

St Lazarus OCCA
1778 NW 3rd St
Miami FL 33125-4562
Phone: 305-649-1519
FAX: 305-649-1199

St Sophia Cathedral GOA
244 SW 24th Rd
Miami FL 33129
Phone: 305-854-2922
FAX: 305-855-1854

St Vladimir ROR
101 NW 46th Ave
Miami FL 33126-5361
Phone: 305-448-7087

Holy Trinity OCA
6033 SW 19th St
1850 SW 60th Ter
Miramar FL 33023-2906
Phone: 305-963-4790

Annunciation GOA
12250 NW 2nd Ave
N Miami FL 33168-4529
Phone: 305-681-1061
FAX: 305-687-0500

St Peter ANT
1811 NW 4th Ct
N Miami FL 33136-1201
Phone: 305-891-0425

St Simeon SOC
175 NW 154th St
N Miami FL 33169-6724
Phone: 305-944-6890

Eastern Orthodox Mission
620 94th Ave BAM
N Naples FL 33963
Phone:

St Sava NGM
PO Box 7978
N Port FL 34287-0978
Phone: 813-475-6811

St Demetrious OCA
140 Price St
Naples FL 34113
Phone: 941-775-8998

St Katharine GOA
7100 Airport Pulling Rd N
Naples FL 33942-1716
Phone: 941-591-3430
FAX: 941-591-3271

St Andrew the First-Called
4633 Glissade Dr OCA
New Port Richey FL 34652-5320
Phone: 813-847-9900

St George GOA
9426 Little Rd
New Port Richey FL 34654-3417
Phone: 813-868-5911
FAX: 813-869-9135

Holy Theotokos VAS
PO Box 301
Odessa FL 33556-0301
Phone:

St Benedict Mission AOM
3357-503 S Orange Ave
Orlando FL
Phone:

St George ANT
24 N Rosalind Ave
137 Wall St
Orlando FL 32801
Phone: 407-422-3230
FAX: 407-425-0683

St Barbara CRC
1533 Wake Forest Rd NW
Palm Bay FL 32907-8632
Phone: 407-952-2418

St Alexis of Wilkes-Barre Mission
St Stephen RC Ch, Bunnell FL OCA
c/o 50 Buttonworth D
Palm Coast FL 32137
Phone: 407-668-6020

Holy Sepulchre VAS
PO Box 2177
Palm Harbor FL 34682-2177
Phone:

St John the Theologian GOA
136 Baldwin Rd
PO Box 1933
Panama City FL 32402-1933
Phone: 904-769-3616

Annunciation GOA
1720 W Garden St
Pensacola FL 32501-4416
Phone: 904-433-2662
FAX: 904-433-9990

St Michael UCU
9201 60th St
Pinellas Park FL 34666-4815
Phone: 813-531-8804

St Nicholas ANT
PO Box 1730
Pinellas Park FL 34664-1730
Phone: 813-545-3797

Holy Trinity GOA
24411 Rampart Blvd
Port Charlotte FL 33949
Phone: 813-624-4896

St James 8CA
1712 SW Garnet St
2201 Airoso Blvd
Port St Lucie FL 34953-1405
Phone: 407-878-0338

Holy Trinity OCA
3265 SR 580
Safety Harbor FL 34695
Phone: 813-791-2273

St Barbara GOA
7671 N. Lockwood Ridge Blvd.
Sarasota FL 34243
Phone: 941-355-2616
FAX: 941-355-0013

St Luke OCCA
8021 Bayhaven Blvd
Seminole FL 33776
Phone: 813-398-1723

St Basil ANT
5200 NE 29th St
Silver Springs FL 34488-1702
Phone: 904-236-2080

Holy Trinity CRC
1120 Elgin Blvd
Spring Hill FL 34608-2110
Phone: 352-686-6050

Holy Trinity GOA
7 Waldo St
PO Box 949
St Augustine FL 32084-2718
Phone:

St Photios National Shrine
41 St George Stgoa
PO Box 1960
St Augustine FL 32084-3607
Phone: 904-829-8205

Holy Theotokos of Vladimir
310 13th Ave NE OCA
St Petersburg FL 33701
Phone: 813-823-2145

S. Stefanos GOA
3600 76th St N
St Petersburg FL 33710-1262
Phone: 813-345-8235
FAX: 813-395-8285

Holy Trinity OCA
301 38th St N
St Petersburg Bch FL 33713-7451
Phone: 813-327-4373

St Andrew ROR
4668 15th Ave S
St Petersburg Bch FL 33711-2326
Phone: 813-321-1639
FAX: 813-347-0672

St Sava SOC
530 77th Ave N
St Petersburg Bch FL 33702-4318
Phone: 813-527-8738

Holy Mother of God GOA
1647 Phillips Rd
Tallahassee FL 32308-5303
Phone: 904-878-0747
FAX: 904-878-0745

St Gregory the Theologian
9615 E Hillsborough Ave
PER
Tampa FL 33610-5927
Phone: 813-628-0026

St John the Baptist GOA
2418 W Swann Ave
Tampa FL 33609-4712
Phone: 813-876-8830
FAX: 813-877-4923

St Nicholas Cathedral GOA
16 Hibicus St
PO BOX 248
Tarpon Springs FL 34689-0248
Phone: 813-937-3540
FAX: 813-937-1739

GEORGIA

St Simeon   OCA
3175 Satterfield Rd
3060 Eads Ct
Titusville FL 32780
Phone: 407-268-8354

Holy Spirit   OCA
1629 Shamrock Blvd
Venice FL 34293
Phone: 813-485-2752

St Catherine   GOA
110 Southern Blvd
W Palm Beach FL 33405-2740
Phone: 561-833-6387
FAX: 561-833-6391

St Mary   ANT
1317 Florida Mango Rd
W Palm Beach FL 33406-5238
Phone: 407-965-5007

St Xenia Skete   VAS
PO Box 260
Wildwood FL 34785
Phone: 707-887-9740
FAX: 707-887-9023

St Sophia GOA
1030 Bradbury Rd
Winter Haven FL 33881
Phone: 941-299-4532

GEORGIA

Joy of All Who Sorrow
OCA
477 Allison Cir
PO Box 264
Alpharetta GA 30201-2130
Phone: 404-667-6407

St Philothea   GOA
1196 S Lumpkin St
Athens GA 30605
Phone:

Annunciation Cathedral
GOA
2500 Clairmont Rd NE
Atlanta GA 30329-2079
Phone: 404-633-5870
FAX: 404-633-6988

St Andrew   UCU
Atlanta GA
Phone: 404-476-0351

St Elias   ANT
2045 Ponce de Leon Ave NE
Atlanta GA 30307-1345
Phone: 404-378-8191
FAX: 404-378-8010

St John the Wonderworker
543 Cherokee Ave SE
VAS
Atlanta GA 30312-3248
Phone: 404-624-1442

St Michael the Archangel
ROR
1160 Reeder Cir NE
Atlanta GA 30306-3311
Phone: 404-875-1447

Tree of Life   VAS
543 Cherokee Ave SE
Atlanta GA 30312-3248
Phone:

Holy Trinity   GOA
953 Telfair St
Augusta GA 30901-2205
Phone: 706-724-1087
FAX: 706-724-3621

Ss. Cyril & Methodius
ROR
3110 Edinburgh Dr
Augusta GA 30909-3316
Phone: 706-738-0698

St George   GOA
401 Newcastle St
Brunswick GA 31520-8241
Phone:

Joy of All Who Sorrow
Church
6728 Campground Rd
ROR
2810 Napa Valley
Cumming GA 30041
Phone: 770-886-7111
FAX: 770-888-2267

St Andrew   UCU
2755 Kenwood Ct
Duluth GA 30136-3683
Phone: 404-476-0351

St Stephen   ANT
1047 Mitchell Rd
Hiram GA 30141
Phone: 770-489-0010
FAX: 770-489-0010

St John the Theologian
Mission
3082 Dempsey Pl
OCA
Lawrenceville GA 30244-4932
Phone: 770-931-0251

Ss. Constantine & Helen
OCA
64 Dickens Rd
Lilburn GA 30247
Phone: 770-935-0871

Holy Cross   GOA
3269 Bloomfield Dr
PO Box 31208
Macon GA 31206-4209
Phone:

St Innocent Mission OCA
St Paul Church, 735 College St
PO Box 18145
Macon GA 31209-8145
Phone: 912-741-6062
FAX: 912-477-3367

Holy Transfiguration GOA
3431 Trickum Rd
Marietta GA 30066-4660
Phone: 770-924-8080
FAX: 770-924-3030

Holy Resurrection   AUX
508 Glenleaf Dr
Norcross GA 30092-6105
Phone: 404-447-0785

Ss. Constantine & Helen
OCA
925 Beaver Ruin Rd
Norcross GA 30093-4802
Phone: 215-635-3720

HAWAII - IOWA - IDAHO - ILLINOIS

St Mary of Egypt   OCA
925 Beaver Ruin Rd
Norcross GA 30093
Phone: 770-923-7790

St Andrew   UCU
7207 Golden Isles Way
Savannah GA
Phone: 912-897-4378

St Mary Magdalene OCA
21 E Bay St
PO Box 15351
Savannah GA 31416-2051
Phone: 912-232-9222

St Paul   GOA
14 W Anderson St
Savannah GA 31401-6738
Phone: 912-236-8256
FAX: 912-236-8257

HAWAII

Iveron Mother of God
ROR
1031 Tenth Ave
Honolulu HI
Phone: 808-484-9047

Ss Constantine & Helen
GOA
930 Lunalilo St
Honolulu HI 96822
Phone: 808-521-7220
FAX: 808-523-0429

St Lazarus   SOC
PO Box 30224
Honolulu HI 96820-0224
Phone: 808-422-8822

St Sophia GMA
88-660 Homestead Rd.
Waianae HI 96792
Phone:

IOWA

St George   ANT
3650 Cottage Grove Ave SE
Cedar Rapids IA 52403-1652
Phone: 319-363-1559
FAX: 319-363-2996

St John the Baptist TOC
3635 Cottage Grove Ave SE
Cedar Rapids IA 52403
Phone: 319-362-8601
FAX: 319-363-4252

St John the Baptist ROR
3635 Cottage Grove Ave SE
Cedar Rapids IA 52403-1612
Phone: 319-362-8601
FAX: 319-363-4252

St George   GOA
35th & Cottage Grove Ave
Des Moines IA 50311
Phone: 515-277-0780
FAX: 515-277-0780

St Elias the Prophet GOA
1075 Rockdale Rd
Dubuque IA 52003-8739
Phone: 319-583-5902

Transfiguration of our Lord
1311 2nd St SW   GOA
Mason City IA 50401-1700
Phone: 515-423-6238

Radcliffe Orthodox Mission
R.R. 1, Box 87   VAS
Radcliffe IA 50230
Phone:

Holy Trinity   GOA
900 6th St
Sioux City IA 51105-1904
Phone: 712-255-5559

St Thomas   ANT
1100 Jones St
Box 1042
Sioux City IA 51105
Phone: 712-258-7166

St Demetrios   GOA
613 W 4th St
Waterloo IA 50702-1501
Phone: 319-232-4773

IDAHO

Orthodox Mission ANT
Boise ID

Ss. Constantine & Helen
GOA
2618 W Bannock St
Boise ID 83702-4705
Phone: 208-345-6147
FAX: 208-345-6147

St Seraphim of Sarov
ROR
872 N 29th St
Boise ID 83702-3122
Phone: 208-345-1553
FAX: 208-377-8865

St. John the Baptist ANT
4750 E 20th Ave
Post Falls ID 83877
Phone: 208-773-2876

Holy Apostles   UIU
PO Box 309
Osburn ID 83849-0309
Phone:

Assumption   GOA
528 N 5th Ave - PO BOX 4567
Pocatello ID 83201-6206
Phone: 208-232-5519

Holy Cross   UIU
1295 N Syringa St
Post Falls ID 83854-9021
Phone:

St Ignatius of Antioch
ANT
1830 Addison East
Twin Falls ID 83301
Phone: 208-734-3664

ILLINOIS

St Athanasios   GOA
1855 5th Ave
Aurora IL 60504-8776
Phone: 630-851-6106
FAX: 630-851-6186

Ss. Constantine & Helen
GOA
405 Huntwood Rd
Belleville IL 62221-8122
Phone: 618-277-0330

St John the Baptist NGM
405 Englewood Ave
Bellwood IL 60104-1745
Phone: 708-544-1524

Holy Dormition PER
304 N 4th St
Benld IL 62009-1306
Phone: 217-835-2202

Orthodox Community OCA
106 W. Chestnut St
Mailing: 907 S Oak St
Bloomington IL 61701
Phone: 309-821-9977

St Andrew UCU
300 E Army Trail Rd
Bloomingdale IL 60108-2158
Phone: 708-894-9717

St Mark GOA
2100 NW 51st St
Boca Raton IL 33431
Phone: 561-994-4822
FAX: 561-998-7875

Nativity of the Virgin Mary
McDyby St. OCA
Buckner IL 62819
Phone: 618-984-2144

Archangel Michael OCA
5037 W 83rd St
Burbank IL 60459-2748
Phone: 708-423-2441

Holy Virgin Protection
Hermitage
407 157th St PRC
Calumet City IL 60409-4703
Phone: 708-862-0868

St Basil DHE
217 S Maple St
Centralia IL 62801-3527
Phone: 618-532-4456

Three Hierarchs GOA
2010 Three Hierarchs Ct
Champaign IL 61820-7232
Phone: 217-352-3452

Annunciation Cathedral
GOA
1017 N. LaSalle Blvd.
Chicago IL 60610
Phone: 312-664-5485
FAX: 312-626-5921

Archangels Michael and
Gabriel
6352 N Paulina St OCA
Chicago IL 60660-1124
Phone: 317-577-7838

Assumption GOA
601 S Central Ave
Chicago IL 60644-5059
Phone: 312-626-3114
FAX: 312-626-3115

Holy Archangel Michael
SOC
9815 S Commercial Ave
Chicago IL 60617-5439
Phone: 312-375-3848

Holy Nativity OCA
6350 N Paulina St
Chicago IL 60660-1124
Phone: 312-743-9648

Holy Resurrection NGM
3062 Palmer Sq.
Chicago IL 60647
Phone: 312-252-4452

Holy Resurrection SOC
5701 N. Redwood Dr.
Chicago IL 60631-2933
Phone: 312-693-3366
FAX: 312-693-7615

Holy Trinity GOA
6041 W Diversey Ave
Chicago IL 60639-1139
Phone: 312-622-5979
FAX: 312-622-8833

Holy Trinity Cathedral
OCA
1121 N Leavitt St
Chicago IL 60622-3502
Phone: 312-486-6064

Pokrov Cathedral UOA
2710 W Iowa St
Chicago IL 60622-4427
Phone:

Ss. Athanasius & John the
Baptist
4200 N Keeler Ave GMA
Chicago IL 60641-2298
Phone: 773-286-3735
FAX: 773-286-3753

Ss. Peter & Paul OCA
53rd St. & S. Western Ave.
Chicago IL 60609
Phone: 708-963-1076

Ss. Raphael & Markella
VAS
Chicago IL
Phone:

St Andrew GOA
5649 N Sheridan Rd
Chicago IL 60660-4803
Phone: 312-334-4515

St Archangel Michael
SOC
9805 Commercial Ave
Chicago IL 60617
Phone: 773-375-3848
FAX: 773-375-3586

St Basil GOA
733 S Ashland Ave
Chicago IL 60607-3103
Phone: 312-243-3738
FAX: 312-243-7961

St Demetrios GOA
2727 W Winona St
Chicago IL 60625-2508
Phone: 312-561-5992

St George BYC
1500 N Maplewood Ave
Chicago IL 60622-1643
Phone: 312-384-5654

St George GOA
2701 N Sheffield Ave
Chicago IL 60614-1326
Phone: 312-525-1793

St George Cathedral OCA
917 N Wood St
Chicago IL 60622-5005
Phone: 312-666-5179

St Mary   OCA
4225 N Central Ave
Chicago IL 60634-1811
Phone: 312-736-1153

St Nicholas   ADA
2701 N Narragansett Ave
Chicago IL 60639-1031
Phone: 312-889-4282

St Nikola NGM
2754 S Central Park Ave
Chicago IL 60623-4632
Phone: 312-522-9643

St Simeon Mirotocivi NGM
3737 E 114th St
Chicago IL 60617-7408
Phone: 312-731-2925

St Sophia BEC
3827 N Lawndale Ave
Chicago IL 60618
Phone: 312-588-1478

St Sophia UCU
6655 W Higgins Ave
Chicago IL 60656-2155
Phone: 312-631-3112

St Stevan of Decani NGM
3543 W Leland Ave
Chicago IL 60625-5834
Phone: 312-539-0818

St Volodymyr Cathedral UCU
2230-50 W Cortez St.
Chicago IL 60622
Phone: 708-596-7316

St George   ANT
1220 S 60th Ct
Cicero IL 60650-1005
Phone: 708-656-2927
FAX: 708-656-1166

St Nicholas   UOA
17624 Maple Ave
Country Club Hills IL 60478-4758
Phone: 708-799-1023

Annunciation   GOA
570 N Union St
Decatur IL 62522-2126
Phone: 217-429-7023

St George   GOA
320 S 2nd St
Dekalb IL 60115-3718
Phone: 815-758-5731

Holy Protection Cathedral ROR
1800 Lee St
Des Plaines IL 60018-2024
Phone: 847-298-4144

St John the Baptist GOA
2350 E Dempster St
Des Plaines IL 60016-4839
Phone: 847-827-5519
FAX: 847-824-3455

Assumption   GOA
4900 Kennedy Dr
E Moline IL 61244-4256
Phone: 309-792-2912

St Sophia GOA
525 Church Rd
Elgin IL 601239307
Phone: 847-888-2822

St Demetrios   GOA
893 N Church Rd
Elmhurst IL 60126-1005
Phone: 708-834-7010

Holy Ancestors of Christ Ss. Joachim & Anna   UOA
1124 Londonberry Ln
Glen Ellyn IL 60137-6110
Phone: 708-495-1807

Ss. Peter & Paul   GOA
1401 Wagner Rd
Glenview IL 60025-2305
Phone: 847-729-2235

St Mary   ANT
PO Box 616
Goshen IL 46527-0616
Phone: 219-534-8410
Ss. Cyril & Methody OCA
4770 Maryville Rd # 1303
Granite City IL 62040-2522
Phone: 618-931-6465

Assumption   GOA
13631 S Brainard Ave
Hegewisch IL 60633-1847
Phone: 312-646-2999

St Nicholas   UOA
17935 Springfield Ave
Homewood IL 60430-2619
Phone: 708-799-1023

All Saints GOA
102 N Broadway St
Joliet IL 60435-7439
Phone: 815-722-1727

St George   SOC
300 Stryker Ave
Joliet IL 60436-1328
Phone: 815-725-5502

St Nicholas   OCA
1018 Barber Ln
Joliet IL 60435-2918
Phone: 815-725-4742

St Sava   NGM
3457 Black Rd
Joliet IL 60435-8400
Phone:

Holy Cross   GOA
7560 S Archer Ave
Justice IL 60458-1151
Phone: 708-594-2040

Annunciation   GOA
296 N Washington Ave
Kankakee IL 60901-3761
Phone: 815-933-5482

St Christopher's Mission CRC
LaSalle IL 61302-0536
Phone: 815-226-8089

New St. George   RMA
17601 Wentworth Ave
Lansing IL 60438-2074
Phone: 708-474-4810

Holy Trinity   BEC
1300 Grand Ave
Madison IL 62060-1254
Phone:

Nativity of Virgin Mary
OCA
416 Ewing Ave.
Madison IL 62060-1456
Phone: 618-451-9995

Holy Taxiarhai & St
Haralambos
7373 Caldwell Ave   GOA
Niles IL 60714
Phone: 847-674-8880

St Michael   CRC
7313 Waukegan Rd
Niles IL 60648
Phone: 312-647-8398

St Nicholas   GOA
10301 S Kolmar Ave
Oak Lawn IL 60453-4845
Phone: 708-636-5460

Assumption   GOA
20401 Western Ave
Olympia Fields IL 60461-1530
Phone: 708-748-3040

Holy Resurrection   OCA
1449 N Quentin Rd
Palatine IL 60067-2057
Phone: 708-358-7291

St Nectarios   GOA
133 S Roselle Rd
Palatine IL 60067-5855
Phone: 708-358-5170

St Spyridon   GOA
12307 S Ridgeland Ave
Palos Heights IL 60463-1855
Phone: 708-385-0787

Ss. Constantine & Helen
GOA
11025-45 S. Roberts Rd.
Palos Hills IL 60465
Phone: 708-974-3400
FAX: 708-974-0179

St Luke the Evangelist
OCA
10700 S. Kean
Palos Hills IL 60465
Phone: 630-243-0893

Ss. Peter & Paul   UCU
8410 W 131st St
Palos Park IL 60464-2122
Phone: 708-448-1350
FAX: 708-361-5179

St Joseph OCA
7900 W 120th St
Palos Park IL 60464-1271
Phone: 708-361-1684

All Saints GOA
1812 N Prospect Rd
Peoria IL 61603-3329
Phone: 309-682-5824

St Vladimir   ROR
Vladimorovo-Lost Lake
Rock City IL 61070
Phone: 815-968-6351

St George   GOA
2930 31st Ave
Rock Island IL 61201
Phone: 309-786-8163
FAX: 309-786-8188

Christ the Saviour   CRC
1802 Pershing Ave
Rockford IL 61109-1246
Phone: 815-226-8089

Ss Constantine & Helen
GOA
108 N 5th St
Rockford IL 61107
Phone: 815-963-8625
FAX: 815-963=8646

St Vladimir   ROR
4859 Huxley Dr
Rockford IL 61101-9003
Phone: 815-968-6351

Protection of the Holy Virgin
Mary
P.O. Box 307   OCA
Royalton IL 62983-0307
Phone: 618-984-2144

St George   ANT
211 E Minnesota St
PO Box 143
Spring Valley IL 61362
Phone: 815-664-4540

St Anthony   GOA
1600 S Glenwood Ave
Springfield IL 62704-3611
Phone: 217-522-7010

St Panteleimon   OCA
7545 W 61st Pl
Summit Argo IL 60501-1617
Phone: 708-458-2575

Ss Constantine & Helen
Orthodox Church   GOA
405 Huntwood Rd
Swansea IL 62226
Phone: 618-277-0330

St Demetrios   GOA
1217 North Ave
Waukegan IL 60085-2941
Phone: 847-623-0190

St Nicholas   SOC
228 N County St
Waukegan IL 60085-4220
Phone: 708-336-9838

Holy Transfiguration ANT
247 N Neltnor Blvd Apt F2H
West Chicago IL 60185-2336
Phone:

Holy Transfiguration ANT
1N075 Woods Ave
Wheaton IL 60187-2983
Phone: 708-510-9934

INDIANA

St Joseph　OCA
412 Crescent St
7900 W 120 St
Wheaton IL 60187
Phone: 708-361-1684
FAX: 708-923-1706

Ss. Anargyroi-St. Nectarios　CHR
11360 S Lawler Ave
Worth IL 60482-2240
Phone: 708-371-1800

INDIANA

Ss Peter & Paul　MOC
9660 Broadway
Crown Point IN 46307
Phone: 219-662-9114

Our Lady Queen of Angels　UAC
4216 Baring Ave
E Chicago IN 46312
Phone:

St George　IND
4019-21 Elm St
E Chicago IN 46312
Phone: 219-398-2333
FAX: 219-836-2909

Holy Ghost　CRC
4413 Olcott Ave
East Chicago IN 46312-2651
Phone: 219-864-9820

St George　NGM
4021 Elm St
East Chicago IN 46312-2816
Phone: 219-397-0240

Holy Ascension　UCU
2902 Evans St
Fort Wayne IN 46806-1436
Phone: 219-440-0269

Holy Trinity　ROR
2402 Smith St
Fort Wayne IN 46803-3250
Phone: 219-432-9742

Holy Trinity　GOA
5420 S Anthony Blvd
Fort Wayne IN 46806-3316
Phone: 219-489-0774

St John Chrysostom　ANT
639 Putnam St
Fort Wayne IN 46808-2430
Phone: 219-424-0615

St Nicholas　OCA
3535 Crescent Ave
Fort Wayne IN 46805-1507
Phone: 219-484-2277

Archangels Michael and Gabriel　OCA
2902 Evans St
Ft Wayne IN
Phone: 317-577-7838

St Mary　RMA
Ft Wayne IN
Phone: 708-895-4810

St Volodymyr　UOD
Drezel & St Anthony
Ft Wayne IN 48606
Phone:

Descent of the Holy Ghost　OCA
750 W 61st Ave
Gary IN 46410-2522
Phone: 219-980-0374

Protection of Virgin Mary　OCA
505 E 45th Ave
Gary IN 46409-2234
Phone: 219-887-4663

Ss Peter & Paul　MOC
51st & Virginia
Gary IN 46409
Phone:

St Clement of Ohrid　OCA
5444 Harrison St
Gary IN 46410-1467
Phone: 219-884-3211

St Elijah Cathedral　SOC
8700 Taft St
Gary IN 46410-6903
Phone: 219-769-2122

St Nicholas　CRC
2582 Newton St
Gary IN 46405
Phone: 219-962-2882

St Sava　NGM
9191 Mississippi St
PO Box 2106
Gary IN 46410
Phone: 219-736-9191
FAX: 219-736-7836

Holy Trinity　UCU
61302 C.R. 21
Goshen IN 46526
Phone: 708-795-0841

Protection　ROR
61355 County Rd 21
Goshen IN 46528-9692
Phone: 219-534-2375

St Mary　ANT
PO Box 616
Goshen IN 46527-0616
Phone: 219-534-8410

St Demetrios　GOA
7021 HOhman Ave
Hammond IN 46324
Phone: 219-932-7347
FAX: 219-932-7136

St Demetrios　GOA
7021 Hohman Ave
Hammond IN 46324-1813
Phone: 219-932-7347

St Michael　UCU
7035 Columbia Ave
Hammond IN 46324
Phone: 219-844-6483
FAX: 219-696-4250

Holy Resurrection　ANT
305 E 6th St
Hobart IN 46342-5135
Phone: 219-942-2592

St Nicholas　CRC
954 State St
Hobart IN 46342
Phone: 219-942-5981

KANSAS - KENTUCKY

Holy Trinity GOA
4011 N Pennsylvania St
Indianapolis IN 46205-2608
Phone: 317-283-3816
FAX: 317-920-0726

Ss. Constantine & Elena
OCA
3237 W 16th St
Indianapolis IN 46222-2704
Phone: 317-638-4162

St George ANT
4020 N Sherman Dr
Indianapolis IN 46226-4464
Phone: 317-547-9356
FAX: 317-547-4520

St Nikola NGM
3626 W 16th St
Indianapolis IN 46222-2502
Phone:

St Stephen BEC
1435 N Medford
Indianapolis IN 46222
Phone:

St Thomas OCA
Kokomo IN
Phone: 317-452-7535

St Clement MOC
5444 Harrison St.
Merillville IN

Ss Constantine & Helen
Cathedral GOA
8000 Madison St
Merrillville IN 46410-5404
Phone: 219-769-2481

Holy Trinity UCU
7396 Johnson Rd
Michigan City IN 46360-9280
Phone: 219-879-7575

St George ANT
303 Grace St
Michigan City IN 46360-4923
Phone: 219-874-5831
FAX: 219-874-4557

St George GOA
528 77th Ave
Schererville IN 46375
Phone: 219-322-6168

St George SOC
905 E Joliet St
Schererville IN 46375-2234
Phone: 219-322-3355
FAX: 219-322-9702

Ss Peter & Paul SOC
59262 Keria Tr
South Bend IN 46614
Phone: 219-291-0937

St Andrew GOA
52455 Ironwood Rd
South Bend IN 46635-1124
Phone: 219-277-4688

St George
1900 S 4th St
Terre Haute IN 47802
Phone: 812-232-5244

St Iakovos GOA
602 E Monroe St
Valoparaiso IN 46383
Phone: 219-462-4052
FAX: 219-531-0702

KANSAS

Holy Trinity OCA
558 Lowell Ave
Kansas City KS 66101-3838
Phone: 913-342-4552

St Archangel Michael
NGM
310 N 72nd St
Kansas City KS 66112-3135
Phone: 913-788-5845

St George SOC
50 S Bethany St
Kansas City KS 66102-5508
Phone: 913-371-1648

St Dionysios GOA
8100 W 95th St
Overland Park KS 66212-3214
Phone: 913-341-7373

Ss Peter & Paul ANT
2516 SW 29TH #F158
Topeka KS 66604-1501
Phone: 913-271-6441

Holy Trinity GOA
805 N Dellrose St
Wichita KS 67208
Phone: 316-681-1165

St George Cathedral
ANT
7515 E 13th St
Wichita KS 67206
Phone: 316-636-4676
FAX: 316-636-5628

St Mary Orthodox Church
ANT
344 S Martinson
Wichita KS 67213-4044
Phone: 316-264-1576

KENTUCKY

Panagia Pantovasilissa
GOA
920 Tates Creek Rd
Lexington KY 40502-2203
Phone: 606-266-1921

St Andrew ANT
1136 Higbee Mill Rd
Lexington KY 40503
Phone: 606-223-5091

Assumption GOA
932 S 5th
Louisville KY 40203
Phone: 502-587-6247

St Michael ANT
3026 Hikes Ln
Louisville KY 40220-2017
Phone: 502-452-1930

St Michael the Archangel
Orthodox Church ANT
3026 Hikes Ln
Louisville KY 40220
Phone: 502-454-3378
FAX: 502-454-3378

LOUSIANA

St John   OCC
Rt 1 Box 333 Highway 3257
Barataria Island LA 70036
Phone: 504-689-2489
FAX: 504-689-2480

Greek Orthodox Community
GOA
PO Box 126
Baton Rouge LA 70821-0126
Phone:

St John the Evangelist
IND
20043 Highway 36
Covington LA 70433
Phone: 504-893-3575

Holy Innocents   OCCA
311 Hickory Ave
Harahan LA 70123
Phone: 504-738-3502
FAX: 504-737-7707

St John the Divine   ANT
5732 Bennie Ln
Lake Charles LA 70605-7144
Phone: 318-474-2004

St Basil   ANT
3916 Hudson St
Metairie LA 70006
Phone: 504-888-8114
FAX: 504-779-0709

Ss. Constantine & Helen
GOA
2011 Forsythe Ave
Monroe LA 71201-3608
Phone: 318-325-1764

Holy Innocents   HOC
311 Hickory Ave
New Orleans LA 70123-4035
Phone: 504-738-3502

Holy Trinity Cathedral
GOA
1200 Robert E Lee Blvd
New Orleans LA 70122-1337
Phone: 504-282-0259
FAX: 504-283-5586

St George   GOA
1719 Creswell Ave
Shreveport LA 71101-4725
Phone: 318-222-5225

MASSACHUSETTS

Holy Resurrection   VAS
64 Harvard Ave
Allston MA 02134-1707
Phone: 617-787-7625

Ss Constantine & Helen
GOA
71 Chandler Rd
Andover MA 01810
Phone: 978-470-0919
FAX: 978-470-0919

St Anthanasius the Great
GOA
735 Massachusetts Ave
Arlington MA 02174-4788
Phone: 781-646-0705
FAX: 781-648-6746

Annunciation Cathedral
GOA
Parker & Ruggles Sts.
Boston MA 02146
Phone: 617-731-6633
FAX: 617-730-2978

Holy Trinity   ADA
245 D St
PO Box 224
Boston MA 02127-1919
Phone: 617-268-8708

Holy Trinity Cathedral
OCA
165 Park Dr
Boston MA 02215-4703
Phone: 617-262-9490

St George's Cathedral
OCA
523 E Broadway
Boston MA 02127-4415
Phone: 617-268-1275
FAX: 617-268-3184

St John the Baptist   OCA
410 W Broadway
Boston MA 02127-2215
Phone: 617-268-3564

Annunciation   GOA
457 Oak St
Brockton MA 02401-1340
Phone: 508-559-0910

Annunciation Cathedral
GOA
162 Goddard Ave
Brookline MA 02146
Phone: 617-731-6633
FAX: 617-730-2978

St Sava   SOC
4 Angela Cl
Burlington MA 01803
Phone:

Ss. Constantine & Helen
GOA
14 Magazine St
Cambridge MA 02139-3965
Phone: 617-876-3601

St Mary   ANT
8 Inman St
Cambridge MA 02139-2407
Phone: 617-547-1234

St George   GOA
1130 Falmouth Rd
Centerville MA 02632-3022
Phone: 508-775-3045
FAX: 508-775-3091

Nativity of the Virgin Mary
OCA
8 Addison St
Chelsea MA 02150-2413
Phone: 508-697-3928

Ss Constantine & Helen GOA
30 Grattan St
PO BOX 112
Chicopee MA 01020-1328
Phone: 413-592-3401

St Nicholas GOA
132 School St
PO BOX 81
Clinton MA 01510-2915
Phone: 508-365-9089

Nativity of the Virgin Mary GOA
811 Jerusalem Rd
Cohasset MA 02025
Phone: 617-383-6380
FAX: 617-383-2975
St John of Damascus ANT
300 West St
Dedham MA 02026-5594
Phone: 617-326-3046

St Luke GOA
400 Prospect St
PO Box 381
E Longmeadow MA 01028-3154
Phone: 413-525-4551

St Demetrios GOA
289 N Main St
Fall River MA 02720-2320
Phone: 508-672-2121
FAX: 508-345-5589

St Michael Mission ANT
PO Box 534
Falmouth MA 02541
Phone: 781-762-4396
FAX: 781-255-1871

Holy Trinity GOA
1319 Main St
Fitchburg MA 01420-6922
Phone: 508-342-1216
FAX: 508-345-5589

Holy Apostles Ss. Peter & Paul GOA
154-156 Winter St
Haverhill MA 01830
Phone: 508-373-3211

St Xenia ROR
55 Wingate St
Haverhill MA 01832-5536
Phone: 508-521-0253

Holy Trinity GOA
410 Main St
Holyoke MA 01040-5610
Phone: 413-533-9880

Assumption GOA
8 Lafayette Rd
PO BOX 6
Ipswich MA 01938-1820
Phone: 508-356-9798

St John the Confessor AUX
244 High St
Ipswich MA 01938-1249
Phone: 508-356-5303

St John the Russian ROR
16 Mt Pleasant Ave
Ipswich MA 01938
Phone: 978-356-1207
FAX: 978-356-0259

St Andrew UCU
24 Orchard Hill Rd
Jamaica Plain MA 02130
Phone: 617-522-3323
FAX: 617-522-6123

St Mark of Ephesus OCA
261 Main St
PO BOX 261
Kingston MA 02364-1910
Phone: 617-585-8907

St George ANT
8 Lowell St
Lawrence MA
Phone: 508-685-4052

St Nicholas GOA
17 Meriam St
Lexington MA 02173
Phone: 781-862-6453
FAX: 781-862-5612

Assumption GOA
72 Butterfield St
PO BOX 1752
Lowell MA 01854-3407
Phone: 508-458-8684

Holy Trinity GOA
Lewis St
Lowell MA 01854
Phone: 508-458-8092
FAX: 508-970-0935

St George ANT
61 Bowers St
44 Bowers St
Lowell MA 01854
Phone: 978-452-4816

Transfiguration of Our Savior GOA
Fr. John Serantos Way
Lowell MA 01854-3599
Phone: 508-458-4321
FAX: 508-458-8726

St George GOA
11 Church St
Lynn MA 01902-4442
Phone: 617-593-6162

Ss Anargyroi GOA
PO Box 381
Marlborough MA 01752-0381
Phone: 508-485-2575

Holy Annunciation OCA
15 Prospect St
PO BOX 604
Maynard MA 01754-1314
Phone: 617-395-7793

St George ANT
103 Pleasant St
Methuen MA 01844-7130
Phone: 508-685-4052

St Xenia of Petersburg ROR
PO Box 147
Methuen MA 01844-0147
Phone: 978-688-1211

Annunciation OCA
37 Washington St
Natick MA 01760-3520
Phone: 508-655-7927

Greek Orthodox Mission MAT
60 Mott St
New Bedford MA 02744-2307
Phone:

House Chapel MAT
60 Mott St
New Bedford MA 02744-2307
Phone:

St George GOA
87 Ashley Blvd
New Bedford MA 02746-1909
Phone: 508-996-5913

Annunciation GOA
Harris and Park Sts
PO Box 575
Newburyport MA 01950-0775
Phone: 508-465-5757

St George ANT
6 Atwood Ave
Norwood MA 02062-4102
Phone: 781-762-4396
FAX: 781-255-1871

St Vasilios GOA
5 Paleologos St
Peabody MA 01960-4496
Phone: 978-531-0777

St George GOA
73 Bradford St
Pittsfield MA 01201-4523
Phone: 413-442-8113

St Nicholas OCA
76 Wahconah St
Pittsfield MA 01201-2607
Phone: 413-442-2669

St Catherine GOA
157 Beale St
Quincy MA 02170-3340
Phone: 617-773-2545

Holy Epiphany ROR
963 South St
Roslindale MA 02131-2309
Phone: 617-327-3663

Holy Protection GMA
22 Cedrus Ave
Roslindale MA 02131-4135
Phone: 617-524-4724
FAX: 617-524-7142

St Anna AUX
852 South St
Roslindale MA 02131-2448
Phone: 617-327-5300

St Mark of Epesus Cathedral AUX
850 South St # 129
Roslindale MA 02131-2448
Phone: 617-469-2380

St Nektarios GOA
39 Belgrade Ave
PO BOX 12
Roslindale MA 02131-3025
Phone: 617-327-1983

St John the Baptist GOA
15 Union Park St
Roxbury MA 02118-2129
Phone: 617-536-5692

St Nicholas OCA
64 Forrester St
Salem MA 01970-4038
Phone: 508-744-5869

Ss Peter and Paul FOCI
PO Box 43
Seekonk MA 02771-0043
Phone:

St Gregory the Theologian
1 Merchant St GOA
Sharon MA 02067-1662
Phone: 617-784-7822
FAX: 617-784-0827

Dormition of the Virgin Mary
29 Central St GOA
Somerville MA 02143-2841
Phone: 617-625-2222
FAX: 617-628-4529

St George GOA
55 North St
PO BOX 25
Southbridge MA 01550-2530
Phone: 508-764-3398

St Michael RMA
16 Roumanian Ave
PO BOX 823
Southbridge MA 01550-2740
Phone: 508-765-5276

St Nicholas OCA
126 Morris St
Southbridge MA 01550-2724
Phone: 508-764-6226

St Ambrose of Milan AOM
PO Box 1016
Southwick MA 01077-1016
Phone: 860-741-0436

Ss Peter & Paul OCA
118 Carew St
Springfield MA 01104-3405
Phone: 413-734-8472

St George Cathedral GOA
8 Plainfield St
Springfield MA 01104-3314
Phone: 413-737-1496

St George ANT
55 Emmonsdale Rd
PO Box 164
W Roxbury MA 02132-0002
Phone: 617-323-0323
FAX: 617-323-6301

Taxiarchai GOA
25 Bigelow Ave
Watertown MA 02172-2041
Phone: 617-924-8182

MARYLAND

Ss Constantine & Helen GOA
PO Box 583
Webster MA 01570-0583
Phone: 508-943-8361

Our Lady of Kazan OCA
Box 212
W Hyannisport MA 02672-0212
Phone: 508-775-8978

St George ANT
55 Emmonsdale Rd
W Roxbury MA 02132-6428
Phone: 617-323-0323
FAX: 617-323-5301

St Nicholas ROR
23 Southworth St
W Springfield MA 01089-2722
Phone: 413-598-0118

St Demetrios GOA
57 Brown St
PO Box 463
Weston MA 02193
Phone: 781-237-5561
FAX: 781-237-8612

Annunciation GOA
70 Montvale Ave
Woburn MA 01801-4254
Phone: 617-935-2424

Assumption of the Virgin Mary OCA
535 Salisbury St
Worcester MA 01609-1307
Phone: 508-756-1690

Holy Resurrection AUX
63 Laurel St
Worcester MA 01605-3069
Phone: 508-752-7813

Ss Peter and Paul OCA
Rochester NY
Box 3142 Main PO
Worcester MA 01613-3142
Phone: 508-754-3451

St George Cathedral ANT
30 Anna St
Worcester MA 01604-1130
Phone: 617-752-9150

St Mary Assumption OCA
535 Salisbury St
Worcester MA 01609
Phone: 508-756-1690
FAX: 508-756-0962

St Nicholas RMA
PO Box 643
Worcester MA 01613-0643
Phone: 508-799-0040
FAX: 508-799-0040

St Spyridon GOA
102 Russell St
Worcester MA 01609-1908
Phone: 508-791-7326
FAX: 508-754-3054

MARYLAND

Ss Constantine & Helen GOA
4 Constitution Ave
Annapolis MD 21401-3513
Phone: 410-263-2550
FAX: 410-280-1625

Annunciation Cathedral GOA
24 W Preston St
Baltimore MD 21201-5700
Phone: 410-727-1831
FAX: 410-727-7602

Holy Transfiguration ROR
2201 E Baltimore St
Baltimore MD 21231-2002
Phone: 410-732-1022

Holy Trinity PER
1723 E Fairmount Ave
Baltimore MD 21231-1516
Phone: 301-732-1824
FAX: None

St Andrew OCA
2028 E Lombard St
Baltimore MD 21231-1923
Phone: 410-276-3422
FAX: 410-947-0629

St Demetrios GOA
PO BOX 28218
Baltimore MD 21234-1006
Phone: 410-661-1090

St Michael UCU
2019 Gough St
Baltimore MD 21231-2616
Phone: 301-327-2840

St Nicholas GOA
520 Ponca St
Baltimore MD 21224-4524
Phone: 410-633-5020
FAX: 410-633-4352

Ss Peter & Paul ANT
7108 Bradley Blvd
Bethesda MD 20817
Phone: 301-365-0932
FAX: 301-365-3217

St George GOA
7701 Bradley Blvd
Bethesda MD 20817-1442
Phone: 301-469-7990
FAX: 301-469-5945

St George OCA
6219 Rockhurst Rd
Bethesda MD 20817-1755
Phone:

St Mark OCA
7124 River Rd
Bethesda MD 20817-4770
Phone: 301-229-6300
FAX: 301-229-1559

St Matthew OCA
PO Box 2003
Columbia MD 21045-1003
Phone: 410-992-0608
FAX: 410-992-7760

Ss Peter and Paul GOA
920 W 7th St St
Frederick MD 21701
Phone: 301-663-0663

MAINE - MICHIGAN

St Catherine the Great
Martyr   OCA
433 Liberty St
Hagerstown MD 21740
Phone: 301-790-2616

St Mary   ANT
909 Shawn Rd
PO Box 594
Hunt Valley MD 21030-0594
Phone: 410-785-5656

St Theodore   GOA
7101 Cipriano Rd
Lanham MD 20706-3808
Phone: 301-552-3540

St Cosmas Aitolos AUX
11812 Randy Ln
Laurel MD 20708-2830
Phone: 301-776-3189

Holy Cross   ANT
105 Camp Meade Rd
Linthicum MD 21090-2142
Phone: 410-362-6620
FAX: 945-7046
FatherGMG@aol.com

St George   GOA
8805 Coastal Hwy
Ocean City MD 21842-2739
Phone: 410-524-0990
FAX: 410-524-6772

Holy Resurrection   CRC
10201 Democracy Blvd
Potomac MD 20854-4439
Phone: 301-299-5120

St Cosmas Aitolos AUX
6300 Kenilworth Ave
Riverdale MD 20737-1210
Phone: 301-776-3189

St John the Theologian
OCA
St Paul Luthern Church
825 Harrington Rd
Rockville MD 20852
Phone: 301-424-7730

St Andrew Cathedral
UCU
15100 New Hampshire Ave
Silver Spring MD 20905-5629
Phone: 301-384-9192

Holy Trinity   UCU
PO Box 44
Whaleyville MD 21872-0044
Phone: 301-835-8661

MAINE

St George   GOA
90 Sanford St
Bangor ME 04401-6132
Phone: 207-945-9588

St Demetrios   GOA
35 Adams St
PO BOX 605
Biddeford ME 04005-2510
Phone: 207-284-5651

St Alexander Nevsky
ROR
33 Mt Vernon St
Gardiner ME 04345-1817
Phone: 207-737-2365

Holy Trinity   GOA
155 Hogan Rd
PO Box 1344
Lewiston ME 04240-2400
Phone: 207-783-6795

Holy Trinity   GOA
133 Pleasant St.
Portland ME 04101
Phone: 207-774-0281

Holy Trinity Chapel OCC
10 Sherman St #2
Portland ME 04101
Phone: 207-761-6583

Holy Cross   UOD
Richmond ME 04357
Phone:

St Alexander Nervsky
ROR
15 Church St
PO Box 45
Richmond ME 04357
Phone: 207-582-8656

Holy Nativity   ROR
967 Broadway
S Portland ME 04106
Phone: 207-767-2330

Holy Nativity   VAS
16 Channel Rd
S Portland ME 04106-5107
Phone:

MICHIGAN

Holy Ascension   OCA
810 Austin Ave
Albion MI 49224-1006
Phone: 517-629-3626

St Nicholas   GOA
414 N Main St
Ann Arbor MI 48104-1134
Phone: 313-769-2945

St Vladimir Mission ROR
9900 Jackson Rd, Dexter MI
PO Box 2072
Ann Arbor MI 48106-2072
Phone: 313-761-2072

Ss Sergius and Herman of
Valaam Mission   ROR
506 Erickson Dr
PO Box 136
Atlantic Mine MI 49905-0136
Phone: 906-487-7013
FAX: 906-487-7013

Ss Constantine & Helen
GOA
1020 W Goguac St
Battle Creek MI 49015-1753
Phone:

St Elias   PER
5066 B Dr S
Battle Creek MI 49017-8313
Phone: 616-979-2146

Christ the Saviour ROR
817 Thresher Ave
Benton Harbor MI 49022-3339
Phone: 616-925-7922

St Mary ANT
3212 12 Mile Rd
Berkley MI 48072-1357
Phone: 313-545-9451

St George GOA
1515 N Woodward Ave
Bloomfield Hills MI 48304-2848
Phone: 810 335-8869
FAX: 810-335-2140

St Andrew ANT
42250 Hayes Rd
Clinton Township MI 48038-3637
Phone: 313-286-7212

Holy Trinity UCU
7108 Normile St
Dearborn MI 48126-1950
Phone: 313-581-8781

St Clement of Ohrid BEC
1900 Ford Rd
Dearborn MI 48128
Phone:

Ss. Peter & Paul Cathedral OCA
750 N Beech Daly Rd
Dearborn Heights MI 48127-3459
Phone: 313-274-9651
FAX: 313-274-9640

All Saints Cathedral OCA
2918 E Hendrie Ave
Detroit MI 48211
Phone:

Annunciation Cathedral GOA
707 E Lafayette Blvd
Detroit MI 48226-2926
Phone: 313-965-2988
FAX: 313-965-2428

Holy Trinity OCA
20500 Anglin
Detroit MI 48234
Phone: 313-366-0677

Incarnation ANT
10331 Dexter Ave
Detroit MI 48206-1420
Phone: 313-361-0110

Romanian Orthodox Archdiocese RMA
19995 Riopelle Ave
Detroit MI 48203
Phone: 313-893-8390

Ss Peter & Paul OCA
3800 Gilbert & Clayton Sts
Detroit MI 48210
Phone: 313-897-3308

St Andrew UOD
5130 Prescott St
Detroit MI 48212-4100
Phone:

St Lazarus-Ravanica Cathedral
4575 E Outer Dr
Detroit MI 48234
Phone: 313-893-6025
FAX: 313-892-6944

St Petka SOC
18040 Van Dyke St
Detroit MI 48234-3651
Phone: 313-893-4858

St Spyridon GOA
19405 Renfrew Rd
Detroit MI 48221-1835
Phone: 313-864-5433

St Vladimir ROR
9900 Jackson Rd
Dexter MI 48130-9426
Phone: 313-761-7311

St Andrew PER
1222 Greencrest Ave
East Lansing MI 48823-2906
Phone: 517-351-4627

All Saints ROR
22312 Kelley Rd
Eastpointe MI 48021
Phone: 810-777-6435

Holy Spirit BAM
14873 Collinson Ave
Eastpointe MI 48021-2861
Phone:

Great Martyr George & St Nectarios CHR
4592 W Jefferson Ave
Ecorse MI 48229-1417
Phone: 313-451-2197

Holy Ascension NGM
4337 W Jeffords St
Ecorse MI 48229
Phone: 313-388-0386

Dormition Cathedral ROR
PO Box 2951
Farmington MI 48333-2951
Phone: 313-939-3490

Holy Cross GOA
25225 Middlebelt Rd
Farmington MI 48336-1381
Phone: 313-477-1677

St Thomas OCA
29150 W 10 Mile Rd
Farmington MI 48336-2814
Phone: 313-471-1059

Dormition Cathedral ROR
2101 Livernois St
Ferndale MI 48021
Phone: 810-478-0270

Assumption GOA
G-3170 W. Beecher Rd
Flint MI 48532
Phone: 810-732-2660
FAX: 810-732-8981

Ss Peter & Paul UOD
715 E Parkway Ave
Flint MI 48505-2961
Phone:

St George ANT
5191 Lennon Rd
Flint MI 48507-1050
Phone: 810-732-0720
FAX: 810-732-0324

Holy Trinity GOA
330 Lakeside Dr NE
Grand Rapids MI 49503-3815
Phone: 616-454-6563

St George ANT
334 La Grave Ave SE
Grand Rapids MI 49503-4534
Phone: 616-454-7558
FAX: 616-454-8174

St Herman of Alaska ROR
648 Ethel Ave SE
Grand Rapids MI 49506-2851
Phone: 616-458-3726

St John Chrysostom PER
40 National NW
Grand Rapids MI 49504
Phone: 616-454-1166
FAX: 616-454-3417

St Nicholas ANT
2148 Boston St SE
Grand Rapids MI 49506-4164
Phone: 616-452-2700

Nativity of the Blessed Virgin Mary OCA
PO Box 309
Grass Lake MI 49240-0309
Phone: 517-522-4800

St James ANT
5921 Bayonne Ave
Haslett MI 48840-9501
Phone: 517-339-2210

St Mary ANT
309 W D St
Iron Mountain MI 49801-3311
Phone: 906-774-3772

St Simon ANT
PO Box 725
Ironwood MI 49938-0725
Phone: 906-774-3772

Nativity of the Blessed Virgin Mary OCA
2522 Grey Tower Rd
Jackson MI 49201-9120
Phone: 517-522-4800

St Demetrius OCA
3043 Seymour Rd
Jackson MI 49201-8829
Phone: 517-784-0116

Annunciation GOA
507 S Westnedge Ave
Kalamazoo MI 49007-5053
Phone: 616-345-5389

Holy Trinity GOA
1701 E Saginaw St
Lansing MI 48912-2316
Phone: 517-482-7315

Holy Transfiguration OCA
36075 7 Mile Rd
Livonia MI 48152-1124
Phone: 313-477-4712

St Mary ANT
18100 Merriman Rd
Livonia MI 48152-4310
Phone: 313-422-0010

Assumption GOA
235 W Ridge St
Marquette MI 49855-4339
Phone: 906-226-6792

St George SOC
2330 N Monroe St
Monroe MI 48161-4252
Phone: 312-241-1169

Annunciation GOA
1194 Terrace St
Muskegon MI 49442
Phone: 616-725-8537

Annunciation GOA
17777 Behner Rd
PO Box 99
New Buffalo MI 49117-0099
Phone: 616-469-0081

Nativity of the Virgin Mary GOA
39851 W Five Mile
Plymouth MI 48170
Phone: 313-420-0131
FAX: 313-420-2559

St Innocent PER
23300 W Chicago
Redford MI 48239-1300
Phone: 313-538-1142

St Michael the Archangel PER
26355 W Chicago
Redford MI 48239-2250
Phone: 313-937-2120

Dormition of the Mother of God Monastery OCA
3389 Rives Eaton Rd
Rives Junction MI 49277-9739
Phone: 517-569-2873

St Mark OCA
400 W Hamlin Rd
Rochester MI 48307
Phone: 248-656-1630

Holy Trinity UOD
1987 S. Wabash
Saginaw MI 48601
Phone:

Holy Trinity UCU
3630 Wilkins St
PO Box 1382
Saginaw MI 48601-4970
Phone: 313-629-5400

St Demetrios GOA
4970 Mackinaw at McCarty
Saginaw MI 48603
Phone: 517-793-8822

MINNESOTA

Assumption GOA
21800 Marter Rd
Saint Clair Shores MI 48080-2464
Phone: 810-779-6111
FAX: 810-282-5700

St George GOA
511 Court St
Sault Ste Marie MI 49783-2103
Phone: 906-632-6351

St George Cathedral OCA
18405 W 9 Mile Rd
Southfield MI 48075-4033
Phone: 313-569-4833

St Mary Protectress Cathedral UCU
20107 Mada & Evergreen Rd
Southfield MI 48075
Phone: 313-356-1636

St George GOA
16300 Dix Toledo Rd
Southgate MI 48195-2970
Phone: 313-283-8820
FAX: 313-282-5700

St Spyridon GMA
23410 Greater Mack
St Clair Shores MI 49080
Phone:

Holy Ghost ROR
38500 Ryan Rd
Sterling Heights MI 48310-2980
Phone: 313-795-3766

St John GOA
11455 Metropolitan Pky
Sterling Heights MI 48312-2937
Phone: 810-977-6080
FAX: 810-977-6081

Holy Ghost ROR
38500 Ryan Rd
Sterling Hts MI 48310
Phone: 810-939-3490

Holy Trinity RMA
1850 E Square Lake Rd
Troy MI 48098-3389
Phone: 313-879-2667

St George ANT
2240 E Maple Rd
Troy MI 48083-4483
Phone: 810-589-0480

St Nicholas OCA
5353 Livernois Rd
Troy MI 48098-3202
Phone: 313-891-7857

St Nicholas GOA
760 W Waffles Rd
Troy MI 48098-4500
Phone: 810-362-9575
FAX: 810-362-9578

Descent of Holy Ghost OCA
31500 Ryan Rd
Warren MI 48092-3763
Phone: 313-979-5193

Mother of God MOC
21740 Ryan Rd
Warren MI 48091-2354
Phone:

St Stevan Decanski NGM
14235 E 11 Mile Rd
Warren MI 48093-4817
Phone: 313-773-1940

Great Martyr George & St Nectarios CHR
34518 Warren Rd Ste 254
Westland MI 48185-2791
Phone: 313-451-2197

Ss Constantine & Helen GOA
36375 Joy Rd
Westland MI 48185-1195
Phone: 313-525-6789
FAX: 313-525-4305

St James ANT
310 S Putnam St
Williamston MI 48895-1312
Phone: 517-339-2130

MINNESOTA

Sts Volodymyr & Olha UCU
1660 Hwy 96 W
Arden Hills MN 55112-5736
Phone: 612-636-0206

St Basil of Ostrog SOC
543 6th St SW
PO BOX 192
Chisholm MN 55719-1935
Phone: 218-254-4874

St Nicholas OCA
402 2nd Ave NW
Chisholm MN 55719-1619
Phone: 218-254-4485

Nativity of the Theotokos NGM
1519 99TH AVE W
Duluth MN 55808-1804
Phone: 218-626-1580

St George SOC
1216 104th Ave W
Duluth MN 55808-1723
Phone: 218-626-1856

Twelve Holy Apostles GOA
632 E 2nd St
Duluth MN 55805-2010
Phone: 218-722-5957
FAX: 218-722-5957

Holy Archangel Michael SOC
701 E 40th St
Hibbing MN 55746-3182
Phone: 218-263-5027

Nativity of Holy Virgin OCA
RR 1 Box 376
Holdingford MN 56340-9621
Phone:

MISSOURI

Resurrection of Christ ROR
1201 Hathaway Ln NE
Minneapolis MN 55432-5720
Phone: 612-574-1001
FAX: 612-574-1001

St George UCU
316 4th Ave SE
Minneapolis MN 55414-1708
Phone: 612-379-1647

St Herman OCA
5355 38th Ave S
Minneapolis MN 55417-2131
Phone: 612-722-2506

St Mary GOA
3450 Irving Ave S
Minneapolis MN 55408-3399
Phone: 612-825-9595
FAX: 612-825-9283

St Mary's Cathedral OCA
1701 Fifth St NE
Minneapolis MN 55413
Phone: 612-781-7667
FAX: 612-781-5047

St Michael UCU
505 4th St NE
Minneapolis MN 55413-2039
Phone: 612-379-2280

St Panteleimon ROR
2210 Franklin Ave SE
Minneapolis MN 55414-3637
Phone: 612-379-7335

Holy Anargyroi SS Cosmos & Damianos
703 W Center St GOA
Rochester MN 55902-6231
Phone: 507-282-1529

St Sava NGM
357 2nd Ave S
S St Paul MN 55075-2608
Phone: 612-451-0775

Falling Asleep of Blessed Virgin Mary OCA
Atwater & Woodbridge Sts

St Paul MN 55117
Phone: 612-489-5618

Holy Trinity OCA
956 Forest St
St Paul MN 55106-3816
Phone: 612-771-5614

Holy Trinity SOC
113 Saratoga St N
St Paul MN 55104-6740
Phone: 612-641-0828

Holy Trinity of the Twin Cities
113 Saratoga St N SOC
St Paul MN 55104-6740
Phone: 612-641-0828

Prophet Elias AUX
1896 Feronia Ave
St Paul MN 55104-3548
Phone: 612-646-5505

Ss Volodymyr & Olha UCU
873 Portland Ave
St Paul MN 55104-7032
Phone: 612-222-0619

St George ANT
1250 Oakdale Ave
St Paul MN 55118-2601
Phone: 612-457-0854

St George GOA
1111 Summit Ave
St Paul MN 55105-2648
Phone: 612-222-6220

St Mary ANT
678 Robert St S
St Paul MN 55107-2935
Phone: 612-224-5151

MISSOURI

Nativity of Holy Virgin OCA
400 Tyler St
Desloge MO 63601
Phone: 314-431-4284

St John Chrysostom ROR
3774 Gravois Rd
PO Box 536
House Springs MO 63051-1355
Phone: 314-677-4333
FAX: 314-376-3223

Annunciation GOA
12001 Wornall Rd
Kansas City MO 64145-1116
Phone: 816-942-9100
FAX: 816-942-9440

Holy Resurrection VAS
PO Box 090492
Kansas City MO 64109-0492
Phone: 826-931-0142

St Theodore of Tarsus OCA
7409 NW Hwy 9
Kansas City MO 64152
Phone: 816-587-9568

Archangel Michael OCA
1901 Ann Ave
Saint Louis MO 63104-2703
Phone: 314-776-4205

Assumption GOA
1755 Des Peres Rd
Saint Louis MO 63131-1405
Phone: 314-966-2255
FAX: 314-966-2416

Christ the Good Shepherd VAS
2309 Thurman Ave
Saint Louis MO 63110-3916
Phone: 314-664-8132

St Basil the Great ROR
3615 McCausland Ave
Saint Louis MO 63109-1126
Phone: 314-645-1905

St John the Theologian SOC
1372 Beverly Ave
Saint Louis MO 63122-4761
Phone: 314-962-2412

MISSISSIPPI - MONTANA - NORTH CAROLINA

St Katherine of Sinai AUX
8400 New Hampshire Ave
Saint Louis MO 63123-2555
Phone: 314-352-2564

St Thomas the Apostle OCA
6501 Nottingham Ave
Saint Louis MO 63109-2659
Phone: 314-353-9785

St Luke SGP
PO Box 735
St Ann MO 60374
Phone: 314-426-2829

St George FOCI
2033 Clock Tower Sq
St Charles MO 63303
Phone:

Holy Trinity AOM
8428 Lackland Rd
St Louis MO
Phone: 314-429-5098

Holy Trinity NGM
1900 -1910 McNair Ave
St Louis MO 63104
Phone: 314-776-3262

Holy Trinity Mission
10204 Whitelock Dr
St Louis MO 63114
Phone:

St Basil the Great ROR
3615 McCausland Ave
St Louis MO 63109-1126
Phone: 314-645-1905

St Michael the Archangel
Orthodox Church OCA
1901 Ann Ave
St Louis MO 63104
Phone: 314-776-4205

St Nicholas GOA
4967 Forest Park Ave
St Louis MO 63108-1495
Phone: 314-361-6924

MISSISSIPPI

Holy Trinity GOA
255 Beauvoir Rd
Biloxi MS 39531-4008
Phone: 601-388-6138

Holy Resurrection OCA
501 W College St
Clinton MS 39056-4117
Phone: 601-924-0292
FAX: 601-924-0644

Holy Trinity & St John the Theologian
1417 W Capitol St GOA
Jackson MS 39203-2122
Phone: 601-355-6325

St Peter ANT
180 St Augustine, Madison MS
PO Box 16652
Jackson MS 39236-6652
Phone: 601-856-3894

St Mary's ANT
PO Box 742
Long Beach MS 39560
Phone: 601-864-1568

St George ANT
2709 Washington St
Vicksburg MS 39180
Phone: 601-636-2483

St Mary Madgalene OCC
125 Hartsie - 150 Angell Ln
Waveland MS 39576
Phone: 228-466-4508
FAX: 228-466-4508

MONTANA

Sts Michael & Florian
Christ's Mission
1206 East Third Street
AOC
Anaconda MT 59711-2704
Phone: 406-563-5426
FAX: 406-563-5426

True Faith Mission AOC
PO Box 674
Anaconda MT 59711-0674
Phone: 406-563-5426
FAX: 406-563-5426

St Elijah SOC
2931 Colton Blvd
PO Box 20842
Billings MT 59102-2003
Phone: 406-259-3466

Holy Trinity SOC
2300 Continental Dr
Butte MT 59701-6506
Phone: 406-723-7889

Ss Constantine & Helen GOA
1101 1st Ave N
Great Falls MT 59401-2621
Phone: 406-452-3670

Annunciation GOA
301 S 6th St W
PO Box 9192
Missoula MT 59801-3936
Phone: 406-726-3445

NORTH CAROLINA

Holy Trinity GOA
227 Cumberland Ave
PO Box 8369
Asheville NC 28814
Phone: 704-253-3754

St Joseph CRC
114 Challedon Dr
Asheville NC 28715
Phone:

St Katherine GOA
2150 W Front St
PO Box 1004
Burlington NC 27216-1004
Phone: 919-226-8243

All Saints ANT
Cary NC
Phone: 919-851-5335

Holy Trinity Cathedral GOA
600 East Blvd
Charlotte NC 28203
Phone: 704-334-4771

NORTH DAKOTA - NEBRASKA

Nativity of the Holy Virgin OCA
1700 Mineral Springs Rd
Charlotte NC 28213
Phone: 704-596-8252

St Barbara GOA
1316 Watts St
PO Box 1149
Durham NC 27702
Phone: 919-682-1414

Ss Constantine and Helen GOA
614 Oakridge Ave
Fayetteville NC 28305
Phone: 910-2010
FAX: 910-2010

St Nicholas ROR
5 Park Ridge Dr
Fletcher NC 28732
Phone: 704-681-8080

Dormition of the Theotokos GOA
800 Westridge Rd
Greensboro NC 27410-4504
Phone: 919-292-8013

St George GOA
808 N Hamilton St
High Point NC 27262-4027
Phone: 919-888-9028

Holy Trinity ROR
533 Lowergate Ln
Kernersville NC 27284
Phone: 910-992-3081

All Saints ANT
7404-M Chapel Hill Rd
Raleigh NC 27607-5043
Phone: 919-851-5335

Holy Trinity GOA
5000 Lead Mine Rd
Raleigh NC 27612-3434
Phone: 919-781-4548
FAX: 919-781-4568

St Gregory the Great OCA
201 St Alban's Dr
Raleigh NC 27609
Phone: 919-781-5477

Ss Peter & Paul PER
St Helena NC 28425
Phone: 919-259-7336

St Nicholas GOA
608 S College Rd
Wilmington NC 28403
Phone: 910-392-4484
FAX: 910-392-4498

Annunciation GOA
435 Keating Dr SW
Winston Salem NC 27104-3907
Phone: 919-765-7145
FAX: 919-659-1643

NORTH DAKOTA

All Saints ANT
1362 9th St N
Fargo ND 58102-2619
Phone: 701-293-0694

St Mary GOA
109 6th St SE
Minot ND 58701-4075
Phone: 701-838-3094

St Peter the Aleut OCA
109 6th St SE
Minot ND 58701-4075
Phone: 701-838-3094

Holy Trinity UCU
RR 1 Box 98
Wilton ND 58579-9801
Phone: 701-734-6494

NEBRASKA

Holy Trinity GOA
1015 W 10th St
PO BOX 998
Grand Island NE 68801-4005
Phone: 308-382-5290

St George ANT
1505 Avenue G
Kearney NE 68847-6274
Phone: 308-234-9456

Annunciation GOA
950 N 63rd St
Lincoln NE 68505-2286
Phone: 402-464-2706

Holy Archangels VAS
1740 W Burnham St
Lincoln NE 68522-9225
Phone: 402-423-8070

Holy Transfiguration VAS
1319 N St Ste 104
Lincoln NE 68347
Phone: 402-438-4566
FAX: 402-438-4758

St Fanourios VAS
1827 S 11th St
Lincoln NE 68502-2211
Phone: 402-438-1332
FAX: 402-438-2595

St John of Kronstadt VAS
2800 Holdrege St
Lincoln NE 68503-1537
Phone:

St Katherine FOCI
353 S 11th St
Lincoln NE 68510
Phone:

St Tikhon DHE
1319 S 11th St
PO Box 22237
Lincoln NE 68502-1220
Phone: 402-476-2676

Three Hierarchs UCU
450 E St
Lincoln NE 68508
Phone: 402-438-5695
FAX: 402-477-2015

Holy Cross RMA
3221 R St
Omaha NE 68107-2531
Phone: 715-455-1553

NEW HAMPSHIRE - NEW JERSEY

St Gabriel VAS
3219 R St
Omaha NE 68107-2531
Phone: 402-423-8070

St John of San Francisco DHE
PO Box 34362
Omaha NE 68134-0362
Phone: 402-572-6360

St John the Baptist GOA
602 Park Ave
Omaha NE 68105-2712
Phone: 402-345-7103

St Mary ANT
10303 Boyd St
Omaha NE 68134-2904
Phone: 402-496-0480
FAX: 402-496-9331

St Nicholas SOC
5052 Harrison St
Omaha NE 68157-2247
Phone: 402-734-4194

St Vincent of Lerins ANT
1717 N 106th St
Omaha NE 68114-1013
Phone: 402-496-2406

St Vincent of Lerins
2502 N 51 St
Omaha NE 68104
Phone: 402-493-8102

NEW HAMPSHIRE

Holy Resurrection OCA
20 Petrograd St
Berlin NH 03570-1216
Phone: 603-752-2254

Holy Resurrection OCA
99 Sullivan St
Claremont NH 03743-2525
Phone: 603-542-6273

Dormition of the Theotokos AUX
4 Union St
Concord NH 03301-4249
Phone: 603-225-4909

Holy Trinity GOA
68 N State St
Concord NH 03301-4330
Phone: 603-225-2961

Annunciation GOA
93 Locust St
PO Box 851
Dover NH 03820-3753
Phone: 603-742-7667

Annunciation Church GOA
93 Locust St
Dover NH 03820
Phone: 603-742-7667

Transfiguration GOA
Sullowey St
Franklin NH 03235
Phone:

St George GOA
70 West St
Keene NH 03431-3373
Phone: 603-352-6424

Taxiarchai GOA
811 N Main St
Laconia NH 03246-2604
Phone: 617-872-8323

Assumption GOA
111 Island Pond Rd
Manchester NH 03109-4807
Phone: 603-623-2045

Ss Peter & Paul PER
306 Beech St
Manchester NH 03103-5437
Phone: 603-623-1700

St George Cathedral GOA
650 Hanover St
Manchester NH 03104-5306
Phone: 603-622-9113
FAX: 603-699-2167

St Nicholas GOA
1168 Bridge St
Manchester NH 03104-5741
Phone: 603-625-6115

St Philip GOA
500 W Hollis St
Nashua NH 03062-1314
Phone: 603-889-4000
FAX: 603-889-3763

St Vasilios GOA
45 Winter St
PO Box 428
Newport NH 03773-1435
Phone: 603-292-1000

St Nicholas GOA
40 Andrew Jarvis Dr
Portsmouth NH 03801-5448
Phone: 603-436-2733

Assumption GOA
45 Tates Brook Rd
Somersworth NH 03878
Phone:

NEW JERSEY

St George GOA
700 Grand Ave
Asbury Park NJ 07712-6629
Phone: 201-775-2777

St Leander's Mission
25 Martin Luther King Blvd
Atlantic City NJ 08401-0027
Phone:

St Nicholas GOA
13 S Mt Vernon Ave
PO Box 641
Atlantic City NJ 08401-6906
Phone: 609-348-3495

Ss Peter & Paul OCA
98 W 28th St
Bayonne NJ 07002-3849
Phone: 201-436-3244

St Mary CRC
90 W 30th St
Bayonne NJ 07002-2802
Phone: 201-436-5549

St Nicholas PER
606 Kennedy Blvd
Bayonne NJ 07002-2758
Phone: 201-339-7488

St Sophia UCU
39 W 22nd St
Bayonne NJ 07002-3701
Phone: 201-436-8350

St Anthony ANT
385 Ivy Ln
Bergenfield NJ 07621-4508
Phone: 203-768-0324

Annunciation OCA
360 Van Zile Rd
Brick NJ 08724-2046
Phone: 908-458-9032

Protection of the Holy Virgin

E Weymouth Rd ROR
RD 2 - Box 358
Buena NJ 08310-9633
Phone: 609-697-2027

St Demetrius Cathedral
UCU
645 Roosevelt Ave
Carteret NJ 07008-2998
Phone: 732-541-1530
FAX: 732-967-2237

Holy Cross OCA
Rte 541 N, Medford NJ 08055
24 Colmar Rd
Cherry Hill NJ 08002
Phone: 609-654-4865
FAX: 609-265-0864

St Thomas GOA
615 Mercer St
Cherry Hill NJ 08002-2635
Phone: 609-665-1731
FAX: 609-665-9207

Assumption of the Holy Virgin
35 Orange Ave OCA
Clifton NJ 07013-2922
Phone: 973-365-9671

Holy Ascension UCU
635-655 Broad St.
Clifton NJ 07013
Phone: 973-471-8131

St George GOA
818 Valley Rd
Clifton NJ 07013-2206
Phone: 973-779-2626

St Mary Protectress UCU
71-83 Washington Ave
Clifton NJ 07011
Phone: 973-546-2473

St Anthony ANT
59 Columbus Rd
Demarest NJ 07627-1401
Phone: 203-768-0324

Holy Trinity BAM
S Jersey Ave
PO Box 255
Dorothy NJ 08317-0255
Phone: 609-697-1063

St Andrew GOA
Sussex Trpk-Randolph Towns
PO Box 336
Dover NJ 07801
Phone: 201-584-0488

Holy Ascension NGM
117 Liberty St
Elizabeth NJ 07202-3414
Phone: 201-354-4134

Ss Peter & Paul PER
159 Stiles St
Elizabeth NJ 07208-1810
Phone: 908-352-1192

St George SOC
654 S Broad St
Elizabeth NJ 07202-2602
Phone: 908-352-8990

St Nicholas CRC
668 S Brook St
Elizabeth NJ 07202
Phone: 908-354-1384

St Nicholas CRC
668 S Broad St
Elizabeth NJ 07202
Phone: 908-354-1384

St John Chrysostom
ANT
358 Mountain Rd
Englewood NJ 07631-3727
Phone: 201-871-1355
FAX: 201-871-7954

Ascension GOA
Anderson Ave & Henry St
Fairview NJ 07022
Phone: 201-945-6448
FAX: 201-945-6453

St Paul the Apostle CRC
24 Burke Rd
RD 3 Box 474, Burke Rd
Freehold Twnsp NJ 07728-8619
Phone: 908-780-3158

Three Saints PER
St Vladimir's Sq; 454 Outwater
Garfield NJ 07026-1426
Phone: 201-772-8973

Elevation of the Holy Cross
PO Box 781 PER
Hackettstown NJ 07840-0781
Phone: 908-852-5611

Mother of God of Zyrovicy
9 River Rd BAM
Highland Park NJ 08904-1705
Phone: 908-247-4490

Kimisis Tis Theotokou
GOA
20 Hillcrest Rd
PO Box 367
Holmdel NJ 07733-0367
Phone: 732-739-1515
FAX: 732-739-1172

Our Lady of Tikhvin ROR
200 Alexander Ave
Howell NJ 07731-3330
Phone: 732-364-3330

St Alexander Nevsky Cathedral
200 Alexander Ave ROR
Howell NJ 07731-8684
Phone: 732-364-3330
FAX: 732-364-5625

St Alexander Nevsky School
200 Alexander Ave ROR
Howell NJ 07731-8684
Phone: 908-370-1881
FAX: 908-364-5625

St George ROR
57 E 3rd St
Howell NJ 07731-8582
Phone: 908-364-4226

Holy Trinity UCU
836 Lyons Ave
680 Stuyvesant Ave
Irvington NJ 07111
Phone: 973-372-6962

Nativity of the Holy Virgin OCA
PO Box 146-316 Cassville Rd
Jackson NJ 08527-0146
Phone: 908-928-3223

St Vladimir Memorial ROR
134 Perrineville Rd
PO Box 143
Jackson NJ 08527-0143
Phone: 908-928-1248

Evangelismos GOA
661 Montgomery St
Jersey City NJ 07306-2411
Phone: 201-432-2488

Ss Peter & Paul OCA
109 Grand St
Jersey City NJ 07302-4428
Phone: 201-434-1986

St Demetrios GOA
524 Summit Ave
Jersey City NJ 07306-2913
Phone: 201-792-0697

St Gregory Palamas OCA
1030 Route 31 North
Lebanon NJ
Mailing: Box 634
Flemington NJ 08822
Phone: 908 788-388
can1735@aol.com

St George ANT
237 Long Hill Rd
Little Falls NJ 07424-2005
Phone: 201-256-8961

St John the Baptist PER
29 Weaver St
Little Falls NJ 07424-1047
Phone: 201-256-0314

Holy Ghost CRC
249 S 7th Ave
Manville NJ 08835-1711
Phone: 908-725-3385

Ss Peter & Paul OCA
605 Washington Ave
Manville NJ 08835-1856
Phone: 908-685-1452

Ss Peter and Paul OCA
605 Washington Ave
Manville NJ 08835-1856
Phone: 908-685-1452
FAX: 908-685-1074

Holy Ascension UCU
652 Irvington Ave
Maplewood NJ 07040-1644
Phone: 973-763-7644

Mother of God 'Joy of All Who Sorrow'
PO Box 398 OCA
Mays Landing NJ 08330-0398
Phone:

Orthodox Mission OCA
Mercer County NJ

Ss Peter & Paul UCU
77 Hogbin Rd
Millville NJ 08332-5202
Phone: 609-825-6720

St Nicholas ROR
129 S 5th St
2113 W Main St
Millville NJ 08332-4643
Phone: 609-293-1700
FAX: 609-825-7952

Christ the Savior PER
103 Horseneck Rd
Montville NJ 07045-9625
Phone: 201-316-8145

St Demetrius GOA
301 St Demetrios St
N Wildwood NJ 08260-0277
Phone: 609-522-0152

Protection of the Holy Virgin
301 Handy St ROR
New Brunswick NJ 08901-2942
Phone: 908-247-4621

Our Lady of Kazan ROR
70 Heller Pkwy
Newark NJ 07104-2204
Phone: 201-482-5627

St Michael ROR
277 Oliver St
280 Van Buren St
Newark NJ 07105-2417
Phone: 973-589-8712

St Nicholas GOA
555 Martin Luther King Jr Blvd
Newark NJ 07102-1244
Phone: 201-623-6211
FAX: 201-623-2238

Holy Trinity GOA
PO Box 769
Northfield NJ 08225
Phone: 609-653-8092
FAX: 609-653-0375

St John Chrysostom OCA
1914 Central Ave
Ocean City NJ 08226-2828
Phone: 609-398-3207

Ss Constantine & Helen GOA
510 Linden Pl
Orange NJ 07050-1602
Phone: 201-674-6600
FAX: 201-674-8330

Christ the Savior OCA
365 Paramus Rd
Paramus NJ 07652-1511
Phone: 201-652-6633

St Athanasios GOA
51 Paramus Rd
Paramus NJ 07652-1320
Phone: 201-368-8881

Ss Cosmas & Damian ROR
44 Van Buren St
Passaic NJ 07055-6706
Phone: 201-471-4485

Ss Cyril & Methodius MOC
124 Hamilton Ave
Passaic NJ 07055-5239
Phone:

Ss Peter & Paul PER
3rd & Monroe Sts
Passaic NJ 07055
Phone: 201-778-0826

St John the Baptist OCA
170 Lexington Ave
Passaic NJ 07055-6205
Phone: 201-473-1928

St John the Baptist SOC
119 Carlisle Ave
Paterson NJ 07501-2517
Phone: 718-389-7296

St Michael's Cathedral ROR
523 Sherman Ave #56
334 Cumberland Ave
Paterson NJ 07502-1323
Phone: 201-595-5816

St Demetrios GOA
PO Box 1068
Perth Amboy NJ 08862-1068
Phone: 908-826-4466
FAX: 908-826-4312

St John the Baptist CRC
145 Broad St
Perth Amboy NJ 08861
Phone: 732-826-4442
FAX: 732-826-1970

St Spiridon ROR
649 Elizabeth St
648 Charles St
Perth Amboy NJ 08861-2808
Phone: 908-826-4818

St John the Baptist OCA
1034 2nd Ave
Phillipsburg NJ 08865-4703
Phone: 908-454-1553

St George GOA
1101 River Rd
Piscataway NJ 08854-5620
Phone: 908-463-1642
FAX: 908-699-9309

Orthodox Chapel of Transfiguration Murray Dodge Hall OCA
109 Rollingmead
Princeton NJ 08540
Phone: 609-924-7368

Holy Trinity OCA
830 Jefferson Ave
Rahway NJ 07065-2618
Phone: 908-574-1234

St John the Baptist CRC
211 W Grand Ave
Rahway NJ 07065-4111
Phone: 908-382-8844

Holy Trinity OCA
120 Dover-Chester Rd
Randolph NJ 07869
Phone: 201-366-8360

St Nicholas ROR
15 Pearl St
Red Bank NJ 07701-1114
Phone: 732-671-5786

Ss Peter & Paul CRC
64 Beach St
Rockaway NJ 07866-3514
Phone: 201-627-1462

St Lucy's Mission AOM
PO Box 302
S Orange NJ 07079
Phone: 973-736-5049

St Stephen the Protomartyr
609 Lane Ave ANT
S Plainfield NJ 07080
Phone: 908-756-0410

Holy Apostles OCA
17 Platt Ave
Saddle Brook NJ 07663-4713
Phone: 201-444-8580

Ss Fanourios & Haralampos
Victor St GMA
Somerset NJ 08873
Phone: 732-214-1727

Nativity of the Blessed Virgin UCU
416 Delmore Ave
S Plainfield NJ 07080-3925
Phone: 908-756-7223

St Stephen ANT
609 Lane Ave
S Plainfield NJ 07080-3516
Phone: 908-756-0410

Ss Peter and Paul OCA
153 Kamm Ave
S River NJ 08882
Phone: 732-257-0102

St Euphrosynia BYC
284 Whitehead Avenue
S River NJ 08882
Phone: 908-257-5007

St Gregory Palamas OCA
Stanton Pl
Stanton NJ 08885
Phone: 908-788-3887

NEW MEXICO - NEVADA

St John the Theologian
Cathedral
353 E Clinton Ave   GOA
Tenafly NJ 07670-2319
Phone: 201-567-5072
FAX: 201-816-0589

St Barbara   GOA
2200 Church Rd
Toms River NJ 08753-8106
Phone: 908-255-5525
FAX: 908-255-8180

Assumption   ROR
106 Jackson St
Trenton NJ 08611-1720
Phone: 609-396-1061

Holy Assumption   UOD
Broad & Market Sts
Trenton NJ 08610
Phone:

Holy Trinity   UCU
824 Adeline St
Trenton NJ 08610-6401
Phone: 609-393-5330

St George   GOA
1200 Klockner Rd
Trenton NJ 08619-3614
Phone: 609-586-4448
FAX: 609-964-6875

St Vladimir   OCA
812 Grand St
Trenton NJ 08610-6429
Phone: 609-393-1234

St Demetrios   GOA
721 Rahway Ave
Union NJ 07083-6633
Phone: 908-964-7957
FAX: 908-964-6875

Holy Trinity   ROR
2211 W Landis Ave
Vineland NJ 08360-3492
Phone: 609-696-1579

St Anthony   GOA
430 W Wheat Rd
Vineland NJ 08360-1911
Phone: 609-696-0917

Holy Name   IND
100 Abbey Ln
W Milford NJ 07480-3909
Phone: 973-838-8795
FAX: 973-838-2228

Holy Resurrection   OCA
285 French Hill Rd
Wayne NJ 07470-3976
Phone: 201-696-6572

Holy Trinity   GOA
250 Gallows Hill Rd
Westfield NJ 07090-1109
Phone: 908-233-8533
FAX: 908-233-0623

St Nicholas   GOA
467 Grandview Ave
Wyckoff NJ 07481-2543
Phone: 201-652-4774
FAX: 201-652-0789

St George   UCU
839 Yardville-Allentown Rd
Yardville NJ 08620
Phone: 609-585-1935

NEW MEXICO

St Anthony the Great
Monastery
Alamagordo NM 88311-1432
CHR
Phone: 505-434-5277

St Peter the Aleut   CHR
Alamagordo NM 88311-1432
Phone: 505-434-5277

Holy Royal Martyrs   VAS
324 Hazeldine Ave SW
Albuquerque NM 87102-4160
Phone: 505-242-6186

St George   GOA
308 High St SE
Albuquerque NM 87102
Phone: 505-247-9411
FAX: 505-248-0804

St Francis Mission   AOC
PO Box 383
Columbus NM 88029
Phone: 505-531-2278

St Nicholas   CHR
Farmington NM 87401
Phone: 505-434-5277

St Benedict   ROR
1714 E Rose Ln
Hobbs NM 88240-3146
Phone: 505-393-4630

Ss Constantine & Helen
CHR
Las Cruces NM
Phone: 505-434-5277

St Juliana of Lazarevo
ROR
855 El Caminito St
PO Box 4353
Santa FE NM 87502-4353
Phone: 505-473-7779

Dormition of All-Holy
Theotokos
885 El Caminito St   OCA
Santa Fe NM 87501-2842
Phone: 505-271-1515

St Elias the Prophet GOA
46 Calle Electra
Santa Fe NM 87505
Phone: 505-466-0515

St Joseph ANT
PO Box 602
Santa Fe NM 87504-0602
Phone: 505-988-9835

St Tikhon ROR
11 Calle Medico # SUITE#1
Santa Fe NM 87505-4724
Phone: 505-982-8871

NEVADA

St Alexios GOA
5300 S El CAmino Rd, Las Vegas NV
Ely NV 89301
Phone:

NEW YORK

St John the Baptist GOA
53005 El Camino Rd
Las Vegas NV 89118-1922
Phone: 702-221-8245
FAX: 702-221-9167

St Michael ANT
5719 Judson Ave
Las Vegas NV 89115-5783
Phone: 702-452-1299
St Paul OCA
5400 Annie Oakley Dr
Las Vegas NV 89120-2024
Phone: 702-898-4800

St Simeon SOC
3950 S Jones Blvd
Las Vegas NV 89103-2205
Phone: 702-367-7783

St Barbara GOA
Fourth St
PO Box 1352
Mc Gill NV 89318-1352
Phone: 702-235-7341

St Anthony GOA
4795 Lakeside Dr
Reno NV 89509-5814
Phone: 702-825-5365

St John the Baptist VAS
661 W Pueblo St
Reno NV 89509-2763
Phone: 702-329-3782

NEW YORK

St George ANT
PO Box 9060
Albany NY 12209-0060
Phone: 518-462-0579

St Sophia GOA
440 Whitehall Rd
Albany NY 12208-1643
Phone: 518-489-4442
FAX: 518-489-0374

Holy Trinity ROR
25-36 37th St
Astoria NY 11103
Phone: 718-726-7870

St Demetrios Cathedral
GOA
30-11 30th Dr
Astoria NY 11102
Phone: 718-728-1754
FAX: 718-728-0079

St Dionysios VAS
PO Box 9001
Astoria NY 11103-0903
Phone: 212-996-0355

St Irene Chrysovalantou
Cathedral
36-07 23rd Ave GMA
Astoria NY 11105
Phone:

St Nicholas OCA
28 Cross St
Auburn NY 13021-2433
Phone: 315-252-3423

St Isidore of Chios CHR
910 Stewart Ave
Bethpage NY 11714-3532
Phone: 516-933-1736

Dormition of the Virgin Mary
53 Baxter St OCA
Binghamton NY 13905-2029
Phone: 607-797-1058

Holy Trinity GOA
214 Court St
Binghamton NY 13901-3605
Phone: 607-723-9662
FAX: 607-798-0963

St Michael CRC
280 Clinton St
Binghamton NY 13950
Phone: 607-797-4471

St John GOA
77 Montauk Hwy
Blue Point NY 11715-1130
Phone: 516-363-6450
FAX: 516-363-6457

Coop City UIU
Hunter Ave.
Bronx NY 10475
Phone:

Zoodochos Peghe GOA
3573 Bruckner Blvd
Bronx NY 10461
Phone: 718-823-2030
FAX: 718-823-0790

Holy Cross GOA
8401 Ridge Blvd
Brooklyn NY 11209-4327
Phone: 718-836-3510
FAX: 716-882-9495

Holy Cross VAS
PO Box 110482
Brooklyn NY 11211-0482
Phone:

Holy Transfiguration
Cathedral
228 N 12th St OCA
Brooklyn NY 11211-1101
Phone: 718-387-1064

Holy Trinity OCA
400 Glenmore Ave
Brooklyn NY 11207-3523
Phone: 718-498-0518

Holy Trinity UOA
185 S 5th St
Brooklyn NY 11211-5303
Phone: 718-388-4723

Kimisis tis Theotokou
GOA
224 18th St
Brooklyn NY 11215-5303
Phone: 718-788-0152
FAX: 718-832-3712

Ss Constantine & Helen
Cathedral
64 Schermerhorn St
GOA
Brooklyn NY 11201-5005
Phone: 718-624-0595
FAX: 718-624-2228

Ss Michael & Gabriel
OCA
355 State St
Brooklyn NY
Mailing: 6655 60th Pl
Flushing NY 11385

St Cyprian & St Justina HOC
PO Box 248
Brooklyn NY 11209-0248
Phone: 718-836-6215

St Cyril's of Turau BAJ
401 Atlantic Ave
Brooklyn NY 11217-1702
Phone: 732-873-8026
FAX: 718-875-0595

St Mary ANT
8100 Ridge Blvd
Brooklyn NY 11209-3528
Phone: 718-238-8008

St Mary Magdalene HOC
PO Box 248
Brooklyn NY 11209-0248
Phone: 718-836-6215

St Michael UOD
16 26th St
Brooklyn NY 11232-1405
Phone:

St Nektarios GMA
340 67th St
Brooklyn NY 11220-5301
Phone: 718-748-7667

St Nicholas GMA
1822 65th St
Brooklyn NY 11204-3812
Phone: 718-232-7358

St Nicholas ANT
355 State St
PO Box 090-147
Brooklyn NY 11209-0003
Phone: 718-855-6225
FAX: 718-855-3608

St Sergius Mission OCA
St Mary's, 8100 Ridge Blvd
217 65th St #1F
Brooklyn NY 11220
Phone: 718-492-5659

Three Hierarchs GOA
1724 Avenue P
Brooklyn NY 11229-1206
Phone: 718-339-0280

Three Hierarchs OCA
7105 Cooper Ave @ Myrtle and 71st
Brooklyn-Glendale NY 11385
Phone: 718-366-1358

Annunciation GOA
146 W Utica St
Buffalo NY 14222
Phone: 716-882-9485
FAX: 716-882-9495

Holy Trinity UCU
200 Como Park Blvd
Buffalo NY 14227-1417
Phone: 716-684-0738

Ss Cyril & Methodius MOC
4785 Lake Ave
Buffalo NY 14219-1311
Phone:

Ss Peter & Paul OCA
45 Ideal St
44 Benzinger St
Buffalo NY 14206-1402
Phone: 716-893-0044
FAX: 716-896-4159

St George OCA
2 Nottingham Ter
Buffalo NY 14216-3636
Phone: 716-873-9106

St George VAS
534 McKinley Pky
Buffalo NY 14220-1739
Phone:

St Nicholas ROR
197 Stanislaus St
Buffalo NY 14212-1560
Phone: 716-896-2729

St Nicola BEC
1496 Kenmore Ave
Buffalo NY 14216-1136
Phone:

St Stephen SOC
177 Weber Rd
Buffalo NY 14218-2837

Phone: 716-823-2846

Holy Trinity UCU
200 Como Park Blvd
Cheektowaga NY 14227
Phone: 716-684-0738

St Mary CRC
81 Fairoaks Ln
Cheektowaga NY 14227
Phone: 716-892-3150

St Nicholas OCA
67 Saratoga St
Cohoes NY 12047-3110
Phone: 518-237-5335

St Mary CRC
254 Sunset Dr
Corning NY 14830-2435
Phone: 607-936-9284

Transfiguration GOA
38-05 98th St
Corona NY 11368
Phone: 718-458-5251
FAX: 718-478-8199

Three Hierarchs PAN
575 Scarsdale Rd
Crestwood NY 10707
Phone: 914-961-8313

St Andrew OCA
1095 Carlls Straight Path
Dix Hills NY 11746-8013
Phone: 516-586-1611

Ss. Peter & Paul OCA
305 Main St.
E Herkimer NY 13350
Phone: 315-866-3272

Holy Trinity OCA
369 Green Ave
E Meadow NY 11554-2309
Phone: 516-483-3649
FAX: 516-486-2963

St Mary UCU
PO Box 305
Eastport NY 11941-0305
Phone: 516-878-8240

St Mary's Dormition Chapel UOA
c/o Ukrainian Youth Association
Ellenville NY 12428
Phone: 914-647-9680

St Mary   OCA
42-14 74th St
Elmhurst NY 11373-1809
Phone: 718-565-2522

Ss Paraskevi & Haralambos
73-05 Grand Ave   VAS
Elmhurst-Maspeth NY 11378
Phone: 718-899-0922

Holy Trinity   OCA
140 Horseheads Blvd
Elmira NY 14903-1934
Phone: 607-732-3980

St Athanasios   GOA
210 Franklin St
Elmira NY 14904-1706
Phone: 607-734-0771

Ss Peter & Paul   ROR
308 N Page Ave
Endicott NY 13760-3938
Phone: 607-745-0881

Ss Peter and Paul   OCA
210 Hill Ave
Endicott NY 13760-2906
Phone: 607-785-4479

St Innocent   OCA
189 Main St, Oneonta NY
210 Hill Ave
Endicott NY 13760-2906
Phone: 518-296-8132

St Mary   CRC
1907 Jenkins St
Endicott NY 13760-3024
Phone: 607-754-8952

St Nicholas   ROR
308 N Page Ave
Endicott NY 13760-3938
Phone: 607-754-0881

Descent of the Holy Spirit OCA
18-69 Gates Ave
Flushing NY 11385-2939
Phone: 718-417-3860

Holy Annunciation   ROR
42-67 147th St
Flushing NY 11355
Phone: 718-359-5373

Ss Michael and Gabriel Mission
St Nicholas Cath, 355 State St OCA
6655 60th Pl
Flushing NY 11385-3220
Phone: 718-386-4978

St Alexander Nevsky ROR
9417 Roosevelt Ave
Flushing NY 11372-7946
Phone: 718-429-7232

St John Chrysostom OCA
7029 45th Ave
Flushing NY 11377-5107
Phone: 718-429-8245

St Mary   OCA
42-14 74th St
Flushing NY 11373-1809
Phone: 718-726-6113

St Nicholas   GOA
196-10 Northern Blvd
Flushing NY 11358-3037
Phone: 718-357-4200
FAX: 718-357-5692

Three Hierarchs   OCA
6332 Forest Ave
Flushing NY 11385-2043
Phone: 718-366-1358

St Basil   GOA
Rt 2; Box 8A
Garrison NY 10524
Phone: 914-424-3500
FAX: 914-424-4172

St Michael   ANT
98 Genesee St
Geneva NY 14456-1726
Phone: 315-789-3060

Ascension Cathedral ROR
Old Tappan Rd
Glen Cove NY 11542
Phone: 516-676-7683

Holy Virgin Protection ROR
14 Alvin St
Glen Cove NY 11542-1810
Phone: 516-676-0539
FAX: 516-676-0539

Intercesson of Holy Virgin & St Sergius
14 Alvin St   ROR
Glen Cove NY 11542-1810
Phone: 516-676-0539
FAX: 516-676-0539

Resurrection   GOA
34 Cedar Swamp Rd
Glen Cove NY 11542-3724
Phone: 516-671-5200
FAX: 516-671-5205

Holy Mother of God Odigitria of Smolensk   BYC
Religious Recreation Center
Belair-
Glen Spey NY 12737
Phone:

Ss Peter & Paul   UCU
PO Box 178
Glen Spey NY 12737-0178
Phone: 914-856-7441

St Nicholas   ROR
PO Box 800
Glenham NY 12527-0800
Phone: 914-831-2164

Ss Theodoroi   GOA
70 Washington St
Gloversville NY 12078-3933
Phone:

St Paraskevi GOA
Shrine Pl
Greenlawn NY 11740
Phone: 516-261-7272
FAX: 516-564-7295

Ss Anargyroi & Taxiarchis
GMA
Main St
Greenport NY 11944
Phone: 516-477-1801

St Paul Cathedral GOA
110 Cathedral Ave
Hempstead NY 11550-2050
Phone: 516-483-5700
FAX: 516-564-8235

St Mary UCU
331 Moore Ave
Herkimer NY 13350-2413
Phone: 315-866-3952

Holy Trinity GOA
20 Field Ave
Hicksville NY 11801-5321
Phone: 516-433-4522
FAX: 516-433-0571

St Mary UCU
40 W Carl St
Hicksville NY 11801-4211
Phone: 718-740-2508

St Michael UCU
59 Partition St
Hudson NY 12534-3111
Phone: 518-828-3121

Kimisis Tis Theotokou
GOA
83 Newport Rd
PO BOX 308
Island Park NY 11558-1012
Phone: 516-432-4086
FAX: 516-433-0571

St Catherine GOA
120 W Seneca St
Ithaca NY 14850-4138
Phone: 607-273-2767

Ss Constantine & Helen
GOA
3757 72nd St
Jackson Hts NY 11372-6144
Phone: 718-639-0611

St Andrew Cathedral
UCU
9034 139th St
Jamaica NY 11435-4214
Phone: 718-297-2407

St Demetrios GOA
84-35 152nd St
Jamaica NY 11432-1620
Phone: 718-291-2420
FAX: 718-526-6775

St Gerasimos VAS
84-41 164th St
Jamaica NY 11432-1734
Phone: 718-523-1859

St Nicholas OCA
181-14 Midland Pkwy
Jamaica Estates NY 11432
Phone: 718-380-5684

St Elia OCA
101 Palmer St
PO Box 1274
Jamestown NY 14702-1274
Phone: 508-754-3451

St Nicholas GOA
PO Box 264
Jamestown NY 14702-0264
Phone: 716-483-0022

Entrance of the Holy Virgin
into the Tem
607 Tecumseh ROR
Jamesville NY 13078-9745
Phone: 315-446-1781

St Nicholas OCA
181-14 Midland Pkwy
Jamiaca Estates NY 11432
Phone: 718-380-5684

St John UCU
1 St John's Pky
Johnson City NY 13790
Phone: 607-797-1584

Community of St Elizabeth
ROR
Jordanville NY 13361
Phone: 315-858-2208

St George GOA
PO BOX 3062
Kingston NY 12401-5342
Phone: 914-331-3522
FAX: 914-338-2942

St Jude FOC
PO Box 32
Lake Katine NY 12449
Phone:

Christ the Savior OCA
3425 Galway Rd @ Paisley
22 Fairlawn Dr
Lathan NY 12110
Phone: 518-885-4681

Holy Trinity MAT
3810 20th Rd
Long Island City NY 11105-1626
Phone:

Ss Constantine & Helen
GOA
35-18 31st Ave #3A
Long Island City NY 11106-4526
Phone: 718-721-3810

St Demetrios Cathedral
GOA
3011 30th Dr
Long Island City NY 11102-1855
Phone: 718-728-1718

St Markella Cathedral
CHR
2268 26th St
Long Island City NY 11105-3152
Phone: 718-932-1592
FAX: 718-274-2875

St John the Baptist AOC
4-20 Green Way Ave
Manorville NY 11949
Phone: 516-878-4172

Transfiguration of Christ GOA
1950 Breakwater Rd PO Box 1162
Mattituck NY 11952
Phone: 516-298-9652

St Demetrios   GOA
24 Kenney Ave
Merrick NY 11566-3934
Phone: 516-379-1368
FAX: 516-379-1368

Holy Cross   GOA
R D 5 Goshen Turnpike
PO Box 109
Middletown NY 10940
Phone: 914-695-1976

Holy Spirit Orthodox Mission
38 Pearl Street   OCA
New Hyde Park NY 11040
Phone: 516-437-5760

Holy Trinity   GOA
10 Mill Rd
New Rochelle NY 10804
Phone: 914-235-6100
FAX: 914-235-0708

All Saints UCU
206 E 11th St
New York NY 10003-7301
Phone: 212-475-9534

Annunciation   GOA
302 W 91st St
New York NY 10024-1002
Phone: 212-724-2070

Christ the Savior   OCA
340 E 71st St
New York NY 10021-5263
Phone: 212-744-8502

Holy Fathers   ROR
524 W 153rd St
New York NY 10031-1001
Phone: 212-281-3992

Holy Trinity Cathedral
UCU
359 Broome St
New York NY 10013-4202
Phone: 212-226-4351

Holy Trinity Cathedral
GOA
319-337 E. 74th St.
New York NY 10021
Phone: 212-288-3215

Mother of God of the Sign Cathedral
75 E 93rd St   ROR
New York NY 10128-1331
Phone: 212-534-1601
FAX: 212-426-1086

Our Lady of Mercy Mission
508 W 166th St   AOM
New York NY
Phone: 212-568=3514

Protection of the Holy Virgin Cathedral OCA
59 E 2nd St
New York NY 10003-9270
Phone: 212-677-4664
FAX: 212-475-7867

Ss Anargyroi   GOA
1547 Saint Nicholas Ave
New York NY 10040-4505
Phone: 212-568-0367

Ss Kiril & Methodi Cathedral
550-A W 50th St   BEC
New York NY 10019
Phone: 212-586-7636

St Barbara   GOA
27 Forsyth St
New York NY 10002-6001
Phone: 212-226-0499

St Demetrios the Physician & Healer Hos   VAS
PO Box 919 Lenox Hill Sta
New York NY 11103
Phone: 212-996-0355

St Dumitru   OCA
50 W 89th St
New York NY 10024-2001
Phone: 212-874-4490

St Eleftherios   GOA
359 W 24th St
New York NY 10011-1501
Phone: 212-924-3919

St George Tropeoforos
GOA
307 W 54th St
New York NY 10019-5101
Phone: 212-265-7808

St George-St Demetrios
GOA
140 E 103rd St
New York NY 10029-5302
Phone: 212-722-6750

St Gerasimos   GOA
153 W 105th St
New York NY 10025-4024
Phone: 212-749-0017

St John the Baptist GOA
143 E 17th St
New York NY 10003-3402
Phone: 212-473-0648

St Mark's Orthodox Monastery
419 E 117 St ROR
New York NY 10035
Phone: 212-289-3071

St Mary   CRC
121 E 7th St
New York NY 10009-5781
Phone: 212-674-1066

St Nicholas   GOA
155 Cedar St
New York NY 10006-1013
Phone: 212-227-0773

St Nicholas   CRC
288 E 10th St
New York NY 10009-4812
Phone: 212-254-6685

St Nicholas Cathedral
PER
15 E 97th St
New York NY 10029-6915
Phone: 212-289-1915

St Sava Cathedral SOC
15 W 25th St
New York NY 10010-2002
Phone: 212-242-9240

St Sava Cathedral NGM
PO Box 687 Cathedral Station
New York NY 10025-0687
Phone: 212-242-9240

St Sergius of Radonezh Chapel
75 E 93rd St ROR
New York NY 10128-1331
Phone: 212-534-1601
FAX: 212-426-1086

St Spyridon GOA
124 Wadsworth Ave
New York NY 10033-4812
Phone: 212-795-5870

St Volodymyr Cathedral UCU
160 W 82nd St
New York NY 10024-5502
Phone: 212-873-8550

St Mary Magdalen OCA
Union Theo Sem 122 & E Broadway
200 E 90th St Apt 22 E-F
New York City NY 10033
Phone: 212-927-0596

St Nicholas GOA
PO BOX 2004
Newburgh NY 12550-4708
Phone: 914-561-2556

St Terese FOCI
84 Liberty St, W.H.
Newburgh NY 12550
Phone:

Holy Trinity OCA
3920 Pine Ave
Niagara Falls NY 14301-2710
Phone: 716-284-9596

St George ANT
MPOB 713
Niagara Falls NY 14302
Phone: 716-297-2668

Holy Virgin Protection ROR
51 Prospect St
38 S Mill St
Nyack NY 10960-3744
Phone: 914-353-1155
FAX: 914-353-4341

St Volodymyr UCU
UNA Foordmore Rd
PO Box 1386
Oliverbridge NY 12461
Phone: 914-626-5641

St John Mission GMA
R.R. 1, Smith Road
Parksville NY 12768-9801
Phone: 914-583-5845

Transfiguration OCA
35 Sickletown Rd
PO Box 759
Pearl River NY 10965
Phone: 914-735-7024

All Saints of Russia PER
RD #2, Box 251
Pine Bush NY 12566
Phone: 914-744-3129

Assumption GOA
430 Sheep Pasture Rd
Port Jefferson NY 11777-2074
Phone: 516-473-0894
FAX: 516-928-5131

Kimisis Tis Theotokou GOA
140 S Grand Ave
Poughkeepsie NY 12603-3010
Phone: 914-452-0772
FAX: 914-452-0114

St Nicholas ROR
100 Livingston St
Poughkeepsie NY 12601-4801
Phone: 914-454-6822

Holy Annunciation AOM
Red Hook NY 12571
Phone: 914-758-6710

Asssumption ROR
119-02 94th Ave.
Richmond Hill NY 11419
Phone: 718-847-0260

St Cyril of Turov
104-29 Atlantic Ave
Richmond Hill NY 11418
Phone: 203-877-0896

Annunciation GOA
962 East Ave
Rochester NY 14607-2241
Phone: 716-244-3377

Protection of the Mother of God
460 East Ave ROR
Rochester NY 14607-1911
Phone: 716-473-4568
FAX: 716-473-4568

St John the Baptist OCA
855 Goodman St S
Rochester NY 14620-2545
Phone: 716-442-6860

St Mary Protectress UCU
3176 Saint Paul Blvd
Rochester NY 14617-3433
Phone: 716-342-1076
FAX: 716-342-1076

St Nicholas UOA
64 Niagara St
Rochester NY 14605-2463
Phone:

St Nicholas UCU
512 N George St
Rome NY 13440-4102
Phone: 315-337-9518

Archangel Michael GOA
108 Warner Ave
Roslyn Hts NY 11577
Phone: 516-625-0900
FAX: 516-625-6244

Our Savior GOA
2195 Westchester Ave E
Rye NY 10580
Phone: 914-967-2838
FAX: 914-967-0164

Our Savior GOA
2195 Westchester Ave
Rye NY 10580
Phone: 914-967-2838
FAX: 914-967-0164

Archangel Gabriel ANT
5 McHugh St
S Glens Falls NY 12803-5236
Phone: 518-792-4985

St George ANT
PO BOX 1344
S Glens Falls NY 12803-4705
Phone: 518-792-2359

Protection of the Holy Virgin ROR
2040 Euclid Ave
Schenectady NY 12306-4102
Phone: 518-456-8228

St George GOA
107 Clinton St
Schenectady NY 12305-2001
Phone: 518-393-0742

St Nicholas OCA
1906 Evva Dr
Schenectady NY 12303-5411
Phone: 518-237-5335

Nativity of Our Lady ROR
2040 Euclid Ave.
Schnectady NY
Phone:

St Seraphim ROR
131-A Carpenter Ave
Sea Cliff NY 11579-1332
Phone: 516-671-2075

Our Lady of Kazan OCA
WIllow Shore Ave
Sea Cliff, LI NY 11579
Phone: 516-671-6616
FAX: 516-671-3720

St Gregory of Nyssa CRC
1100 Hicksville Rd
Seaford NY 11783-1603
Phone: 516-541-8977

St John the Theologian Mission
158 W End Ave OCA
Shirley NY 11967
Phone: 516-281-5960

Kimisis Tis Theotokou GOA
P.O. Box 2550
Southampton NY 11969-2550
Phone: 516-283-6169

Icon of the Mother of God "Otrada"
385 S Pascack Rd ROR
Spring Valley NY 10977-6804
Phone: 914-623-4696

St John the Baptist OCA
West and Church Streets
PO Box 498
Spring Valley NY 10977
Phone: 914-425-0259

Holy Trinity-St. Nicholas GOA
1641 Richmond Ave
Staten Island NY 10314
Phone: 718-494-0658
FAX: 718-494-2037

St Irenaeus Chapel OCA
2099 Forest Ave
Staten Island NY 10303
Phone: 718-720-8800
FAX: 718-447-8095

St Sergius of Radonezh Chapel
6850 N Hempstead Tpk, Oyster B
PO Box 675 OCA
Syosset NY 11791
Phone: 516-922-0550
FAX: 516-922-0954

Ss Peter & Paul OCA
401 Hamilton St
Syracuse NY 13204-1915
Phone: 315-468-1715
FAX: 315-477-1915

St Elias ANT
4988 Onondaga Rd
Syracuse NY 13215-1932
Phone: 315-488-0388

St George MOC
5083 Onandaga Rd.
Syracuse NY 13215
Phone:

St Michael OCA
Cornei Oswego # Fabius
PO Box 125
Syracuse NY 13215-0128
Phone: 315-468-0442

St Sergius & St Herman VAS
6421 Franklin Park Dr
Syracuse NY 13057
Phone:

St Sophia GOA
325 Waring Rd
Syracuse NY 13224-2254
Phone: 315-446-5222

St Basil GOA
909 River St
Troy NY 12180-1243
Phone: 518-273-8923

St Nicholas UCU
376 Third St
Troy NY 12180
Phone: 518-274-5482

St John the Baptist ANT
560 Uniondale Ave
Uniondale NY 11553-2202
Phone: 516-485-8934

St Michael UCU
237 Maple Ave
Uniondale NY 11553
Phone: 516-669-7402

... UCU
...er St
... 13501-1407
Pho... 315-733-9339

Ss Peter & Paul UCU
815 Hamilton St
Utica NY 13502-4003
Phone: 315-732-2895

St George ANT
1104 Brinkerhoff Ave
Utica NY 13501
Phone: 315-735-7465

St John of Kronstadt
ROR
1009 Conkling Ave
Utica NY 13501-3131
Phone: 315-797-6539

Theotokos of Great Grace
IGO
Cathedral
1101 Howard Ave
Utica NY 13501
Phone: 315-798-4457
igoa@borg.com

St Sergius of Radonezh
ROR
Tolstoy Farm - Lake Rd
PO Box B
Valley Cottage NY 10989-0599
Phone: 914-268-6551

Annunciation GOA
1 Hellenic Ctr
Vestal NY 13850-3503
Phone: 607-797-0824

St Nicholas GOA
200 Great East Neck Rd
W Babylon NY 11704
Phone: 516-587-1150
FAX: 516-587-1253

St Demetrius MOC
234 Telephone Rd
W Henrietta NY 14586-9758
Phone:

Ss Peter & Paul UCU
64 Higbie Ln
W Islip NY 11795-3924
Phone: 516-422-4453

Ss Constantine & Helen
GOA
1 Mary Crest Rd.
W Nyack NY 10994
Phone: 914-623-4023

St Martin Chapel OCA
Office of Cadet Chaplains
W Point NY 10996
Phone:

St Markella GOA
1960 Jones Ave N
Wantagh NY 11793-3352
Phone: 516-783-5760
FAX: 516-783-4958

St Gregory the Theologian
1824 Rt 376 OCA
Wappingers Falls NY 12590
Phone: 914-462-3887

St Luke UCU
3290 Warners Rd
Warners NY 13164-9761
Phone: 315-468-3472
FAX: 315-468-1981

St Vasilios GOA
516 Franklin St
Watertown NY 13601-3406
Phone: 315-788-4920

St Basil OCA
21 Archibald St
6 Lansking Ave
Watervliet NY 12189-1845
Phone: 518-271-7070

Holy Cross GOA
150-05 12th Ave
Whitestone NY 11357
Phone: 718-767-2943

St Nicholas OCA
14-65 Clintonville St
Whitestone NY 11357
Phone: 718-767-7292

St Theodore ROR
96 Los Robles St
Williamsville NY 14221-6721
Phone: 716-634-6721

Assumption GOA
PO Box 454
Windham NY 12496-0454
Phone: 518-734-4631

Ss Peter & Paul ROR
Ulster Heights Rd
Woodbourne NY 12788
Phone: 914-434-8723

Ss Fanourios & Gerasimos
Cathedral
44-02 48th Ave VAS
Woodside NY 11377
Phone: 718-786-4495
FAX: 718-786-7887

St John Chrysostom
OCA
70-29 45 Ave
Woodside NY 11377
Phone: 718-429-8245

St Nicholas RMA
45-03 48th Ave
Woodside NY 11377
Phone: 718-784-4453

St Toma VAS
44-02 48th Ave
Woodside NY 11377
Phone:

Holy Transfiguration of Christ
PO BOX 121
Woodstock NY 12498
Phone: 914-679-2569

Holy Transfiguration of Christ
on Mount
Mead Mountain Rd AOM
Woodstock NY 12498
Phone: 914-657-3315

St John the Theologian
OCA
PO Box 274
Yaphank NY 11980-0274
Phone: 516-475-7146

OHIO

Holy Trinity OCA
46 Seymour St
Yonkers NY 10701
Phone: 914-965-6815
FAX: 914-966-2466

Prophet Elias GOA
15 Leroy Ave
Yonkers NY 10705
Phone: 914-963-3638
FAX: 914-963-5757

St Mary CRC
485 N Broadway
Yonkers NY 10701
Phone: 914-963-5549

Taxiarchai Chapel GOA
3 Lehman Ter
Yonkers NY 10705
Phone: 914-476-3374
FAX: 914-476-1744

Virgin Mary ANT
77 High St
Yonkers NY 10703
Phone: 914-476-1072
FAX: 914-476-1072

OHIO

Annunciation GOA
129 S Union St
Akron OH 44304-1590
Phone: 330-434-0000

Ascension HOC
Box 72102
Akron OH 44372
Phone: 330-867-3685

Presentation of Our Lord
OCA
3365 Ridgewood Rd
Akron OH 44333-3117
Phone: 330-666-8054
FAX: 330-668-9999

St Archangel Michael
SOC
2552 Pickle Rd
Akron OH 44312-5304
Phone: 216-644-1571

St Demetrius NGM
3106 Ridgewood Rd
PO Box 151
Akron OH 44333-3266
Phone: 216-666-7852

St George ANT
3204 Ridgewood Rd
Akron OH 44333-3116
Phone: 216-666-7116
FAX: 216-456-6207

St Mary CRC
1357 Coventry St
Akron OH 44306-2651
Phone: 330-724-5828

St Prophet Elia OCA
64 W Wilbeth Rd
Akron OH 44301-2414
Phone: 216-724-7129

St Nicholas OCA
1035 E Grant St
Alliance OH 44601-3208
Phone: 216-499-3432

All Saints OCA
1395 County Hwy 75
Amsterdam OH 43903-9801
Phone: 614-543-3671

St Clement of Ohrid MOC
38665 French Creek
Avon OH 44011
Phone: 216-934-6060

Great Martyr George
BAM
558 W Tuscaworas
Barberton OH 44203
Phone:

Ss Peter & Paul NGM
3532 Clark Mill Rd
Barberton OH 44203-1032
Phone: 216-763-3968
FAX: 216-745-0189

St Nicholas CRC
PO Box 777
Barton OH 43905-0777
Phone: 614-695-9533

Ss Cyril & Methodius
OCA
527 44th St
Bellaire OH 43906-1406
Phone: 614-676-2366

St Matthew ANT
192 Prospect St
Berea OH 44017-2522
Phone: 216-826-0662

Archangel Michael OCA
5025 Mill Rd
Broadview Heights OH
44147-2216
Phone: 216-526-5192

St Sava NGM
2151 Wallings Rd
Broadview Hgts OH 44147
Phone: 216-237-2260

St Stephen Church of
Millenium
1905 Pearl Rd UCU
Brunswick OH 44212-3201
Phone: 216-237-6238

Virgin of All Who Sorrow Icon
2030 Hathaway Dr ROR
Brunswick OH 44212-4028
Phone: 216-225-5615

Christ the Savior OCA
282 S 5th St
Byesville OH 43723-9799
Phone: 513-422-1213

Archangel Michael GOA
401 12th St
Campbell OH 44405-1454
Phone: 330-755-3596
FAX: 330-755-6114

St John the Baptist OCA
301 Struthers-Liberty Rd
Campbell OH 44405
Phone: 330-755-4931

Holy Assumption OCA
2027 18th St NE
Canton OH 44705-2175
Phone: 330-455-9146
FAX: 330-445-9182

Holy Cross   ANT
5015 Ridge Ave SE
PO BOX 8034
Canton OH 44707-1127
Phone: 216-484-1284

Holy Trinity   GOA
4705 Fairhaven Ave NW
Canton OH 44709-1348
Phone: 216-494-8770

St George   ANT
1118 Cherry Ave NE
Canton OH 44704-1036
Phone: 216-455-8482

St George   SOC
4663 Wayview St NW
Canton OH 44720-7044
Phone: 216-494-7888

St George the Great Martyr
114 30th St NW   OCA
Canton OH 44709
Phone: 330-492-4592
FAX: 330-492-5993

St Haralambos   GOA
251 25th St NW
Canton OH 44709-3923
Phone: 216-454-7278

Christ the Savior / Holy Spirit
OCA
4285 Ashland Ave
Cincinnati OH 45212-3127
Phone: 513-351-0907

Holy Trinity-St. Nicholas
GOA
7000 Winton Rd
Cincinnati OH 45224-1331
Phone: 513-591-0030
FAX: 513-591-0034

St Andrew   RMA
837 Dayton St
Cincinnati OH 45214-2225
Phone: 513-681-6230

St George   NGM
5830 Glenview Ave
Cincinnati OH 45224-2814
Phone: 513-542-4452

St George   ROR
4905 Myrtle Ave
Cincinnati OH 45242-6134
Phone: 513-791-6540

St. Ilija   MOC
8465 Wuest Rd
Cincinnati OH 45247
Phone: 513-385-4880

St James ROR
9158 Winton Rd
Cincinnati OH 45231-3830
Phone: 513-729-1600

Annunciation   GOA
2187 W 14th St
Cleveland OH 44113-3609
Phone: 216-861-0116

Falling Asleep of Blessed
Virgin Mary
3256 Warren Rd   OCA
Cleveland OH 44111-1144
Phone: 216-941-5550

Holy Resurrection   ROR
6201 Detroit Ave
Cleveland OH 44102-3007
Phone: 216-651-2879

Mother of God of Zyrovicy
3517 W 25th St   BAM
Cleveland OH 44109-1950
Phone: 216-749-5756

Ss Boris and Gleb   IND
1416 W 57th St
Cleveland OH 44102
Phone: 419-433-7655

Ss Constantine & Helen
Cathedral
3352 Mayfield Rd   GOA
Cleveland OH 44118-1330
Phone: 216-932-3300
FAX: 216-932-0825

St E Premte   OCA
10716 Jasper Rd
Cleveland OH 44111-5346
Phone: 216-941-1508

St George   ANT
2587 W 14th St
Cleveland OH 44113-4408
Phone: 216-781-9020

St Mary Romanian   OCA
3256 Warren Rd
Cleveland OH 44111
Phone: 216-941-5550
FAX: 216-941-3068

St Panteleimon   UCU
3747 W 135th St
Cleveland OH 44111-4427
Phone: 216-251-1064

St Theodosius Cathedral
OCA
8200 Biddulph Rd
Cleveland OH 44144-3203
Phone: 216-741-1310

Virgin of All Who Sorrow Icon
1350 W 69th St   ROR
Cleveland OH 44102-2016
Phone: 216-225-5615

Annunciation Cathedral
GOA
555 N High St
Columbus OH 43215-2068
Phone: 614-224-9020
FAX: 614-224-5032

Dormition MCI
3564 Medway Ave
Columbus OH 43213-1643
Phone:

St Gregory of Nyssa
OCA
271 Brevoort Rd
Columbus OH 43214-3825
Phone: 614-268-4186

St Mary
MOC
120 S Napoleon Ave
Columbus OH 43213
Phone: 614-231-7851

St Nectarios of Aegina VAS
1618 S Champion Ave
Columbus OH 43207-1308
Phone:

St Stephen of Decani SOC
1840 N Cassady Ave
Columbus OH 43219-1519
Phone: 614-475-0922

Annunciation   GOA
500 Belmonte Park N
Dayton OH 45405-4705
Phone: 513-224-0601
FAX: 513-224-0173

St Paul the Apostle OCA
2382 Kennedy Ave
Dayton OH 45420
Phone: 937-254-7900
FAX: 937-254-0800

St Paul the Apostle OCA
2382 Kennedy Ave
Dayton OH 45420-3167
Phone: 937-254-7900
FAX: 937[254-0800

Presentaton of Our Lord OCA
3365 Ridge Rd
Fairlawn OH 44333
Phone: 330-666-8054
FAX: 330-668-9999

St Thomas   BEC
555 S Cleveland-Massilon Rd
Fairlawn OH 44333
Phone: 330-666-8006

St Nikola MOC
5305 Masillon Rd
Green OH 44232
Phone:

Holy Assumption OCA
114 E Main St
Lakeside Marblehead OH 43440-2224
Phone: 419-798-4591

Ss Peter & Paul   OCA
12711 Madison Ave
Lakewood OH 44107-4936
Phone: 216-521-0923

St Nicholas Pro-Cathedral UCU
2101 Quail St
Lakewood OH 44107-5219
Phone: 216-226-5506

Ss Cyril & Methodius BEC
31 East
Lorain OH 44055
Phone:

Ss Cyril & Methodius OCA
1795 E 31st St
Lorain OH 44055-1719
Phone: 216-277-5195

Ss Peter & Paul   OCA
Gary Ave & 32nd St
Lorain OH 44055
Phone: 216-277-5281

St George   SOC
3335 Grove Ave
Lorain OH 44055-2051
Phone: 216-781-9020

St Mary UCU
2304 E 34th St
Lorain OH 44055-2028
Phone: 630-980-5796

St Nicholas   GOA
2000 Tower Blvd
Lorain OH 44053-3034
Phone: 216-960-2992

Ss Constantine & Helen GOA
265 W 3rd St
Mansfield OH 44903-7200
Phone: 419-526-0129

St Andrew   OCA
16069 Maple Park Dr
Maple Heights OH 44137-4220
Phone: 216-475-9365

Zoodochos Peghe GOA
314-316 N 5th St
Martins Ferry OH 43935
Phone: 614-633-3707

Holy Spirit Chapel   OCA
PO Box 540
Massillon OH 44648-0540
Phone: 216-833-3135

St George   GOA
364 1st St SE
PO Box 438
Massillon OH 44646
Phone: 216-832-3659

St Nikola
5305 Massilon Rd, Box 905
Massilon OH 44648
Phone: 216-896-2323

St Nicholas   OCA
9650 Johnnycake Ridge Rd
Mentor OH 44060-6708
Phone: 216-946-9571

Ss Constantine & Helen GOA
2500 Grand Ave
Middletown OH 45044-4712
Phone: 513-422-2312

St Andrew   OCA
PO Box 273
Mingo Jct OH 43938
Phone: 614-535-0397

St Nicholas   OCA
755 S Cleveland Ave
Mogadore OH 44260-1521
Phone: 216-628-1333

St Matthew   ANT
10383 Albian Rd
N Royalton OH 44133
Phone: 440-582-5673

St Paul GOA
4548 Wallings Rd
N Royalton OH 44133-3121
Phone: 216-237-8998
FAX: 216-237-8999

St John Chrysostom OCA
135 S Chestnut Ave
Niles OH 44446-1544
Phone: 216-369-3908

St Innocent OCA
25151 Mitchell Dr
North Olmsted OH 44070-3440
Phone: 216-979-9622

Christ the Saviour CRC
10000 State Rd
North Royalton OH 44133-1938
Phone: 216-886-4609

Holy Trinity UCU
9672 State Rd
North Royalton OH 44133-1930
Phone: 216-237-0101

St Matthew ANT
10383 Albion Rd
PO BOX 33183
North Royalton OH 44133-1408
Phone: 216-826-0662

Holy Trinity OCA
6822 Broadview Rd
Parma OH 44134-4805
Phone: 440-524-4859

St Sava Cathedral SOC
6306 Broadview Rd
Parma OH 44134-3169
Phone: 216-749-0064

St Sergius ROR
6520 Broadview Rd
Parma OH 44134-4802
Phone: 216-447-1015

St Vladimir's Cathedral UCU
5913 STte Rd
Parma OH 44134
Phone: 440-885-1509

St Volodymyr Cathedral UCU
5913 State Rd
Parma OH 44134-2864
Phone: 216-885-1509

Christ the Saviour CRC
9115 Ridge Rd
Pasrma OH 44129
Phone: 216-886-4609

Holy Trinity AUX
579 Pickerington Hills Dr
Pickerington OH 43147-1368
Phone: 614-833-1170

Marcha Monastery SOC
5095 Broadview Rd
Richfield OH 44286-9480
Phone: 216-659-4027

Bunavestire Cathedral RMA
3300 Wooster Rd
Rocky River OH 44116-4168
Phone: 216-356-1126

St Demetrios GOA
22909 Center Ridge Rd
Rocky River OH 44116-3047
Phone: 216-331-2246

St Mark NGM
1434 Lake Breeze Rd
Sheffield Lake OH 44054-2526
Phone: 216-949-7719

Assumption of the Blessed Virgin
1127 E High St GOA
PO Box 1694
Springfield OH 45505-1121
Phone: 513-322-8169

Holy Resurrection SOC
530 N 4th St
Steubenville OH 43952-1934
Phone: 614-282-4463

Holy Transfiguration OCA
206 10th St
Steubenville OH 43952-2203
Phone: 614-282-2493

Holy Trinity GOA
300 S 4th St
PO BOX 788
Steubenville OH 43952-2931
Phone: 614-282-9835

St Elias ANT
4940 Harroun Rd
Sylvania OH 43560
Phone: 419-882-4037
FAX: 419-882-4954

Holy Trinity Cathedral GOA
740 N Superior St
Toledo OH 43604-1739
Phone: 419-243-9189

St George ANT
3754 Woodley Rd
Toledo OH 43606-1159
Phone: 419-475-7054
FAX: 419-475-3502

St George Cathedral OCA
137 Oswald St
Toledo OH 43605-2110
Phone: 419-691-8913

St George Cathedral ANT
3754 Woodley Rd
Toledo OH 43606-1159
Phone: 419-475-7054
FAX: 419-475-3502

Our Lady of Kazan ROR
218 W Market St
Urbana OH 43078-2021
Phone: 513-653-5179

Holy Resurrection OCA
1836 North Rd NE
Warren OH 44483-3653
Phone: 216-372-1159

St Demetrios GOA
429 High St NE
PO Box 4214
Warren OH 44481-1226
Phone: 216-394-9021

St Elija NGM
PO Box 2304
Warren OH 44484-2304
Phone: 216-369-8092

St John the Baptist OCA
2220 Reeves Rd NE
Warren OH 44483-4330
Phone: 216-372-3895

St Matrona of Chios CHR
425 Kenworth NE
Warren OH 44483
Phone: 718-932-1592

St Nicholas CRC
2053 North Rd
Warren OH 44485
Phone: 216-372-6240

St Innocent OCA
25800 Hilliard Blvd
Westlake OH 44145-3312
Phone: 216-979-9622

Holy Ghost OCA
18 S Richview Ave
Youngstown OH 44509-2731
Phone: 216-792-9119

Holy Trinity OCA
626 Wick Ave
Youngstown OH 44502-1215
Phone: 216-746-4424

Holy Trinity SOC
39 Laird Ave
Youngstown OH 44509-2517
Phone: 216-792-2022

Nativity of Christ PER
727 Miller St
Youngstown OH 44502
Phone: 216-788-0151
FAX: 216-788-9361

Old Holy Trinity NGM
420 N Raccoon Rd
Youngstown OH 44515-1520
Phone: 216-799-0075

Ss Peter and Paul UCU
1025 N Belle Vista Ave
Youngstown OH 44509
Phone: 330-799-3830

St John the Forerunner
Orthodox Church
4955 Glenwood Ave GOA
Youngstown OH 44512
Phone: 330-788-5257
FAX: 330-788-5257

St Mark ANT
3560 Logan Way
Youngstown OH 44505-1644
Phone: 216-759-8383

St Michael CRC
125 Steel St
Youngstown OH 44509-2536
Phone: 216-799-8133

St Nicholas GOA
220 N Walnut St
Youngstown OH 44503-1623
Phone: 216-743-5493

OKLAHOMA

Ss Cyril & Methodius OCA
3rd & Modoc
Hartshorne OK 74547
Phone:

St Mary UCU
PO Box 793
Jones OK 73049-0793
Phone: 405-632-4501

St Benedict ROR
1124 N Macarthur Blvd
Oklahoma City OK 73127-4327
Phone: 405-672-1441

St Elias ANT
2101 NW 16th St
Oklahoma City OK 73107-4924
Phone: 405-524-2625
FAX: 405-528-1832

St Elijah Orthodox Christian Church ANT
15000 N May Ave
Oklahoma City OK 73132
Phone: 405-755-7804
FAX: 405-755-7807

St George Greek Orthodox Church GOA
2101 NW 145 St
Oklahoma City OK 73134
Phone: 405-751-1885
FAX: 405-751-1889

St James ROR
9612 N 151st E Ave
Owasso OK 74055-4848
Phone: 918-274-9612

Holy Trinity GOA
1222 S. Guthrie Ave
Tulsa OK 74119
Phone: 918-583-0417

St Antony ANT
2645 E 6th St
Tulsa OK 74104
Phone: 918-584-7300
FAX: 918-584-7300

St Photios HOC
PO Box 52015
Tulsa OK 74152
Phone:

OREGON

St Anne Missiion OCA
2309 NW Scenic Dr
PO Box 1366
Albany OR 97321-0545
Phone: 541-928-9240
FAX: 541-928-6982

Greek Orthodox Parish of Portland Metro
16752 SW Amy Lane GOA
Beaverton OR 97007
Phone: 503-259-0331

Dormition CHU
Donald OR 97020
Phone:

St George GOA
202 Hillview #1
PO Box 70132
Eugene OR 97401-0107
Phone: 541-683-3519
FAX: 541-683-1044

St Paul the Apostle VAS
135 E 13th Ave
Eugene OR 97401-3516
Phone:

Holy Transfiguration MOR
12929 Bethlehem Dr NE
Gervais OR 97026-9721
Phone:

St Nicholas CHU
Gervais OR 97026
Phone:

St Innocent ROR
719 Welsh St
Medford OR 97501-2301
Phone: 541-772-0851
FAX: 541-772-0349

Annunciation OCA
13515 SE Rusk Rd
Milwaukie OR 97222
Phone: 503-659-5593
FAX: 503-659-1119

New Martyrs of Russia
ROR
13848 S Union Hall Rd
Mulino OR 97042-9763
Phone: 503-632-7040

Descent of Holy Spirit OCA
20607 Hwy 214
Oregon City OR 97045-9170

Annunciation OCA
13515 SE Rusk Rd
Portland OR 97222-3212
Phone: 503-659-3646
FAX: 503-659-1119

Holy Apostles OCA
2053 NW Overton
Portland OR 97209-1600
Phone: 503-222-3469
FAX: 503-916-8789

Holy Trinity GOA
3131 NE Glisan
Portland OR 97232
Phone: 503-234-0468
FAX: 503-236-8379

PENNSYLVANIA

Nativity of the Most Holy
Theotokos 16838 SE Kelly St
SOC
Portland OR 97236-1430
Phone: 503-760-2330

Nativity of the Theotokos
AUX
5209 SE 64th St
Portland OR 97206-4645
Phone: 503-285-3881

St George ANT
5834 SE Lincoln St
Portland OR 97266-2150
Phone: 503-761-7292

St John the Baptist UCU
8014 SE 16th Ave
3007 NE Schuyler
Portland OR 97212
Phone:

St Mary OCA
2210 SW Dolphin St
Portland OR
Phone: 503-254-8376

St Nicholas OCA
2210 SW Dolph Ct
Portland OR 97219-4138
Phone: 503-245-2403

St Raphael VAS
2057 NW Overton St
Portland OR 97209-1620
Phone:

Our Lady of Tikhvin MAR
St. Benedict OR 97373
Phone:

Holy Spirit - Paraclete
SGP
20012 Williams Hwy
Williams OR 97544-9500
Phone: 503-846-6935

Our Lady of Kursk Chapel
1250 Hardcastle Ave
PER
Woodburn OR 97071
Phone: 503-981-1627

St Nicholas CHU
Woodburn OR 97071
Phone:

Theotokos of Kursk UCU
1250 Hardcastle Ave
Woodburn OR 97071-3624
Phone:

PENNSYLVANIA

Holy Resurrection OCA
17 E Kirmar Ave
Alden Staton PA 18634
Phone:

Kimisis Tis Theotokou
GOA
2111 Davidson St
Aliquippa PA 15001-2706
Phone: 412-375-5341
FAX: 412-378-3162

St Elijah SOC
12200 Irwin St
Aliquippa PA 15001
Phone: 412-375-4074
FAX: 412-375-1018

Protection of Blessed Virgin
Mary
703 N 6th St CRC
Allentown PA 18102-1607
Phone: 215-439-9589

St George ANT
1011 Catasauqua Ave
Allentown PA 18102-5001
Phone: 215-439-9972

St Mary's Cathedral UOA
1031 Fullerton Ave
Allentown PA 18102-5007
Phone: 215-439-4810

St Alexander Nevsky
Cathedral
1600 Guyton Rd OCA
Allison Park PA 15101-3250
Phone: 412-366-4647
FAX: 412-366-4647

Holy Trinity GOA
1433 13th Ave
Altoona PA 16601-3339
Phone: 814-943-0091

Ss Peter & Paul OCA
2027 13th Ave
Altoona PA 166012419
Phone: 814-946-9482

St George ANT
519 58th St
Altoona PA 16602-1122
Phone: 814-944-7187

Holy Ghost OCA
210 Maplewood Ave
Ambridge PA 15003-2516
Phone: 412-741-5008
FAX: 412-741-5008

Holy Trinity GOA
2930 Beaver Rd
Ambridge PA 15003-1418
Phone: 412-266-5336

St John's Orthodox Church
450 Glenwood Dr CRC
Ambridge PA 15003
Phone: 412-266-2879

St Vladimir UCU
313 9th St
Ambridge PA 15003-2350
Phone: 412-266-8330

Holy Virgin UCU
1701 Kenneth Ave
Arnold PA 15068
Phone: 412-335-1302

St John the Evangelist
ANT
221 Oakville Rd
Beaver Falls PA 15010-1209
Phone: 412-847-1111

Holy Resurrection OCA
Mary St.
Belle Vernon PA 15012
Phone: 412-929-9194

St Basil the Great ROR
RD #3 (Ridge Rd) - Box 187a
Belle Vernon PA 15012-0548
Phone: 412-929-2878
FAX: 412-326-4410

Holy Annunciation OCA
1228 2nd Ave
Berwick PA 18603-1604
Phone: 717-752-3184

St Nicholas OCA
980 Bridle Path Rd
Bethlehem PA 18017-3120
Phone: 215-867-0402

St Nicholas GOA
1607 W Union Blvd
Bethlehem PA 18018-3416
Phone: 610-867-1327
FAX: 610-867-9487

St Nicholas OCA
980 Bridle Path Rd
Bethlehem PA 18017-3120
Phone: 610-867-0402
FAX: 610-866-3282

St John the Baptist OCA
PO Box 464
Black Lick PA 15716-0464
Phone: 724-248-3288

St John the Baptist OCA
801 Blaire Rd; Black Lick
Blairsville PA 15717
Phone: 412-248-3822

St Andrew UCU
300 Main St
Blakely PA 18447
Phone: 717-383-0530

St Ignatius ANT
RR 1 Box 307
Bolivar PA 15923-9603
Phone: 412-238-9565

St Michael CRC
146 3rd St
Braddock PA 15104-1145
Phone: 412-271-2725

St George ANT
610 Dewey Ave
Bridgeville PA 15017
Phone: 412-221-2277

St Luke GOA
35 N Malin Rd
Broomall PA 19008
Phone: 610-353-1592
FAX: 610-353-8714

Holy Resurrection OCA
118 Main St
Brownsville PA 15417-2331
Phone: 412-785-4245

St Ellien ANT
500 Spring St
Brownsville PA 15417
Phone: 412-785-9431

St Ellien ANT
506 Spring St
Brownsville PA 15417-1739
Phone: 412-785-9431

St Anthony ANT
400 S 6th Ave
Butler PA 16001-5633
Phone: 412-287-6893

Holy Trinity ROR
630 American St
California PA 15419-1402
Phone: 412-938-7216

Holy Trinity Cathedral
GOA
1000 Yverdon Dr
Camp Hill PA 17011-1239
Phone: 717-763-7441
FAX: 717-763-7458

All Saints GOA
411 Blaine Ave
Canonsburg PA 15317-2107
Phone: 412-745-5205
FAX: 412-745-3599

St John the Baptist OCA
601 Boone Ave
Canonsburg PA 15317-1410
Phone: 412-745-9776
FAX: 412-745-8216

St Basil   ROR
33 Midland St
Carbondale PA 18407-1245
Phone: 717-282-2314

St George   SOC
RR 1 Box 91
Carmichaels PA 15320-9503
Phone: 412-966-7428

Intercession of the Holy
Virgin
214 Mansfield Blvd   OCA
Carnegie PA 15106-2433
Phone: 412-276-6234

Ss Peter & Paul   UCU
200 Walnut St
Carnegie PA 15106-2442
Phone: 412-279-2111

St John the Wonderworker
PO Box 510   ROR
Carnegie PA 15106-0510
Phone: 412-684-8043

Holy Trinity   OCA
1023 5th St
Catasauqua PA 18032-2202
Phone: 610-264-0822

Holy Assumption   OCA
635 Sunshine Ave
Central City PA 15926-1230
Phone: 814-754-4054

Ss Peter & Paul   OCA
Boswell PA
635 Sunshine Ave
Central City PA 15926
Phone: 814-754-4054

Ss Peter & Paul   CRC
149 Wheeler St
Central City PA 15926-1043
Phone: 814-754-4442

Ss Peter and Paul   OCA
Pine Hill PA
635 Sunshine Ave
Central City PA 125926
Phone: 814-754-4054

Holy Trinity   OCA
1000 Lookout Ave
Charleroi PA 15022-2024
Phone: 724-483-4441

St Michael   PER
335-37 Fairmount Ave, Phila
103 Hilldale Rd
Cheltenham PA 19012
Phone: 215-635-0509

Assumption of the Blessed
Virgin Mary
2412 W 3rd St   UCU
Chester PA 19013-2308
Phone: 215-494-7853

St Mary's UCU
2412 W 3rd St
Chester PA 19013
Phone: 610-494-7853

St Nicholas   PER
2513 W Fourth St
Chester PA 19013
Phone: 610-497-3860

St Anthony   GOA
421 Miller Ave
PO BOX 31
Clairton PA 15025-1719
Phone: 412-621-0581

St Mary   SOC
524-526 3rd St
Clairton PA 15025
Phone: 412-929-8052

St Basil   OCA
1107 Sunset Dr
Clarks Summit PA 18411
Phone: 717-937-4899

St Michael   CRC
65 Morris St
Clymer PA 15728-1224
Phone: 412-254-4343

St Mary (Nativity)   OCA
1st & Phillips Sts
Coaldale PA 18218-1602
Phone: 717-645-2087

St Nicholas   OCA
Oak St & 1st Ave
354 Sherry Ln
Coatesville PA 19320
Phone: 610-380-8741

Holy Ascension   OCA
5th Ave
Box 428
Colver PA 15927
Phone: 814-946-9482

Holy Resurrection   OCA
716 Atlantic Ave, Forest Hills
PO Box 1769
Cranberry Twp PA 16066
Phone: 412-271-4738

St Michael   OCA
PO Box 92
Curtisville PA 15032-0092
Phone: 724-265-1005

St Andrew   OCA
PO Box 147
Dallas PA 18612-0147
Phone: 717-675-1541

St Mary   CRC
522 Main St
Dickson City PA 18519-1524
Phone: 717-489-7023

St John the Baptist   UCU
PO Box 81
Dixonville PA 15734-0081
Phone: 412-349-4821

St Nicholas   OCA
1 St Nicholas Dr
Donora PA 15033
Phone: 724-379-4827

Ss Peter and Paul   OCA
108 N Third St
DuBois PA 15801-3158
Phone: 814-375-0459

St Nicholas   OCA
507 Catherine St
Duquesne PA 15110
Phone: 412-466-1180

St Nicholas OCA
507 Catherine St
Duquesne PA 15110
Phone: 412-466-1180

Presentation of Christ GOA
PO Box 87
E Pittsburgh PA 15112-0087
Phone: 412-824-5540
FAX: 412-824-9740

St John CRC
211 Cable Ave
E Pittsburgh PA 15112
Phone: 412-824-0246

Evangelismos GOA
20th St. & Hay Terrace
Easton PA 18042
Phone: 610-253-8147

Ss Peter and Paul OCA
25636 N Mosiertown Rd
Edinboro PA 16412
Phone: 814-734-3801

St Nicholas PER
8442 Pageville Rd
Edinboro PA 16412-3544
Phone: 814-756-4548

St John the Baptist OCA
93 Zerby Ave
Edwardsville PA 18704
Phone: 717-287-7186

Annunciation GOA
7921 Old York Rd
Elkins Park PA 19027-2306
Phone: 215-635-0316
FAX: 215-635-8301

Descent of Holy Ghost OCA
323 Ashbourne Rd
Elkins Park PA 19027-2601
Phone: 215-637-4285

Holy Trinity OCA
1709 Moravia St
PO Box 222, Short Ave,
Elport
Ellwood City PA 16117
Phone: 724-758-9745

St Elias OCA
425 Cherry Way
Ellwood City PA 16117-2064
Phone: 330-452-1940

St John the Baptist CRC
528 1st Ave
Ellwood City PA 16117-1105
Phone: 412-652-7602

Ss Peter & Paul UCU
PO Box 147
Elmora PA 15737-0147
Phone: 814-948-6718

St Paul ANT
45 S 4th St
Emmaus PA 18049-3844
Phone: 610-965-2298

Holy Trinity OCA
631 Parade St
Erie PA 16503-1111
Phone: 814-459-2599

Koimisis Tis Theotokou GOA
4376 W Lake Rd
Erie PA 16505-1416
Phone: 814-459-4390

Nativity of Christ ROR
721 E Front
109 German St
Erie PA 16507
Phone: 814-459-8515
FAX: 814-459-8515

St Nicholas CRC
1115 East Ave
Erie PA 16503-1533
Phone: 814-452-4176

Evangelismos GOA
1007 Washington St
Farrell PA 16121-1871
Phone: 412-342-2070

Holy Resurrection OCA
716 Atlantic Ave
Forest Hills PA 15221
Phone: 412-271-4738

Holy Ascension OCA
209 S Lehigh Ave
Frackville PA 17931-2211
Phone: 717-874-3162

Ss Peter & Paul UOA
921 Walnut St
Freeland PA 18224-1325
Phone: 717-636-0291

St Michael CRC
451 Fern St
Freeland PA 18224-1808
Phone: 717-636-2085

Ss Peter and Paul OCA
RD 1, Urey
Glen Campbell PA 15742
Phone: 814-375-0459

St Michael ANT
601 Wirsing Ave
Greensburg PA 15601-5347
Phone: 412-834-1311

Christ the Savior OCA
5501 Locust Ln
Harrisburg PA 17109-5623
Phone: 717-872-8834
FAX: 717-545-5054

Holy Annunciation BEC
721 N Front St
Harrisburg PA 17113-2130
Phone: 717-939-7525

St Nicholas SOC
601 S Harrisburg St
Harrisburg PA 17113-1219
Phone: 717-939-0251

St John the Baptist CRC
PO Box 203
Hawk Run PA 16840-0203
Phone: 814-342-0163

St Joseph of Masramures OCA
314 W Broad St
Hazelton PA 18201-6105
Phone: 718-366-9053

Holy Cross   OCA
950 Maple Dr
Hermitage PA 16148-2333
Phone: 724-346-9937
FAX: 724-342-3113

St George   SOC
PO BOX 1052
Hermitage PA 16148-3514
Phone: 412-342-2600

Ss Peter & Paul   CRC
419 S Main St
Homer City PA 15748-1550
Phone: 412-479-3656

St Gregory   OCA
214 E 15th Ave
Homestead PA 15120-1705
Phone: 412-461-2426

St Nicholas   CRC
903 Ann St
Homestead PA 15120-1615
Phone: 412-461-3264

Epiphany of Our Lord
CRC
85 Penn St
Huntington PA 16652
Phone: 412-258-5072

Nativity of the Theotokos (St Mary's)
PO Box 158 OCA
Irvona PA 16656
Phone: 814-672-3846

St Michael the Archangel
OCA
PO Box 158
Irvona PA 16656
Phone: 814-672-3846

Ss. Cyril & Methodius
OCA
520 Scott Ave
Jeannette PA 15644-1719
Phone: 724-523-3628

St Michael   UCU
112 13th St
Jeannette PA 15644-2013
Phone: 412-523-8849

St Sophia - Ss Faith, Hope, & Agape GOA
900 S Trooper Rd
Jeffersonville PA 19403
Phone: 610-650-8960
FAX: 215-855-5577

Nativity of the Blessed Virgin Mary 5222 Front St CRC
Jenners PA 15546
Phone: 814-629-9177

St Mary's CRC
190 Front St
Jenners PA 15546
Phone: 814-629-5292

St Michael   OCA
Walnut & Hudson Sts
305 Walnut St
Jermyn PA 18433
Phone: 717-876-1241

American Carpatho-Russian Orthodox Dioc.   CRC
312 Garfield St
Johnson PA 15906
Phone: 814-539-9143
FAX: 814-536-4699

Christ the Saviour Seminary / Mount Chri   CRC
225 Chandler Ave
Johnstown PA 15906-2103
Phone: 814-539-0116

Ss Peter and Paul   UCU
St Clair Rd
PO Box 1233
Johnstown PA 15907
Phone: 814-536-8387

St George   NGM
PO Box 1096
Johnstown PA 15907
Phone:

St John the Baptist OCA
427 1st St
Johnstown PA 15909-1907
Phone: 814-539-8613
FAX: 814-539-8841

St Mary   GOA
435 Somerset St
Johnstown PA 15901-2529
Phone: 814-535-5056

St Mary   ANT
111 Alberta Ave
Johnstown PA 15905-3002
Phone: 814-255-4077
FAX: 814-255-2148

St Nicholas   SOC
971-1001 St Clair Rd
Johnstown PA 15905
Phone: 814-255-1853

St John the Baptist OCA
PO Box 131
Lake Ariel PA 18436
Phone: 717-937-4860

Annunciation   GOA
64 Hershey Ave
Lancaster PA 17603-5402
Phone: 717-394-1735
FAX: 717-394-0991

St Nicholas   CRC
125 W Bertsch St
Lansford PA 18232-1908
Phone: 717-645-4311

St Stephen   CRC
720 Mission Rd
Lawson Hts PA 15650
Phone: 412-539-1109

Holy Resurrection   NGM
122 E Weidman St
Lebanon PA 17046-3952
Phone: 717-272-8132

Ss Peter & Paul   CRC
1313 Randall Ave
Levittown PA 19057-5023
Phone: 215-943-8222

Ss Peter & Paul   ANT
PO Box 638
Ligonier PA 15658-0638
Phone: 412-238-3677

St John the Baptist CRC
RD 1 Box 241-I
Ligonier PA 15658
Phone: 412-238-9783

St Stephen CRC
RD 1; Box 241-I
Ligonier PA 15658
Phone: 412-238-9783

St Vladimir OCA
211 Main St
Lopez PA 18628
Phone: 717-928-8909

Holy Ascension OCA
752 N 2nd St
Lykens PA 17048-1403
Phone: 717-453-7927

Ss Peter & Paul UCU
21 Evergreen Dr
Lyndora PA 16045-1309
Phone: 412-287-4448
FAX: 412-287-4448

St Andrew OCA
201 Penn Ave
Lyndora PA 16045-1056
Phone: 724-285-6010

Nativity of the Theotokos
OCA
PO Box 158
Madera PA 16661
Phone: 814-672-3846

Nativity of the Blessed Virgin Mary 309 S Washington St
OCA
Masontown PA 15461-2031
Phone: 724-583-9740

St John the Baptist ROR
706 Hill St
Mayfield PA 18433-2015
Phone: 717-876-0730
FAX: 717-876-2534

St Sava SOC
901 Hartman St
Mc Keesport PA 15132-1526
Phone: 412-672-1872

Holy Trinity OCA
223 S Kennedy Dr
McAdoo PA 18237-1713
Phone: 717-929-2733

St Mary UCU
116 Ella St
McKees Rocks PA 15136-2730
Phone: 412-331-2362

St Mary's UCU
116 Ellis St
McKees Rocks PA 15136
Phone: 412-331-2362

St Nicholas OCA
320 Munson Ave
McKees Rocks PA 15136-2722
Phone: 412-331-1053

Annunciation GOA
1128 Summit Ave.
McKeesport PA 15131
Phone: 412-673-1224

Dormition ROR
330 Shaw Ave
McKeesport PA 15132-2917
Phone: 412-672-3444

Holy Dormition ROR
330 Shaw Ave
McKeesport PA 15132-2917
Phone: 412-672-3444

St Michael's Orthodox Church
424 9th Ave CRC
McKeesport PA 15132-4001
Phone: 412-678-0517

St Sava
SOC
901 Hartman St
McKeesport PA 15132
Phone: 412-672-1872
Fr.Stevo@aol.com

St John Chrysostom
ANT
26 Winding Hill Dr
Mechanicsburg PA 17055-5642
Phone: 717-795-7170

St George GOA
30 E Forge Rd
Media PA 19063-0366
Phone: 610-459-0366

St Herman of Alaska
OCA
1855 Middletown Rd,
Gradyville
692 Meadowbrook Ln
Media PA 19063
Phone: 610-459-5310

St George SOC
30 Tenth St
Midland PA 15059
Phone: 412-643-1396
FAX: 412-643-1396

Ss Peter & Paul OCA
558 Sunbury St
Minersville PA 17954-1016
Phone: 717-544-2690

St George UCU
336 N Front St
Minersville PA 17954-1417
Phone: 717-544-4553

St John the Divine OCA
42 McKee Ave
Monessen PA 15062-1227
Phone: 742-684-3932

St Michael ANT
141 Pennslyvania Blvd
Monessen PA 15062
Phone: 412-684-7460

St Nicholas UCU
17 Reed Ave
Monessen PA 15062-1236
Phone: 412-684-3614

St Spyridon GOA
Reeves Ave
PO Box 327
Monessen PA 15062-0327
Phone: 412-684-4841
FAX: 412-684-3889

Nativity of the Blessed Virgin Mary 508 High St OCA
Monongahela PA 15063-2530
Phone: 724-925-7129

St Nicholas CRC
314 6th St
Monongahela PA 15063-2620
Phone: 412-258-5072

St Archangel Michael NGM
PO BOX 392
Monroeville PA 15146-2912
Phone: 412-373-2726

St Nicholas SOC
2110 Haymaker Rd
Monroeville PA 15146-4322
Phone: 412-372-4454

St Michael OCA
131 N Willow St
Mount Carmel PA 17851-1122
Phone: 717-339-1200

Ss Peter and Paul CRC
Sherman St
PO Box 495
Mount Union PA 17066
Phone: 814-542-2207
FAX: 814-542-9299

Three Pillars of Orthodoxy
Mill St & Zion Rd AUX
Mt Holly Springs PA 17065
Phone: 717-486-5642

Ss Peter & Paul CRC
20 W Sherman St
Mt Union PA 17066-1166
Phone:

Christ the Saviour ROR
11 W Kirmar Ave
Nanticoke PA 18634-2001
Phone: 717-822-3358

Holy Resurrection OCA
17 E Kirmar Ave
Nanticoke PA 18634-3607
Phone: 717-735-0546

St John the Baptist OCA
Front and Welles St
106 Welles Sts.
Nanticoke PA 18634
Phone: 717-735-2263

Holy Ascension UCU
980 Caroline St
Nanty Glo PA 15943-1309
Phone: 412-349-4821

St John the Baptist CRC
9 W Railroad St
Nesquehoning PA 18240-1514
Phone: 717-669-6523

Holy Trinity UCU
940 Rose Ave
New Castle PA 16101-4408
Phone:

St Elias ANT
915 Lynn St
New Castle PA 16101-4374
Phone: 412-658-1712

St George GOA
315 W Englewood Ave
New Castle PA 16105-1805
Phone: 412-654-8521

St Nicholas CRC
205 E Reynolds St
New Castle PA 16101-4716
Phone: 412-652-7602

Annunciation of the Virgin Mary
805 Walnut St GOA
New Kensington PA 15068-5648
Phone: 412-339-2003

Holy Virgin UCU
1701 Kenneth Ave
New Kensington PA 15068-4220
Phone: 412-335-1302

St George ANT
1150 Leishman Ave
New Kensington PA 15068-5605
Phone: 412-335-9988
FAX: 412-335-5223

St George ANT
1150 Leishman Ave
New Kensington PA 15068-5605
Phone: 412-335-9988

St John the Baptist OCA
150 Elmtree Rd
New Kensington PA 15068-4636
Phone: 724-337-8162

Holy Trinity OCA
915 S Mill St
RR 1 Box 14
New Salem PA 15468-9702
Phone: 724-245-9251

Assumption of the Virgin Mary
1301 Newport Ave UCU
Northampton PA 18032
Phone: 610-262-2882
FAX: 610-266-4105

Dormition of the Theotokos
12 Washington Ave GOA
Oakmont PA 15139
Phone: 412-828-2888
FAX: 412-828-4144

St Michael OCA
512 Summer St
Old Forge PA 18518-1327
Phone: 717-457-3703

St Stephen Protomartyr ROR
St Stephens Ln
PO Box 181
Old Forge PA 18518
Phone: 717-457-3384

All Saints OCA
210 Susquehanna Ave
Olyphant PA 18447-1513
Phone: 717-489-0942

St Andrew UCU
300 Main St
Olyphant PA 18447-1236
Phone: 717-383-0530

St Nicholas OCA
Lackawanna & Gravity Sts
Olyphant PA 18447
Phone: 717-489-3891

Nativity of the Virgin Mary
414 French St OCA
Osceola Mills PA 16666
Phone: 814-339-7569

St Mary Nativity OCA
414 French St
Osceola Mills PA 16666-1218
Phone: 814-339-7569

St George PER
730 Church St
Palmerton PA 18071-1514
Phone: 215-635-0509

Ss Peter & Paul OCA
1005 N 5th Ave
352 Main St
Patton PA 16668
Phone:

Assumption of the Holy Virgin
28th St & Snyder Ave
OCA
PO Box 20083
Philadelphia PA 19145-0383
Phone: 215-468-3535
FAX: 610-461-1031

Evangelismos GOA
6501-05 Bustleton Ave
Philadelphia PA 19149
Phone: 215-743-7982

Holy Trinity RMA
9865 Jeanes St
Philadelphia PA 19115-1910
Phone: 215-671-1075

Joy of All Who Sorrow ROR
560 N 20th St
Philadelphia PA 19130-3231
Phone: 215-568-6788

Ss Peter & Paul OCA
9230 Bustleton Ave
Philadelphia PA 19115-4211
Phone: 215-676-3311

St Andrew UOD
1070 69th Ave
Philadelphia PA 19126-2913
Phone:

St Andrew's Cathedral PER
709 N 5th St
Philadelphia PA 19123-2803
Phone: 215-627-3338

St Basil the Great VAS
4526 Mercer St
Philadelphia PA 19137-1712
Phone:

St George Cathedral GOA
256 S 8th St
Philadelphia PA 19107-5731
Phone: 215-627-4389
FAX: 215-627-4394

St John Chrysostom OCA
5 Franklin Plaza, 237 N 17th St
Philadelphia PA 19103-1292
Phone: 215-563-0979

St Mary Protectress UCU
12th St & Oak Lane Ave
Philadelphia PA 19126
Phone: 215-424-9692

St Michael's Cathedral MAT
1334 W Rising Sun Ave
Philadelphia PA 19140
Phone: 215-221-5180
FAX: 215-223-9888

St Nicholas OCA
817 N 7th St
PO Box 16459 - Spring Garden Sta
Philadelphia PA 19122
Phone: 215-922-3037
FAX: 215-592-9201

St Nicholas SOC
1231-39 N Hancock St
Philadelphia PA 19123
Phone: 215-425-2128

St Stephen Cathedral OCA
8598 Verree Rd
Philadelphia PA 19111-1367
Phone: 215-745-3232

St Vladimir Cathedral UCU
6740 N 5th St
Philadelphia PA 19126-3025
Phone: 215-927-2287

Nativity of St John the Baptist
420 Laura St OCA
Philipsburg PA 16866-2520
Phone: 814-342-2011

Holy Ghost CRC
Starr Street, Phoenix Park
PO Box 66
Phoenixville PA 19460
Phone: 610-933-3336
FAX: 610-933-3336

Holy Assumption OCA
105 S 19th St
Pittsburgh PA 15203-1833
Phone: 412-431-6428

Holy Cross GOA
123 Gilkeson Rd
Pittsburgh PA 15228
Phone: 412-833-3355
FAX: 412-833-3357

Holy Resurrection OCA
716 Atlantic Ave
Pittsburgh PA 15221-4204
Phone: 412-271-4738

Holy Trinity GOA
302 W North Ave
Pittsburgh PA 15212-4626
Phone: 412-321-9282
FAX: 412-321-7272

Holy Trinity Cathedral SOC
4920 Clairton Blvd
Pittsburgh PA 15236-2102
Phone: 412-882-3900
FAX: 412-882-6391

Intercession of the Holy Virgin
334 Rockfield Rd OCA
Pittsburgh PA 15243-1408
Phone: 412-276-6234

St Andrew the First-Called Apostle s.
600 Dunster St ICA
PO Box 79059
Pittsburgh PA 15216-0059
Phone: 412-531-4707
FAX: 412-778-2820

St George ANT
3400 Dawson St
Pittsburgh PA 15213
Phone: 412-681-2988
FAX: 412-831-5554

St John the Baptist CRC
2695 Woodland Ave
Pittsburgh PA 15222
Phone: 412-766-3460

St Michael OCA
43 Reed St
Pittsburgh PA 15219-3380
Phone: 412-261-2314

St Nicholas Cathedral GOA
419 S Dithridge St
Pittsburgh PA 15213-3509
Phone: 412-682-3866
FAX: 412-683-4960

St Sava NGM
185 Knox Ave
Pittsburgh PA 15210-2079
Phone:

St Vladimir's UCU
1810 Sidney St
Pittsburgh PA 15203
Phone: 412-431-0687

St Volodymyr UCU
1810 Sidney St
Pittsburgh PA 15203-1718
Phone: 412-431-9758

St Michael OCA
915 Blair St
Portage PA 15946-1909
Phone: 814-736-3051

Holy Trinity OCA
Mervin & Juniper Sts.
Pottstown PA 19464
Phone: 610-323-4183

St Innocent Mission ROR
850 Vaughn Rd
Pottstown PA 19465-8022
Phone: 610-323-9349

Ss Constantine & Helen GOA
1001 E Wyomissing Blvd
Reading PA 19611-1763
Phone: 610-374-7511

St Gregory Mission OCA
N Fifth and Elm St
Reading PA 19601
Phone:

St Herman of Alaska OCA
133 W Broad St
Reading PA 19607-2501
Phone: 215-777-3553

St Matthew GOA
N 5th & Elm Sts
Reading PA 19601
Phone: 215-372-1031

St Nicholas PER
241-243 S 3rd St
Reading PA 19602
Phone: 215-375-2946

St Basil OCA
Simpson PA
PO Box 130
S Canaan PA 18459
Phone:

Annunciation GOA
505 N Washington Ave
Scranton PA 18509-3208
Phone: 717-342-0566

Ss Peter & Paul PER
1720 Academy St
Scranton PA 18504-2309
Phone: 717-343-8128

St Michael UCU
540 N Main Ave
Scranton PA 18504-1875
Phone: 717-343-7165

St Nicholas CRC
621 Vine St
Scranton PA 18510-2008
Phone: 717-344-5917

St John the Baptist CRC
725 Cedar Ave
Sharon PA 16146-2521
Phone: 412-346-4457

St John the Baptist UCU
385 Clark St
Sharon PA 16146-2401
Phone: 412-342-9324

St Herman of Alaska OCA
133 W Broad St
Shillington PA 19607
Phone: 610-777-3553

St Basil   ROR
33 Midland St
Simpson PA 18407-1245
Phone: 717-282-2314

Holy Ghost   UCU
Westmoreland and Penna. Ave
PO Box 3
Slickville PA 15684-0003
Phone: 724-468-5581
RobertP525@aol.com

St Volodymyr   UCU
PO Box 106
Smithmill PA 16680-0106
Phone: 814-378-5041

St Philip   ANT
1970 Clearview Rd
Souderton PA 18964-1020
Phone: 215-721-4947

Assumption of the Blessed Virgin Mary
49 Nicholas St   OCA
St Clair PA 17970
Phone: 717-544-2690

St Michael   CRC
106 N Morris St
St Clair PA 17970-1061
Phone: 717-429-0670

Holy Trinity   OCA
119 S Sparks St
State College PA 16801
Phone: 814-231-2855
FAX: 814-861-8019

Holy Cross   GOA
135 Stokes Ave
Stroudsburg PA 18360-2337
Phone: 717-421-5734
FAX: 717-421-0469
Frtheodor@sunlink.net

Holy Trinity   OCA
Trinity Ct & Chipperfield Dr
PO Boc 832
Stroudsburg PA 18360
Phone: 717-421-4455
FAX: 717-347-2064

St George   CRC
745 S Keyser Ave
Taylor PA 18517-9613
Phone: 717-562-1170

Holy Nativity of the Mother of God
767 Washington Ave
AOM
Tyrone PA 16686
Phone: 814-684-9411

Ss Peter & Paul   OCA
RR 2
Uniondle PA 18470-9802
Phone: 717-488-2523

St Demetrios   GOA
229 Powell Ln
Upper Darby PA 19082-3328
Phone: 215-352-7212

St George   ANT
8210 W Chester Pike
Upper Darby PA 19082-2829
Phone: 610-853-1171

Ss Constantine & Helen   GOA
167 Lincoln Ave
Vandergrift PA 15690
Phone: 412-568-2998

Ss Peter & Paul   OCA
3rd St
PO Box 204
Vintondale PA 15961-0204
Phone: 814-736-3051

Holy Resurrection   OCA
118 Main St
W Brownsville PA 15417
Phone: 724-837-8957

St Herman of Alaska   OCA
403 Moore Rd
Wallingford PA 19086-7049
Phone: 215-876-6077

Protection of the Virgin Mary
1232 N 14th St   CRC
Whitehall PA 18052-6007
Phone: 215-432-0272

Annunciation   GOA
32 E Ross St
Wilkes Barre PA 18701-2304
Phone: 717-823-4805

Christ the Saviour   ROR
558 Main St
Wilkes Barre PA 18706-2126
Phone: 717-822-3358

Holy Resurrection Cathedral
591 N Main St   OCA
Wilkes Barre PA 18705-1731
Phone: 717-822-7725

Holy Trinity   OCA
401 E Main St
Wilkes Barre PA 18705-3925
Phone: 717-825-6540

St John the Baptist   OCA
93 Zerby Ave
Wilkes Barre PA 18704-3214
Phone: 717-287-7186

St Mary Dormition   ANT
905 S Main St
Wilkes Barre PA 18702-3470
Phone: 717-824-5016

St Nicholas   PER
58 Seneca St
Wilkes Barre PA 18702-6152
Phone: 717-823-0905

St Mary (Dormition) ANT
905 S Main St
Wilkes-Barre PA 18702
Phone: 717-824-5016

Holy Assumption   OCA
Ganister PA 16693
RD 1 Box 230C
Williamsburg PA 16693
Phone: 814-942-9482

Elevation of the Holy Cross
1725 Blair Street   OCA
Williamsport PA 17701-2732
Phone: 717-322-3020

RHODE ISLAND - SOUTH CAROLINA

St Theodore the Tyro VAS
126 Allison Rd
Willow Grove PA 19090-3113
Phone:

Ss Peter and Paul CRC
RD 2 Box 6
Windber PA 15963
Phone: 814-467-7444

St Michael CRC
PO Box 47
Wood PA 16694-0047
Phone: 814-635-3752

St Mark OCA
452 Durham Rd
Wrightstown PA 18940-9633
Phone: 215-860-9640

Annunciation GOA
2500 Pine Grove Rd
York PA 17403
Phone: 717-741-4200
FAX: 717-741-4200

St John Chrysostom ANT
2397 N Sherman St
York PA 17402
Phone: 717-757-6360

Holy Ascension SOC
24 N 3rd St
Youngwood PA 15697-1608
Phone: 412-925-6353

RHODE ISLAND

Annunciation GOA
175 Oaklawn Ave
Cranston RI 02920-9320
Phone: 401-942-4188
FAX: 401-942-3020

Dormition of the Holy Theotokos OCA
71 Manville Hill Rd
Cumberland RI 02864-2317
Phone: 401-658-0874

Holy Mother of God AOC
37 Shippee School House Rd
Foster RI 02825
Phone: 401-647-2867

St Spyridon GOA
Thames and Brewer streets
PO Box 427
Newport RI 02840-0004
Phone: 401-846-0555

Assumption GOA
97 Walcott St
Pawtucket RI 02860-3205
Phone: 401-725-3127

Christ the Saviour Monastery

27 Whiteman St ROR
PO Box 1272
Pawtucket RI 02860-4901
Phone: 401-725-1692

St Mary ANT
249 High St
Pawtucket RI 02860-2115
Phone: 401-726-1202

St John the Baptist OCA
501 E School St
Woonsocket RI 02895-1375
Phone: 401-766-3343

St Michael UCU
74 Harris Ave
Woonsocket RI 02895-1843
Phone: 401-762-3939

SOUTH CAROLINA

Holy Trinity GOA
30 Race St
Charleston SC 29403-4606
Phone: 803-577-2063
FAX: 803-722-2331

Holy Trinity GOA
1931 Sumter St
Columbia SC 29201-2503
Phone: 803-252-6758

Transfiguration GOA
2990 S Cashua Dr
Florence SC 29501-6327
Phone: 803-662-5471

St George GOA
15 DeCamp St
Greenville SC 29601
Phone: 864-233-8531
FAX: 864-421-9182

St John of the Ladder OCA
314 Lloyd St
Greenville SC 29601-1408
Phone: 803-878-5815

Holy Resurrection GOA
PO Box 22888
Hilton Head Island SC 29925-2888
Phone: 912-352-4019

St John the Baptist GOA
3301 33rd Ave N
PO Box 2247
Myrtle Beach SC 29578-2247
Phone: 803-448-3773
FAX: 803-946-7597

St Nicholas GOA
697 Asheville Hwy
Spartanburg SC 29303-2934
Phone: 864-585-5961
FAX: 864-596-4455

Ss Cyril & Methodius ROR
123 W Richardson Ave
123 W Richardson Ave - PO BOX 932
Summerville SC 29484-0932
Phone: 803-871-1160
FAX: 803-871-1165

Good Samaritan VAS
199 Lang Fort Rd
Travelers Rest SC 29690
Phone:

SOUTH DAKOTA - TENNESSEE - TEXAS

Holy Apostles   OCA
931 Lucas St N
W Columbia SC 29169-7004
Phone: 803-926-8744

St Silouan Retreat   OCA
6102 Rockefeller Rd
Wadmalaw Is SC 29487
Phone: 843-559-1404
FAX: 843-559-1404

SOUTH DAKOTA

Holy Enlighteners   AUX
514 S Duluth Ave
Sioux Falls SD 57104-4327
Phone: 605-331-4938

St Seraphim of Sarov   ROR
1606 S Duluth Ave
Sioux Falls SD 57105-1713
Phone: 605-338-5922

Transfiguration   GOA
1936 S Summit Ave
Sioux Falls SD 57105-2726
Phone: 605-334-5301

TENNESSEE

Ss Peter & Paul   AUX
8111 Vaden Dr
Brentwood TN 37027-7306
Phone: 615-377-6477

Holy Trinity   GOA
306 Westwood Pl, Private Dr #2
Bristol TN 37620-2926
Phone: 423-652-7553

Annunciation   GOA
722 Glenwood Dr
Chattanooga TN 37404
Phone: 615-629-4881

St Ignatius   ANT
4671 Peytonsville Rd
Franklin TN 37064-7614
Phone: 615-791-0658

St George   GOA
4070 Kingston Pike
Knoxville TN 37919-5245
Phone: 423-522-5043
FAX: 423-521-2633

Annunciation / Agape Community
1180 Orthodox Way ROR
Liberty TN 37095-9801
Phone: 615-536-5239
FAX: 615-536-5945

Annunciation   GOA
573 N Highland St
Memphis TN 38122-5107
Phone: 901-327-8177

St John   ANT
1663 Tutwiler Ave
Memphis TN 38107
Phone: 901-274-4119
FAX: 901-274-6519

St Seraphim's   VAS
3174 Carnes Ave
Memphis TN 38111
Phone: 901-327-7221
FAX: 901-323-4830

Holy Trinity   GOA
4905 Franklin Rd
Nashville TN 37220-1517
Phone: 615-333-1047

St Basil Cathedral   HOC
355 Tusculum Rd
Nashville TN 37211-6101
Phone: 615-834-1936

TEXAS

St John the Prodromos   GOA
1101 Bell St
Amarillo TX 79106-4215
Phone: 806-355-0683

Holy Name of Mary   IND
715 W Mary St
Austin TX 78704
Phone: 512-326-1111
FAX: 512-416-6556

St Elias   ANT
408 E 11th St
Austin TX 78701-2617
Phone: 512-476-2314
FAX: 512-858-1630

St John the Forerunnner   ANT
3605 Adelphi Ln
Austin TX 78727
Phone: 512-719-4104
FAX: 512-833-6602

Transfiguration   GOA
414 St Stephen's School Rd S
PO Box 160632
Austin TX 78716
Phone: 512-329-6363

St Michael   ANT
690 N 15th St
Beaumont TX 77702-1403
Phone: 409-838-4951

Ss Constantine & Helen   ANT
3755 Walnut Hill Ln
2203 Southern Cir
Carrollton TX 75006
Phone: 972-416-3324

Falling Asleep of Virgin   OCA
3801 Glade Rd
Colleyville TX 76034-4830
Phone: 817-545-0753

St Nicholas   GOA
502 S Chaparrel St
PO Box 343
Corpus Christi TX 78401-3501
Phone: 512-883-9843

St Sava   SOC
16900 Cypress Rosehill Rd
Cypress TX 77429-1420
Phone: 713-373-1769

Holy Trinity   GOA
13555 Hillcrest Rd
Dallas TX 75240-5412
Phone: 214-991-1166
FAX: 214-661-1717

Orthodox Mission DHE
4690 S Counts Blvd
Dallas TX 75211-3705
Phone:

St Barbara OCA
PO Box 191109
Dallas TX 75219
Phone: 817-294-0325
FAX: 214-526-7170

St Gregory ANT
PO Box 140772
Dallas TX 75214-0772
Phone: 214-823-7830

St Nicholas ROR
3617 Abrams Rd, Dallas TX
2102 Summit Dr
Dallas TX 75070-2608
Phone: 972-529-2754

St Seraphim of Sarov
Cathedral
4112 Throckmorton St
OCA
Dallas TX 75219-3002
Phone: 214-528-3741

St George ANT
915 N Florence St
El Paso TX 79902-4301
Phone: 915-532-7845

St Nicholas GOA
245 S Festival
El Paso TX 79912-5802
Phone: 915-833-0882

St John the Baptist GOA
303 Cullum Dr
Euless TX 76040-4625
Phone: 817-283-2291

St Demetrios GOA
2022 Ross Ave
Fort Worth TX 76106-8169
Phone: 817-626-5578
FAX: 817-626-5538

Assumption GOA
1824 Ball St
PO Box 655
Galveston TX 77550
Phone: 409-762-7591

Ss Constantine & Helen
SOC
4109 Ave L PO Box 3280
Galveston TX 77550-3942
Phone: 409-762-4363

Ss Constantine & Helen
NGM
6914 Yupon St
Galveston TX 77551-1730
Phone: 409-744-3966

Annunciation Cathedral
GOA
3511 Yoakum Blvd
Houston TX 77006-4388
Phone: 713-526-5377
FAX: 713-526-1010

Christ the Teacher Mission
HUS
406 Settles St, Big Spring TX
3011 Roe Dr
Houston TX 77087-2409
Phone: 713-645-0843
FAX: 713-645-0104

Holy Comforter IND
PO Box 271688
Houston TX 77277-1688
Phone: 713-728-3750

Holy Myrrh-Bearers HUS
3011 Roe Dr
Houston TX 77087-2409
Phone: 713-645-0843
FAX: 713-645-0104

St Basil the Great GOA
1304 Langham Creek Dr
#312
Houston TX 77084
Phone: 281-647-0147
FAX: 281-647-0147

St Demitrios VAS
10107 Silver City Dr
Houston TX 77064-5306
Phone:

St George ANT
5311 Mercer at Bissonnet
Houston TX 77005-2125
Phone: 713-665-5252
FAX: 713-665-0514

St John Chrysostom
Cathedral
3011 Roe Dr HUS
Houston TX 77087
Phone: 713-645-0843
FAX: 713-645-0104

St Juvenaly of Alaska
CYP
6530 Kernel St
Houston TX 77087-1514
Phone:

St Vladimir ROR
24 Tidwell Rd
Houston TX 77022-1906
Phone: 713-695-3223

St Sava SOC
19149 Glenway Falls
Katy TX 77449
Phone: 713-373-1769

Orthodox Mission Parish
FOCI
1402 N Valley Pkwy #504
Lewisville TX 75067
Phone:

St Andrew GOA
6001 81st St
PO Box 93705
Lubbock TX 79493-3705
Phone: 806-798-1828

Holy Annunciation OCA
3500 W Wadley Ave
Midland TX 79707-5748
Phone:

St George the Great Martyr
784 W Sam Houston St
OCA
Pharr TX 78577-5228
Phone: 512-781-6114

St Sava OCA
PO Box 865081
Plano TX 75086-5081
Phone: 214-494-2623

St George GOA
3146 Thomas Blvd
Port Arthur TX 77642-4961
Phone: 409-983-7360

UTAH - VIRGINIA

Holy Trinity ROR
Rt 1 Box 115A
Rochelle TX 76872
Phone: 915-463-5538
FAX: 915-463-5612

Assumption GOA
2702 Oak Forest
San Angelo TX 76903-7224
Phone: 915-653-6074

St Anthony the Great
OCA
103-105 Carolina St.
San Antonio TX 78210
Phone: 210-533-2492

St Ignatius IND
4135 Bretton Ridge
San Antonio TX 78217
Phone: 210-654-7887

St Sophia GOA
2504 N St Mary's St
San Antonio TX 78212
Phone: 210-735-5051
FAX: 210-735-5649

St Anthony the Great
ANT
18823 Mirror Lake Dr
Spring TX 77388-5855
Phone: 713-350-6784

St Nicholas GOA
617 N 17th St
Waco TX 76707-3522
Phone: 817-754-6519

Holy Cross GOA
3804 Old Seymour Rd.
Wichita Falls TX 76309
Phone: 817-692-0860

UTAH

Mission of Greater Salt Lake City
516 E 13800 S OCA
Draper UT 84020-9292
Phone: 801-572-5323

Transfiguration GOA
674 42nd St
Ogden UT 84403-2851
Phone: 801-399-2231

Assumption GOA
61 S 2nd St
PO Box 688
Price UT 84501-0688
Phone: 801-637-0704
FAX: 801-637-2211

Holy Trinity Cathedral
GOA
279 S 300 W
Salt Lake City UT 84101-1703
Phone: 801-328-9681
FAX: 801-328-9688

Prophet Elias GOA
5335 Highland Dr
Salt Lake City UT 84117-7633
Phone: 801-277-2693

Ss Peter & Paul ANT
PO Box 17896
Salt Lake City UT 84117-0896
Phone: 801-272-7920

St Nicholas of Myra ROR
9589 S Kilmvir Circle
South Jordan UT 84065
Phone: 801-569-0881

Mid-Valley Eastern Orthodox Community OCA
7723 S 1530 W
PO Box 1054
W Jordan UT 84084
Phone: 801-567-0501

St George AUX
1538 W 7800 S
West Jordan UT 84088-4105
Phone: 801-562-4508

VIRGINIA

Holy Cross OCA
5150 Leesburg Pike
Alexandria VA 22302-1030
Phone: 703-671-1919

Nativity of Our Lord CRC
8916 Center St
4317 Dahill Pl
Alexandria VA 22312-1230
Phone: 703-335-8752

St George OCA
800 S Buchanan St
Arlington VA 22204-1442
Phone: 703-761-4316

Holy Wisdom AUX
4561 Dumfries Rd
Catlett VA 22019-1712
Phone: 703-788-3074

Transfiguration GOA
100 Perry Dr
PO BOX 94
Charlottesville VA 22902-4340
Phone: 804-295-5337

St Peter GOA
116 Jefferson Ave
PO BOX 3392
Danville VA 24541-1922
Phone: 804-793-5382

St Katherine GOA
3149 Glen Carlyn Rd
Falls Church VA 22041-2430
Phone: 703-671-1515

Nativity of the Theotokos
GOA
102 Caison Rd Rt 603
PO Box 8418
Fredericksburg VA 22404-8418
Phone: 540-371-6791

St Elpis GOA
107 Memorial Ave
PO Box 1204
Hopewell VA 23860-2540
Phone: 804-458-4142

St George GOA
1724 Langhorne Rd
PO BOX 2061
Lynchburg VA 24503-3120
Phone: 804-384-7585

VERMONT - WASHINGTON

St Luke   OCA
6801 Georgetown Pike
PO BOX 178
Mc Lean VA 22101-2148
Phone: 703-893-1759

St Seraphim of Sarov
AUX
2036 Cully Dr
Mechanicsville VA 23111-3812
Phone: 804-750-8348

All Saints of North America
RR 2 Box 162 ROR
Middlebrook VA 24459-9625
Phone: 540-434-8944

Ss Constantine & Helen
GOA
60 Traverse Rd
Newport News VA 23606-3507
Phone: 757-872-8119
FAX: 757-874-6958

Annunciation   GOA
7220 Granby St
Norfolk VA 23505
Phone: 804-440-0500
FAX: 804-423-6429

Dormition of the Theotokos
1065 E Bayview Blvd
OCA
PO Box 14073
Norfolk VA 23518
Phone: 757-587-6369

Dormition of the Theotokos
1051 E Bayview Blvd
OCA
Norfolk VA 23503-3956
Phone: 804-587-6369

Holy Trinity   OCA
P.O. Box 3708
Reston VA 22090-1708
Phone: 703-758-7914

Ss Constantine and Helen
GOA
30 Malvern Ave
Richmond VA 23221
Phone: 804-355-3687
FAX: 804-342-1947

St Andrew   VAS
1629 Brook Rd
Richmond VA 23220-1801
Phone: 804-266-3364

St Cyprian of Carthage
OCA
8419 Zell Ln
Richmond VA 23227-4110
Phone: 804-288-9363

Holy Trinity   GOA
30 Huntington Blvd NE
Roanoke VA 24012
Phone: 540-362-3601
FAX: 540-362-3638

St Ambrose of Milan
OCA
8115 Williamson Rd
Roanoke VA 24019-6949
Phone: 703-982-7710

St Ignatius of Antioch
ROR
822 Gammon Rd
5600 Albright Dr
Virginia Beach VA 23464-6702
Phone: 804-479-1714

St Nicholas   GOA
621 First Colonial Rd
Virginia Beach VA 23451-6121
Phone: 757-422-5600

Dormition of the Virgin Mary
GOA
1700 Amherst St
Winchester VA 22601
Phone: 540-667-1416

Protection of the Mother of God
15111 Catalpa Ct   OCA
Woodbridge VA 22193-5351
Phone: 703-670-0867

VERMONT

Dormition of the Mother of God
30 Ledge Rd   GOA
Burlington VT 05401-4026
Phone: 802-862-2155

St Nicholas   GOA
8 Cottage St
PO Box 939
Rutland VT 05701
Phone:

Holy Trinity   OCA
90 Park St
Springfield VT 05156-3025
Phone: 802-885-2615

WASHINGTON

Apostolic Mission   AOC
PO Box 2217
Battle Ground WA 98604
Phone: 360-263-3340

St Sophia GOA
510 E Sunset Dr
Bellingham WA 98225-1926
Phone: 206-734-8745

St Paul   ANT
21226 Poplar Way
Brier WA 98036-8916
Phone: 206-771-1816

St Innocent   ANT
7592 Oat Cole Rd
Everson WA 98247-9542
Phone: 206-966-3937

Prophet Elias   AUX
5977 Paradise Rd
Ferndale WA 98248-9431
Phone: 206-380-6238

St Sava   SOC
14619 239th Pl SE
Issaquah WA 98027
Phone: 206-391-2240

Holy Nativity   UCU
Kelso WA 98626
Phone:

WISCONSIN

Orthodox Mission Pasrish FOCI
PO Box 1302
Kettle Falls WA 99141
Phone:

St Paul   ANT
21226 Poplar Way, Brier WA
PO Box 437
Lynnwood WA 98046
Phone: 425-771-1916
FAX: 425-670-0414

St Nektarios   GOA
627 W Bonneville
PO BOX 1161
Pasco WA 99301-5432
Phone: 509-547-3968

St Herman of Alaska
VAS
552 Hastings Ave
Port Townsend WA 98368-6121
Phone:

St Herman of Alaska
IND
1404 30th St
Port Townsend WA 98368
Phone: 360-385-6303
FAX: 360-385-6303

Holy Trinity / Holy Resurrection
PO Box 1332   OCA
Puyallup WA 98371
Phone: 206-848-7505

Raft Island Camp   GOA
Raft Island WA
Phone: 206-244-2511

New Iveron   DHE
HC 65 Box 146A
Riverside WA 98849-9613
Phone:

Assumption   GOA
1804 13th Ave
Seattle WA 98122-2515
Phone: 206-323-8557

Holy Trinity   UCU
Seattle WA 98102
Phone: 206-524-3496

Ss Sergius & Herman
VAS
4619 S Brandon St
Seattle WA 98118-2355
Phone:

St Demetrios   GOA
2100 Boyer Ave E
Seattle WA 98112-2115
Phone: 206-325-4347
FAX: 206-328-1119

St Innocent   DHE
1838 S King Hwy
Seattle WA 98144-2229
Phone: 206-726-7972

St Nectarios   HOC
19399 Ashworth Ave N
Seattle WA 98133-9410
Phone: 206-522-4471
FAX: 206-523-0550

St Nicholas Cathedral
ROR
1714 13th Ave
Seattle WA 98122-2513
Phone: 206-322-9387

St Spiridon Cathedral
OCA
400 Yale Ave N
Seattle WA 98109-5431
Phone: 206-624-5341

Holy Trinity   GOA
1703 N. Washington
Spokane WA 99205-4769
Phone: 509-328-9310

St Nicholas   GOA
1523 S Yakima Ave
Tacoma WA 98405
Phone: 253-272-0466
FAX: 253-572-3245

St Andrew's   HOC
10403 NE 74th St
Vancouver WA 98662
Phone:

Holy Trinity/Holy Resurrection   OCA
Long St.
Wilkeson WA 98396
Phone: 206-848-7505

Holy Cross   ANT
706 Stewart St.
Yakima WA 98902-4473
Phone: 509-575-0145

WISCONSIN

St Nicholas   GOA
3333 N French Rd
Appleton WI 54911-8936
Phone: 414-734-2305

St Patrick SGP
PO Box 704
Baraboo WI 53913-0704
Phone: 608-356-2808

St John the Baptist CYP
18426 Chezik Rd
Blue River WI 53518-9425
Phone: 608-537-2978

Holy Trinity   OCA
523 1st St
Clayton WI 54004
Phone: 715-948-2493

St Mary   OCA
Cornucopia WI 54827
511 1st St
Clayton WI 54004
Phone: 715-948-2493

St Nikola NGM
3802 E Squire Ave - PO BOX 564
Cudahy WI 53110-1517
Phone: 414-747-9246

St Matthew   OCA
Crypt Chapel, St Norbert's Abbey, 1
DePere WI 54115
Phone: 414-432-0840

Holy Trinity GOA
198 N Macy St
PO Box 11
Fond Du Lac WI 54935-3360
Phone: 414-921-4264

Holy Trinity UCU
3669 County Hwy W
Granton WI 54436
Phone: 715-743-2769

St Matthew OCA
1226 Redwood Dr
PO Box 652
Greenway WI 54305-0652
Phone: 920-490-7900
FAX: 920-432-0840

St Nicholas OCA
4313 18th Ave
Kenosha WI 53140-2707
Phone: 414-657-3415

St Elias ANT
716 Copeland Ave
La Crosse WI 54603-2656
Phone: 608-782-8641

Holy Assumption OCA
N1249 County Road F
Lublin WI 54447-9634
Phone: 715-669-3855

Holy Trinity UCU
683 N 7th Ave.
Lublin WI 54447
Phone: 612-789-0456

Assumption GOA
11 N 7th St
Madison WI 53704
Phone: 608-244-1001
FAX: 608-244-1565

Madison Orthodox Mission
VAS
157 Farrell St
Madison WI 53714-2277
Phone:

St Nicholas ANT
3906 W Mequon Rd - PO
BOX 114
Mequon WI 53092-2728
Phone: 414-241-9041

St Nicholas ANT
1235 W Baldwin Ct
Mequon WI 53092-5909
Phone: 414-241-9041

Annunciation GOA
9400 W Congress St
Milwaukee WI 53225-4812
Phone: 414-461-9400

Holy Trinity ROR
1136 W Madison St
Milwaukee WI 53204-2217
Phone: 414-383-1477

Holy Trinity ROR
1136 W Madison St
Milwaukee WI 53204-2217
Phone: 414-383-1477

Ss Constantine & Helen
GOA
2160 N Wauwatosa Ave
Milwaukee WI 53213-1743
Phone: 414-778-1555

Ss Cyril & Methodius
OCA
2505 S 30th St
Milwaukee WI 53215-2829
Phone: 414-671-5819

St Mary Protectress UCU
1231 W Scott St
Milwaukee WI 53204-2230
Phone: 414-672-9285

St Sava Cathedral SOC
3201 S 51st St
Milwaukee WI 53219-4514
Phone: 414-545-4080

St Andrew OCA
@ St Matthias Episcopal
Church, 403
Minocqua WI 54548
Phone: 715-669-3855

St James Hermitage
505 Half Ave
Prairie Farm WI 54762
Phone: 715-455-1553

Dormition of the Theotokos
1335 S Green Bay Rd
GOA
Racine WI 53406
Phone: 414-632-5682
FAX: 414-632-3358

Kimisis Tis Theotokou
GOA
1335 S Green Bay Rd
Racine WI 53406-4405
Phone: 414-632-5682

St George SOC
6108 Braun Rd
Racine WI 53403-9409
Phone: 414-554-7998

St George NGM
826 State St
Racine WI 53404-3344
Phone: 414-634-9512

St Spyridon GOA
1427 S 10th St
Sheboygan WI 53081-5337
Phone: 414-452-2585

St Croix Orthodox Mission
PO Box 142 OCA
St Croix Falls WI 54024
Phone: 715-646-2146

St John the Baptist OCA
RR 2
Stanley WI 54768-9802
Phone:

Holy Trinity UCU
Thorp WI 54771
Phone: 612-789-0456

Ss Constantine and Helen
GOA
2160 Wauwatosa Ave
Wauwatosa WI 53213
Phone: 414-778-1555
FAX: 414-778-1117

WEST VIRGINIA

St Nicholas   ANT
211 S Heber St
Beckley WV 25801-5424
Phone: 304-252-5821

St George   ANT
Lee & Court Sts
PO Box 2044
Charleston WV 25327-2044
Phone: 304-346-0106
FAX: 304-346-0146

St John   GOA
3512 Maccorkle Ave SE
Charleston WV 25304-1420
Phone: 304-925-3906

St Spyridon   GOA
340 S 2nd St - PO BOX 1703
Clarksburg WV 26301-3716
Phone: 304-624-5331

Assumption of the Blessed
Virgin Mary
Box 221   CRC
Elkhorn WV 24831
Phone: 304-862-3312

Dormition of the Mother of God
PO Box 221   CRC
Elkhorn WV 24831-0221
Phone: 304-862-3313

St Andrew the Apostle   CRC
501 Cleveland Ave
Fairmont WV 26554-1602
Phone: 304-366-8523

Holy Spirit   ANT
2109 10th Ave
Huntington WV 25703-2005
Phone: 304-529-6693

St George   GOA
701 11th Ave
Huntington WV 25701-3213
Phone: 304-522-7890

St George   GOA
701 Eleventh Ave
PO Box 2822
Huntington WV 25727-2822
Phone: 304-522-7890

Assumption   GOA
447 Spruce St
Morgantown WV 26505-5525
Phone: 304-292-9048

Holy Trinity   MAT
51 Fairfield Manor
Morgantown WV 26505-8011
Phone: 304-284-0045

Nativity of the Blessed Virgin Mar
19 W Park Ave CRC
Morgantown WV 26505-4524
Phone: 304-296-4319

Ss Peter & Paul   OCA
1109 Morton Ave
Moundsville WV 26041-2444
Phone: 614-535-1379

Entrance into the Temple Mission
Rt 2 - Box 2343   ROR
Wayne WV 25570-9755
Phone: 304-849-3553

All Saints GOA
3528 West St
Weirton WV 26062-4525
Phone: 304-797-9884

St Nicholas   OCA
604 Colliers Way
Weirton WV 26062-5006
Phone: 304-723-9746

St John the Divine   GOA
2215 Chapline St
Wheeling WV 26003-3842
Phone: 304-233-0757

WYOMING

Holy Trinity   GOA
1350 E C Rd
PO Box 11465
Casper WY 82602
Phone: 307-237-9969

Diocese of the Rocky Mountains & Midwest
AOC
2817 Forst Dr
Cheyenne WY 82001
Phone: 307-637-7768

Ss Constantine & Helen   GOA
501 W 27th St
PO Box 112
Cheyenne WY 82001-3030
Phone: 307-635-5929

Ss Anargyroi Cosmas & Damian/St John
54 Harriman Rd   GOA
Harriman WY 82059
Phone: 307-638-6642
FAX: 307-638-0611

Holy Trinity   GOA
405 N St
Rock Springs WY 82901-5408
Phone: 307-362-2930

St George   GOA
12th St & Robertson
Worland WY 82041
Phone:

PUERTO RICO

San Miguel   VAS
Arroyo PR 00615
Phone:

Our Lady of Peace   OCC
Calle Albacete #509
Rio Piedras PR 00932
Phone: 809-250-0647

St Mark of Ephesus OCC
PO Box 21195 65th Inf Sta
Rio Piedras PR 00928
Phone: 809-752-1374

St Spyridon   ECP
RJ13 Via Amazonas
Trijillo Alto PR 00976-6010
Phone: 787-760-7476

Mission Congregation   OCC
c/o Michael Mansour
Bridgetown PR
Phone: 809-429-7818

Parishes and Missions in Canada

ALBERTA

Archangel Michael OCA
Ewanowich; Box 425
Andrew AB T0B 0C0
CANADA
Phone: 403-365-3521

Nativity of the Holy Virgin
Ewanchuk; Box 148 OCA
Andrew AB T0B 0C0
CANADA
Phone:

St Tikhon of Moscow
OCA
PO Box 255
Andrew AB T0B 0C0
CANADA
Phone: 403-365-2340

St Mary's Convent ROR
PO Box Bluffton
Bluffton AB T0C 0M0
CANADA
Phone: 403-843-6434

All Saints ROR
905 8th Ave. N.E.
Calgary AB T2E 0S2
CANADA
Phone: 403-230-7015

Mother of God Keeper of the
Portal 639 9th Ave. N.E. AUX
Calgary AB T2E 0W4
CANADA
Phone: 403-276-4347

Nativity of the Holy Virgin
Mary
4727 17th Ave NW OCA
Calgary AB T3B 4P4
CANADA
Phone: 403-288-4699

St Demetrios GOA
1 Tamarac Crescent SW
Calgary AB T3C 3B7
CANADA
Phone: 403-249-8876

St Simeon Mirotocivi
SOC
2001 31st Ave SW
Calgary AB T2T 1T3
CANADA
Phone: 403-244-3586

St Vladimir UOC
400 Meredith Rd
Calgary AB T2E 5A6
CANADA
Phone:

All Saints GOA
5824 118th Ave
Edmonton AB T5W 1E4
CANADA
Phone: 403-471-2781

Holy Trinity ROR
10902 96th St. N.W.
Edmonton AB T5H 2K3
CANADA
Phone: 403-429-1925

Ss Constantine & Helen
RMA
9005 - 132nd Ave
Edmonton AB T5E 0Y1
CANADA
Phone: 403-475-1422

St Andrew UOC
9755 64th Ave NW
Edmonton AB T6E 0J4
CANADA
Phone:

St George GOA
10831 124th St
Edmonton AB T5K 1R2
CANADA
Phone: 403-452-7329

St Herman of Alaska
OCA
10320 147th St
Edmonton AB T5N 3C3
CANADA
Phone: 403-454-8335

St John UOC
10945 107th St
Edmonton AB T5K 1G4
CANADA
Phone:

St Michael UOC
8541 89th St NW
Edmonton AB T6C 3K4
CANADA
Phone:

St Phillip ANT
15804 98th Ave
Edmonton AB T5P 0G8
CANADA
Phone: 403-489-7943

St Sava SOC
12904 112th St
PO Box 71040 N
Edmonton AB T5E 6J8
CANADA
Phone: 403-455-2147

St Vladimir Cathedral
ROR
6824 128th Ave NW
Edmonton AB T5C 1S7
CANADA
Phone: 403-476-2381

Holy Apostle Andrew
ROR
4823 7th Ave
Edson AB T7E 1K8
CANADA
Phone: 403-325-2357

Greek Orthodox Community
PO Box 85 GOA
Jasper AB T0E 1E0
CANADA
Phone: 403-852-3137

St Michael OCA
Staciuk; RR 1
Lamont AB T0B 2R0
CANADA
Phone:

Holy Dormition ROR
906 9th Ave N
Lethbridge AB T1H 1E9
CANADA
Phone: 205-251-6694

Holy Trinity UOC
1417 9th Ave
Lethbridge AB T1J 0P6
CANADA
Phone:

St Sava SOC
PO Box 794
Lethbridge AB T1J 3Y6
CANADA
Phone: 403-244-3586

Dormition Skete ROR
PO Box 104
Wildwood AB T0E 2M0
CANADA
Phone: 403-325-2357

Holy Apostle Andrew
ROR
PO Box 104
Wildwood AB T0E 2M0
CANADA
Phone: 403-325-2357

Holy Ascension OCA
Katarenchuk; RR 1
Willingdon AB T0B 4R0
CANADA
Phone:

Ss Peter & Paul OCA
Shapka; RR 1
Willingdon AB T0B 4R0
CANADA
Phone:

BRITISH COLUMBIA

Ss Peter & Paul UOC
7137 Grand Hwy
Burnaby BC V5G 1M2
CANADA
Phone:

St Nicholas ROR
4764 Parker St
Burnaby BC V5C 3E3
CANADA
Phone: 604-873-8110

St Peter the Aleut OCA
3107 40th St SW
Calgary BC T2W 5G3
CANADA
Phone: 403-242-6754

Descent of the Holy Spirit
UCU
37323 Hawkins Rd
Dewdney BC V0M 1H0
CANADA
Phone: 604-826-9336

Holy Nativity UCU
37323 Hawkins Rd
Dewdney BC V0M 1H0
CANADA
Phone: 604-826-9336

Nemanjic Institute for Serbo-Byzantine S
37323 Hawkins Rd UCU
Dewdney BC V0M 1H0
CANADA
Phone: 604-826-9336
FAX: 604-820-9758

St Michael the Archangel
UCU
37323 Hawkins Rd
Dewdney BC V0M 1H0
CANADA
Phone: 604-826-9336

St Symeon UCU
37323 Hawkins Rd
Dewdney BC V0M 1H0
CANADA
Phone: 604-826-9336

St Tikhon UCU
37323 Hawkins Rd
Dewdney BC V0M 1H0
CANADA
Phone: 604-826-9336

Theotokos 'Joy of Canada'
Cathedral UCU
37329 Hawkins Rd
Dewdney BC V0M 1H0
CANADA
Phone: 604-826-9336

Greek Orthodox Community
756 Ridgeview Terr GOA
Kamloops BC V2B 4G9
CANADA
Phone:

Metamorfosis GOA
71 Finch St
Kitimat BC V8C 1T1
CANADA
Phone: 604-632-7475

St Herman of Alaska
OCA
216th St & Glover Rd
Langley BC
CANADA
Phone: 604-588-6166

St Nicholas UCU
4828 216A St
Langley BC
CANADA
Phone:

Mar Elias OCA
1398 Ewen Ave
New Westminster BC V3M 5E7
CANADA
Phone: 604-941-8498

St George RMA
1932 - 8th Ave
New Westminster BC V3M 2T4
CANADA
Phone: 604-522-4360

Greek Orthodox Community
486 Alder St GOA
Penticton BC V2A 6S6
CANADA
Phone:

Koimisis   GOA
511 Tabor Blvd
Prince George BC V2M 6W7
CANADA
Phone: 604-564-2766

Greek Orthodox Church of
Surrey and Fras   GOA
PO BOX 55514
Surrey BC V3R 0J7
CANADA
Phone: 604-583-0554

St Herman of Alaska   OCA
13268-99A Ave
Surrey BC V3T 1G4
CANADA
Phone: 604-588-8911

Holy Annunciation   RMA
1805 Larch St
Vancouver BC V6K 3N9
CANADA
Phone:

Holy Resurrection   OCA
75 E 43rd Ave
Vancouver BC V5W 1S7
CANADA
Phone: 604-325-1922

Holy Trinity   ROR
2733 E 2nd Ave
Vancouver BC V5Y 2G4
CANADA
Phone: 604-254-2571

Holy Trinity   OCA
75 E 43rd Ave
Vancouver BC V5W 1S7
CANADA
Phone:

Holy Trinity   UOC
126 E 10th St
Vancouver BC V5Y 2G4
CANADA
Phone:

St Archangel Michael   NGM
1806 E Hastings St
Vancouver BC V5L 1T2
CANADA
Phone: 604-253-8121

St George   GOA
4500 Arbutus St
Vancouver BC V6J 4A2
CANADA
Phone: 604-266-7148

St Michael   VAS
1736 E 32nd Ave
Vancouver BC V5N 3B6
CANADA
Phone:

St Nicholas   GOA
4641 Boundary Rd
Vancouver BC V5T 2L5
CANADA
Phone: 604-438-6432

St Nicholas   ROR
810 East 13th St
Vancouver BC V5T 2L5
CANADA
Phone: 604-873-8110

St Sava   SOC
505 E 63rd Ave
Vancouver BC V5X 2K3
CANADA
Phone: 604-321-6572

Hellenic Orthodox Community of Victoria   GOA
420 Linden Ave #201
Victoria BC V8V 4G3
CANADA
Phone: 604-382-5650

St Sophia ROR
947 Meares St
Victoria BC V8V 3J5
CANADA
Phone:

St Mary   UOC
13512 108th Ave
Walley BC
CANADA
Phone: 604-581-2768

MANITOBA

Holy Ghost   UOC
2204 MacDonald Ave.
Brandon MB R7A 6A2
CANADA
Phone:

Holy Ascension Monastery Cemetery
34 3rd Ave NW #1   OCA
Dauphin MB
CANADA
Phone:

St George   UOC
810 Main St E
Dauphin MB R7N 0E7
CANADA
Phone:

Ss. Peter & Paul   UOA
Box 78
Ethelbert MB R0L 0T0
CANADA
Phone: 204-742-3349

St George   UOC
52 Hill St
Flin Flon MB R8A 1G5
CANADA
Phone:

St Demetrios   UOA
213 Claremont Ave
Gardenton MB R0E 0M0
CANADA
Phone:

St Lavrentius the Martyr   OCA
Hwy 286
Minitonas MB
CANADA
Phone:

St Stephen the First Martyr
219 1st St NW   OCA
Roblin MB R0L 1P0
CANADA
Phone: 204-937-4673

St Nicholas the Wonder-worker
PO Box 512   AUX
Russell MB R0J 1W0
CANADA
Phone: 204-773-2364

St Nicholas   OCA
County Hwy 250 N
Sandy Lake MB R0J 1X0
CANADA
Phone:

Sclater Cemetery   OCA
Box 1093
Swan River MB R0L 1Z0
CANADA
Phone:

St Demetrios   UOA
Pohychuk, Box 245
Vita MB R0A 2K0
CANADA
Phone:

Committee of Concerned Orthodox
3 Prestwood Pl   PAN
Winnipeg MB R3T 4Y9
CANADA
Phone:

Holy Ascension   CYP
197 Euclid Ave
Winnipeg MB R2W 2X5
CANADA
Phone:

Holy Resurrection   ROR
732 Alfred Ave
Winnipeg MB R2W 1Y9
CANADA
Phone: 204-586-4152

Holy Trinity Cathedral   UOC
1175 Main St
Winnipeg MB R2W 3S4
CANADA
Phone:

Holy Trinity Sobor   OCA
643 Manitoba Ave
Winnipeg MB R2W 2H1
CANADA
Phone: 204-589-6223

St Demetrios   GOA
2255 Grant Ave
Winnipeg MB R3P 0S2
CANADA
Phone: 204-889-8723

St Demetrius   RMA
103 Furby St
Winnipeg MB R3C 2A4
CANADA
Phone: 204-775-6472

St George   OCA
121 Harvard Ave E
Winnipeg MB R3T 4Y9
CANADA
Phone: 204-269-3743

St Ivan Suchavsky Cathedral
939 Main St   UOA
Winnipeg MB R2W 3P2
CANADA
Phone: 204-942-3655

St Mary   ANT
903 Winnipeg Ave
Winnipeg MB R3E 0S1
CANADA
Phone: 204-775-9084

St Mary Cathedral   UOC
840 Burrows Ave
Winnipeg MB R2X 0R4
CANADA
Phone:

St Michael   UOC
110 Disraeli St
Winnipeg MB R2W 3J5
CANADA
Phone:

St Michael's   UOC
16 Miami Pl
Winnipeg MB R5T 3T9
CANADA
Phone: 204-261-0361
FAX: 204-261-3797

St Sava SOC
226 Atlantic Ave
Winnipeg MB R2W 0R2
CANADA
Phone: 204-582-1389

St Nicholas   OCA
5635 Henderson Hwy - Box 2 Grp 35
Winnipeg (North Winnipeg) MB R3C 2E7
CANADA
Phone: 204-786-3262

NEW BRUNSWICK

St Nicholas   GOA
33 Dorchester St
St John NB E2L 3H7
CANADA
Phone: 506-642-1258

NEWFOUNDLAND

Greek Orthodox Community of Newfoundland   GOA
PO Box 6302; Station C
St John's NF A1C 5X3
CANADA
Phone: 709-579-0612

NOVA SCOTIA

Holy Protection   GMA
Box 119
Bear River NS B0S 1B0
CANADA
Phone:

Ss Anargyroi   GOA
15 Marconi St
Glace Bay NS B1A 2P2
CANADA
Phone: 902-849-9554

St Anthony ANT
2455 Windsor St
Halifax NS B3K 5B9
CANADA
Phone: 902-422-5056

St George GOA
38 Purcell's Cove Rd
Halifax NS B3N 1R4
CANADA
Phone: 902-479-1271

ONTARIO

Holy Trinity GOA
PO Box 483
Belleville ON K8N 5B2
CANADA
Phone: 613-968-3327

Hellenic Community of
Brantford
475 Park Rd N GOA
PO Box 651
CANADA
Brantford ON N3R 7K8
Phone: 519-759-7353

Analipsis GOA
PO Box 1521
Brockville ON K6V 6E6
CANADA
Phone: 613-345-5525

St Nectarios GOA
PO Box 34A
Chatham ON N7M 5K1
CANADA
Phone: 519-352-6266

Greek Orthodox Community

436 2nd St W GOA
Cornwall ON K6G 1H1
CANADA
Phone: 613-933-1000

St George UOC
804 McKenzie Ave
Ft Frances ON P9A 2C4
CANADA
Phone:

Holy Resurrection GOA
Mantle; RR 1
Goulais River ON P0S 1E0
CANADA
Phone:

Panagia GOA
Mantle; RR 1
Goulais River ON P0S 1E0
CANADA
Phone:

St George UOC
16 Adelaide St
Grimsby ON L3M 4G3
CANADA
Phone:

Hellenic Canadian Community
PO Box 1591 GOA
Guelph ON N1H 6R7
CANADA
Phone: 519-836-8101

Holy Resurrection RMA
278 McNab St N
Hamilton ON L8L 1B1
CANADA
Phone: 416-529-1663

Holy Trinity UOA
73 Mohawk Rd E
Hamilton ON
CANADA
Phone:

Holy Veil of the Theotokos
77 Sanford Ave S ROR
Hamilton ON L8M 2G7
CANADA
Phone: 905-529-7043

Koimisis GOA
233 E 15th St
Hamilton ON L9A 4G1
CANADA
Phone: 416-385-9815

St Demetrios GOA
22 Head St
Hamilton ON L8R 1P9
CANADA
Phone: 416-529-9651

St Nicholas Cathedral SOC
153 Nash Rd S
Hamilton ON L8K 4J9
CANADA
Phone: 416-560-0563

St Nikola NGM
1415 Barton St E
Hamilton ON L8H 2W6
CANADA
Phone: 416-549-0876

St Naum of Ohrid MOC
235 Kensington Ave N
Hamilton ON L8V 1P7
CANADA

St Vladimir UOC
851 Barton St E
Hamilton ON
CANADA
Phone:

Our Lady of Smolensk ROR
Birch Rd. near Jackson Point
Jackson Point ON L0E 1L0
CANADA
Phone: 416-763-6822

Canadian Orthodox
Messenger
43 Newcourt Pl OCA
Kingston ON K7M 6Y1
CANADA
Phone:

Koimisis GOA
121 Johnson St
Kingston ON 37763
CANADA
Phone: 613-546-9841

St Gregory of Nyssa
OCA
@Queens University
Kingston ON
CANADA
Phone: 613-542-5832

Holy Trinity SOC
700 Fischer Hallman Rd
Kitchener ON N2E 1K3
CANADA
Phone: 519-578-2715

Ss. Peter & Paul   GOA
527 Bridgeport Rd E
Kitchener ON N2K 1N6
CANADA
Phone: 519-579-4703

St George Martyr   NGM
PO Box 473 Sta C
Kitchener ON N2G 4A2
CANADA
Phone: 519-884-0311

St John the Baptist   OCA
126 Madison St S
Kitchener ON N2G 3M4
CANADA
Phone: 519-576-8953

Holy Transfiguration   ANT
4647 Colonel Talbot Rd
Lambeth ON N0L 1S3
CANADA
Phone: 519-432-1461

St Mary   UOC
2529 Buckingham Dr
Leamington ON N8H 3L2
CANADA
Phone:

Christ the Saviour   ROR
140 Fairview Ave
London ON N6C 4T8
CANADA
Phone: 519-433-7458

Holy Cross   OCA
1320 Wilton Ave
London ON N6G 1H6
CANADA
Phone: 519-434-8572

Holy Trinity   UOC
151 King Edward Ave
London ON N6A 4L9
CANADA
Phone:

Holy Trinity   GOA
1114 Richmond St
London ON N6A 4L9
CANADA
Phone: 519-438-7951

St Sava   SOC
Bostwick Rd @ 401
PO Box 62
London ON N6C 3C7
CANADA
Phone: 519-652-2771

St Dimitrija Solunski   MOC
199-201 Main St
Markham ON L3P 1Y4
CANADA

Canadian Serbian Monastery
7470 McNiven Rd   SOC
Milton ON
CANADA
Phone: 416-878-1909

Prophet Elias   GOA
4030 Dixie Rd
Mississauga ON L4W 1M4
CANADA
Phone: 416-238-9491

St Barbara   GOA
352 Michelle Row
Mississauga ON L5A 2Z7
CANADA
Phone: 416-848-6069

St Ilija   MOC
Box 337, Streetsville Station
Mississauga ON L5M 2B9
CANADA

Christ the Saviour   CRC
26 Bowmoor Ave
Nepean ON K2E 6M4
CANADA
Phone: 613-727-7790

Christ the Saviour Mission
26 Bowmoor Ave   CRC
Nepean ON K2E 6M4
CANADA
Phone: 613-727-0897

St Xenia of Petersburg
ROR
3501 Carling Ave
Nepean ON K2H 9R0
CANADA
Phone: 613-726-8123

St Archangel Michael
NGM
4992 Huron St
Niagara Falls ON L2E 2J5
CANADA
Phone: 416-358-7363

St George   SOC
6085 Montrose Rd S
Niagara Falls ON 14305
CANADA
Phone: 416-356-0090

St John of Rila   ROR
4871 Willmott St
Niagara Falls ON L2E 1Z5
CANADA
Phone:

Ss Peter & Paul   SOC
PO Box 7408
Oakville ON L6J 6L6
CANADA
Phone: 416-829-0659

St John of San Francisco
AOM
340 Gallawa Dr
Orleans ON K1F 1W3
CANADA
Phone: 613-841-8867
FAX: 613-841-7190

Holy Cross-St. Nektarios
GOA
Heliotis; RR 2
Orillia ON L3Y 6H2
CANADA
Phone:

Evangelismos-St Gerasimos-St Nektarios
261 Bloor St E   GOA
Oshawa ON L1H 3M3
CANADA
Phone: 416-728-5965

St Mary   UOC
261 Bloor St E
Oshawa ON L1G 1G9
CANADA
Phone:

Annunciation / St Nicholas Cathedral 55 Clarey Ave   OCA
Ottawa ON K1S 2R6
CANADA
Phone: 613-236-5596

Christ the Saviour   CRC
@ All Saints Anglican Church, 347 Ri
Ottawa ON
CANADA
Phone: 613-727-7790

Holy Assumption   UOC
1000 Byron Ave
Ottawa ON K2A 0J3
CANADA
Phone:

Holy Trinity Sobor   OCA
58 Arthur St
Ottawa ON K1R 7B9
CANADA
Phone: 613-230-4113

Koimisis   GOA
1315 Prince of Wales Dr
Ottawa ON K2C 1N2
CANADA
Phone: 613-225-8545

Orthodox Campus Ministry   PAN
University of Ottawa, PO Box 450, S
Ottawa ON K1N 6N5
CANADA
Phone: 613-564-5741
FAX: 613-564-5683

Protection of the Holy Virgin
99 Stonehurst Ave ROR
Ottawa ON K1Y 4R7
CANADA
Phone: 613-722-6247

St Elias   ANT
700 Ridgewood Ave
Ottawa ON K1V 6N1
CANADA
Phone: 613-738-2222

St Matthew   RMA
289 Spencer St
Ottawa ON K1Y 2R1
CANADA
Phone: 313-893-0385

St Nicholas   OCA
253 Echo Dr
Ottawa ON K1N 1C4
CANADA
Phone: 613-565-0275

St Stephen   SOC
361 Dominion Ave
Ottawa ON K2A 2H1
CANADA
Phone: 613-729-0244

St Vladimir's Russian Senior Residence
89 Stonehurst Ave   ROR
Ottawa ON K1Y 4R6
CANADA
Phone: 613-729-0159

Yvonne S. Lysack, M.A., Counseling & Edu   PAN
7-297 Sunnyside Ave
Ottawa ON K1S 0R9
CANADA
Phone: 613-730-0242

Greek Orthodox Community
526 Alfred St   GOA
Pembroke ON K8A 3L7
CANADA
Phone:

Greek Orthodox Community
PO Box 1985   GOA
Peterborough ON K9J 7X7
CANADA
Phone: 705-742-5664

St George   ANT
9116 Bayview Ave
Richmond Hill ON L4C 7B5
CANADA
Phone: 416-731-7210

St Panteleimon   GOA
1-81 Granton Dr
Richmond Hill ON L4B 2N5
CANADA
Phone: 416-472-2452

Holy Trinity   UOC
14 Lisgar St
Sarnia ON N7T 7C2
CANADA
Phone:

St Demetrios   GOA
204 N East St
Sarnia ON N7T 6X7
CANADA
Phone: 519-336-1420

St John   GOA
1385 Warden Ave
Scarborough ON M1R 2S3
CANADA
Phone: 416-759-9259

St Nicholas   GOA
3840 Finch Ave E
Scarborough ON M1W 4R6
CANADA
Phone: 416-291-4367

Bishop's Chapel of St Silouan the Athon
Box 179   OCA
Spencerville ON K0E 1X0
CANADA
Phone: 613-658-2901
FAX: 613-925-1521

Canadian Orthodox Messenger
PO Box 179   OCA
Spencerville ON K0E 1X0
CANADA
Phone:

St Charalambos   GOA
Antoniou; RR 2
St Ann's ON L0R 1Y0
CANADA
Phone: 416-386-6224

St Katherine GOA
124 Queenston St
St Catherines ON L2R 2Z6
CANADA
Phone: 416-685-3028

Ss Peter & Paul NGM
515 Antwerp St
Sudbury ON P7B 4M9
CANADA
Phone: 705-674-2578

St George GOA
99 Shappert St
Sudbury ON P3B 3J2
CANADA
Phone: 705-566-1059

St Nicholas GOA
486 Ester Rd
Sudbury ON P3E 5C4
CANADA
Phone: 705-522-5181

St Vladimr UOC
190 Baker St
Sudbury ON P3A 5P3
CANADA
Phone:

Holy Trinity GOA
651 Beverly St
Thunder Bay ON P7B 5X1
CANADA
Phone: 807-623-1033

St George SOC
1237 John St
Thunder Bay ON P7B 2A4
CANADA
Phone: 807-767-8359

St Mary UOA
716 Pacific Ave
Thunder Bay ON P7A 7E4
CANADA
Phone: 807-767-3515

Agioi Anargyroi GOC
281 Jones Ave
Toronto ON M4M 3A7
CANADA
Phone:

Christ the Savior Sobor
OCA
823 Manning Ave
Toronto ON M6G 2W9
CANADA
Phone: 416-534-1763

Evangelismos GOA
136 Sorauren Ave
Toronto ON M6R 2E4
CANADA
Phone: 416-537-2665

Greek Community of
Metropolitan Toronto
GOA
30 Thorncliffe Park Dr
Toronto ON M4H 1H8
CANADA
Phone: 416-425-2485

Holy Resurrection ROR
213 Winona Dr
Toronto ON M6C 3S3
CANADA
Phone: 416-233-1543

Holy Trinity BEC
201 Monarch Park Ave
Toronto ON M4J 4R9
CANADA
Phone: 416-423-6929

Holy Trinity ROR
23 Henry St
Toronto ON M5T 1W9
CANADA
Phone: 416-265-5651

Holy Trinity-Panagia
Grigoroussa
54 Clinton St GOA
Toronto ON M6G 2Y3
CANADA
Phone: 416-537-1351

Metamorphosis GOA
40 Donlands Ave
Toronto ON M4J 3N6
CANADA
Phone: 416-465-2345

Mother of God of Prussa
AUX
461 Richmond St E
Toronto ON M5A 1R1
CANADA
Phone: 416-364-8918

Mother of God the Life-
Giving Spring CYP
47 Thorncliffe Park Dr 1124

Toronto ON M4H 1J5
CANADA
Phone:

Orthodox Campus Fellow-
ship
University of Toronto, #706 - 2350
Toronto ON M6P 4B1
CANADA
Phone:

Orthodox Fellowship of St.
Cyprian #706 - 2350 Dundas
St W
Toronto ON M6P 4B1
CANADA
Phone:

Orthodox Way GOA
27 Teddington Park Ave
Toronto ON M4N 2C4
CANADA
Phone: 416-462-0833
FAX: 416-485-5919

Ss Constantine & Helen
GOA
1 Brookhaven Dr
Toronto ON M6M 4N6
CANADA
Phone: 416-241-2470

Ss Cyril & Methodius
BEC
237 Sackville
Toronto ON M5A 3G1
CANADA
Phone:

St Andrew   UOC
30 O'Hara St
Toronto ON M6K 2P8
CANADA
Phone:

St Archangel Michael
NGM
212 Delaware Ave
Toronto ON M6H 2T1
CANADA
Phone: 416-531-0275

St Clement of Ohrid MOC
76 Overlea Blvd
Toronto ON M4H 1C5
CANADA
Phone: 416-421-7451

St Demetrios   GOA
30 Thorncliffe Park Dr
Toronto ON M4H 1H8
CANADA
Phone: 416-425-2485

St Demetrius   UOC
3338 Lakeshore Blvd W
Toronto ON M8W 2S8
CANADA
Phone:

St Euphrosynia   BYC
1008 Dovercourt Rd
Toronto ON M6H 2X8
CANADA
Phone: 416-536-4449

St George   OCA
247 Rosethorn Ave
Toronto ON M6M 3K9
CANADA
Phone: 416-651-1321

St George   OCA
17 Regent St
Toronto ON M6M 3K9
CANADA
Phone: 416-366-1810

St George   GOA
115 Bond St
Toronto ON M5B 1Y2
CANADA
Phone: 416-977-3342

St Irene Chrysovalantou
GOA
66 Cough Ave
Toronto ON M4K 3N8
CANADA
Phone: 416-465-8213

St Joseph of Arimathea
AUX
1223 Dovercourt Rd
Toronto ON M6H 2Y1
CANADA
Phone: 416-537-8300

St Kosmas Aitolos   GMA
2817 St Clair Ave E
Toronto ON M4B 1N3
CANADA
Phone:

St Kyrilla of Turov   BAM
524 St Clarens Ave
Toronto ON M6H 3W7
CANADA
Phone: 416-530-1025

St Nectarios Cathedral
AUX
1223 Dovercourt Rd
Toronto ON M6H 2Y1
CANADA
Phone: 416-537-7283

St Sava   SOC
203 River St
Toronto ON M5A 3P9
CANADA
Phone: 416-967-9885

Three Hierarchs   SOC
5A Stockbridge Ave
Toronto ON M8Y 4M6
CANADA
Phone: 416-231-4409

St Ilija   NGM
PO Box 130
West Lorne ON N0L 2P0
CANADA
Phone:

All Saints GOA
3125 Bayview Ave
Willowdale ON M2K 1G2
CANADA
Phone: 416-221-4611

Orthodox Light   AUX
28 Flintwood Ct
Willowdale ON M2J 3P2
CANADA
Phone:

All Saints RMA
1242 McEwan Ave
Windsor ON N9B 2G7
CANADA
Phone: 519-252-2269

Descent of the Holy Ghost
RMA
2895 Seminole St
Windsor ON N8Y 1Y1
CANADA
Phone: 519-948-0818

Dormition of the Theotokos -
'Gracanica'
1960 Meldrum Rd   SOC
Windsor ON N8W 4E2
CANADA
Phone: 519-945-8555

Holy Cross   GOA
65 Ellis St E
Windsor ON N8X 2G8
CANADA
Phone: 519-252-3435

Holy Trinity   ROR
1410 Drouillard Rd
Windsor ON N8Y 2R9
CANADA
Phone: 519-945-2862

St Dimitrije   NGM
2690 Seminole St
Windsor ON N8Y 1X7
CANADA
Phone:

St George Cathedral
RMA
1960 Tecumseh Rd E
Windsor ON N8W 1E1
CANADA
Phone: 519-258-1824

St Ignatius of Antioch
ANT
283 St Rose St
Windsor ON N8S 1X1
CANADA
Phone: 519-945-2280

St John the Divine OCA
1094 Drouillard Rd
Windsor ON N8Y 2P8
CANADA
Phone: 313-263-0986

St Nicholas
5225 Howard Ave
Windsor ON N9H 1Z5
CANADA

St Vladimir UOC
1905 Alsace Ave
Windsor ON N8W 1M5
CANADA
Phone:

Belarusan Autocephalous
Orthodox Church BAM
524 St Clarance Ave
Toronto ON M6H 3W7
CANADA
Phone: 416-530-1025

St Paul the Apostle UCU
Windsor ON N9E 2X8
CANADA
Phone: 519-966-3905

QUEBEC

St Irene Chrysovalantou
GOC
1474 Chamedy
Chamedy PQ H2E 1A7
CANADA
Phone:

Demosthenes Ecole
Primaire
3730 boul Levesque GOA
Chomedey-Laval PQ H7V
1E8
CANADA
Phone: 514-686-1800

Ecole Primaire Socrates,
Socrates V 938 Emerson Dr
GOA
Chomedey-Laval PQ H7W
3Y5
CANADA
Phone: 514-681-5142

Holy Cross GOA
4865 Du Souvenir
Chomedey-Laval PQ H7W
1E1
CANADA
Phone: 514-973-3773

St Nicholas GOA
3780 Du Souvenir
Chomedey-Laval PQ H7V
1X3
CANADA
Phone: 514-688-2080

Ss Constantine & Helen
GOA
20 Brunswick Rd
Dollard Des Ormeaux PQ
H9B 2N8
CANADA
Phone: 514-684-6462

St Sergius of Radonezh
OCA
RR 2
Labelle PQ J0T 1H0
CANADA
Phone:

Saint-Jean le Martyr ROR
660 Ave 6iem
Lachine PQ H8S 2Y3
CANADA
Phone: 514-637-4189

Holy Transfiguration Skete
240 Chemin Noel; RR 3
OCA
Magog PQ J1X 2W4
CANADA
Phone:

Holy Transfiguration
Monastery
RR 1 ROR
Mansonville PQ J0E 1X0
CANADA
Phone: 514-292-3102

American Orthodox Mission
8893 St-Hubert HOC
Montreal PQ H2M 2K8
CANADA
Phone: 514-384-6391

Archangels GOA
11801 Elie Blanchard Blvd
Montreal PQ H4J 1R7
CANADA
Phone: 514-334-6868

Catechetical School of St
Anna
7870 Birnam CHR
Montreal PQ H3N 2T5
CANADA
Phone: 514-276-8408

Ecole Primaire Socrates
GOA
5777 Wilderton Ave
Montreal PQ H3S 2V7
CANADA
Phone: 514-738-2421

Evangelismos GOA
777 St Roch St
Montreal PQ H3N 2K3
CANADA
Phone: 514-340-3552

Evangelismos/St Nektarios
4520 Hutchinson GOC
Montreal PQ H2V 4A1
CANADA
Phone:

Fraternite Missionaire de St
Serafin OCA
1605 Blvd Henri Bourassa
Oest #308
Montreal PQ H3M 3B5
CANADA
Phone: 514-493-8915

Hagia Sophia   AUX
898 St Roch
Montreal PQ P0B 3M7
CANADA
Phone:

Hellenic Community of
Montreal
5777 Wilderton Ave GOA
Montreal PQ H3S 2V7
CANADA
Phone: 514-738-2421

Holy Trinity   GOA
7570 Tenasse St Rock
Montreal PQ H3Z 2J7
CANADA
Phone:

Holy Trinity   SOC
351 Melville Ave
Montreal PQ H3Z 2J7
CANADA
Phone: 514-932-8529

Koimisis GOA
7700 De L'Epee St; Park Ext
Montreal PQ H3N 2E6
CANADA
Phone: 514-340-3555

Pan-Orthodox Alliance
Romiosini PAN
8012 Querbes
Montreal PQ H3N 2C1
CANADA
Phone: 514-273-3954

Saint-Seraphim de Sarov
ROR
8011 Champagneur Ave
Montreal PQ H3N 2K4
CANADA
Phone: 514-271-5823

Ss Peter & Paul Sobor
OCA
1175A rue Champlain
Montreal PQ H2L 2R7
CANADA
Phone: 514-522-2801

St Benoit de Nursie OCA
1605 Blvd Henri Bourassa
Oest #308
Montreal PQ H3M 3B5
CANADA
Phone: 514-321-3591

St George   GOA
2455 Cote St Catherine Rd
Montreal PQ H3T 1A8
CANADA
Phone: 514-340-3550

St George   ANT
575 Jean-Talon St E
Montreal PQ H3T 1A8
CANADA
Phone: 514-276-8533

St John the Baptist RMA
1841 Masson St
Montreal PQ H2H 1A1
CANADA
Phone: 514-527-3314

St Markella   GOA
5390 St Urbain St
Montreal PQ H2T 2X1
CANADA
Phone: 514-270-4513

St Mary UOC
2246 Rosemount Blvd
Montreal PQ H2G 1T6
CANADA
Phone:

St Nicholas   ANT
80 de Castelnau St E
Montreal PQ H2R 1P2
CANADA
Phone: 514-270-9788

St Sophia UOC
6270 12th Ave
Montreal PQ H1X 3A5
CANADA
Phone: 514-727-2236
FAX: 514-728-9834

The Sign of the Theotokos
OCA
CP 1390; Place Bonaventure
Montreal PQ H5A 1H3
CANADA
Phone: 514-934-5093

Virgin Mary   ANT
CP 532; Succ Ahuntsic
Montreal PQ H3L 3P1
CANADA
Phone: 514-858-7004

St Benoit de Nursie OCA
2014 St Urbain St
Montreal North PQ H1H 4X1
CANADA
Phone: 514-337-0559

Cathedrale de Saint-
Nicholas ROR
422 Boul Saint-Joseph O
Outremont PQ H2V 2P5
CANADA
Phone: 514-276-8322

Evangelismos   GOA
17 St Cyrille St E
Quebec City PQ G1R 2A3
CANADA
Phone: 418-523-8564

Notre Dame de Kazan
ROR
3836 Sunshine Ave
Rawdon PQ J0K 1S0
CANADA
Phone:

Ecole Primaire Socrates,
Socrates III 11 Eleventh St
GOA
Roxboro PQ H8Y 1K6
CANADA
Phone: 514-685-1833

Ecole Primaire Socrates,
Socrates IV
5220 Grande Allee GOA
St Hubert PQ J3Y 1A1
CANADA
Phone: 514-656-4832

St John the Baptist GOA
4350 Montee St Hubert
St Hubert PQ J3Y 1V1
CANADA
Phone: 514-676-4027

St Marina GOA
5220 Grande Allee
St Hubert PQ J3Y 1A1
CANADA
Phone: 514-656-4832

St Dionysios   GOA
7707 LaSalle Blvd
Ville LaSalle PQ H8P 1Y5
CANADA
Phone: 514-364-5442

Ecole Primaire Socrates,
Socrates I   GOA
275 Houde St
Ville St Laurent PQ H4N 3J3
CANADA
Phone: 514-340-3562

Sign of the Theotokos
OCA
330 Clarke Ave
Westmount PQ
CANADA
Phone: 514-934-5093

Our Savior   BAM
1973 Romiti Rue
Laval PQ H7T 1J7
CANADA
Phone: 514-688-9783

SASKATCHEWAN

Descent of the Holy Ghost
OCA
504 6th Ave E
PO Box 285
Assiniboia SK S0H 0B0
CANADA
Phone: 306-642-3201

Orthodox Christian Centre,
Inc.
Box 3512 OCA
Ft Qu'Appelle SK
CANADA
Phone:

Holy Trinity   OCA
PO Box 12
Kayville SK S0H 2C0
CANADA
Phone:

St Mary / Ss Peter & Paul
RMA
PO Box 74
Kayville SK S0H 2C0
CANADA
Phone: 306-475-2345

All Saints UOC
PO Box 3520
Melfort SK S0E 1A0
CANADA
Phone:

St Michael   OCA
Box 28
Montmartre SK S0G 3M0
CANADA
Phone: 306-424-2067

Holy Trinity   OCA
725 9th Ave SW
Moose Jaw SK S6H 5X2
CANADA
Phone: 306-692-7582

St John   UOC
972 108th St
North Battleford SK S9A 2B9
CANADA
Phone:

Holy Trinity   UOC
305 6th St
Prince Albert SK S6V 7P3
CANADA
Phone:

Holy Ghost   UOC
1920 Toronto St
Regina SK S4P 1M8
CANADA
Phone:

Holy Trinity   SOC
928 11th Ave
Regina SK S4N 0K7
CANADA
Phone:

St George   OCA
2005 Edgar St
Regina SK S4N 3K5
CANADA
Phone: 306-352-0112

St Michael   UOA
2075 McDonald St
Regina SK S4N 2Y4
CANADA
Phone: 306-522-9004

St Nicholas   OCA
1770 St John St
PO Box 36
CANADA
Regina SK S4P 2Z5
Phone: 306-523-5935

St Paul   GOA
3000 Argyle St
Regina SK S4S 2B2
CANADA
Phone: 306-586-6402

Holy Resurrection   OCA
2202 Lorne Ave
Saskatoon SK S7J 0R9
CANADA
Phone: 306-665-3155
FAX: 306-477-3718

Koimisis   GOA
1020 Dufferin Ave
Saskatoon SK S7H 2C1
CANADA
Phone: 306-244-2802

St Vincent of Lerins   ANT
224 25th St W
Saskatoon SK S7M 0C4
CANADA
Phone: 306-934-1695

Ss Peter & Paul   OCA
PO Box 356
St Walbourg SK S0M 2T0
CANADA
Phone:

Holy Assumption   OCA
Stenen SK S0A 3X0
CANADA
Phone: 306-548-4280

Lifegiving Font   GOA
301 N Railway St E
Swift Current SK S9H 1C6
CANADA
Phone: 306-773-3735

Assumption   UOA
PO Box 113
Verigin SK S0A 4H0
CANADA
Phone: 306-542-3385

Ss Anargyroi   GOA
160 Betts Ave
Yorkton SK S3N 1M5
CANADA
Phone: 306-773-3735

St Mark   OCA
160 Betts Ave
Yorkton SK S3N 3R2
CANADA
Phone: 306-786-6216
FAX: 306-783-2153

Parishes and Missions in Mexico and the Carribean

Annunciation ECP
PO Box N-823; West St
Nassau
BAHAMAS
Phone: 809-322-4382

St Michael the Archangel
ECP
30/32 Macaw Ave
Belmopan
BELIZE
Phone: 501-823-284
FAX: 501-823-633

St Benedict
ECP
22 Coconut Ave
San Ignacio
BELIZE
Phone: 501-922-382
FAX: 501-823-633

Orthodox Mission OCC
Box 90
San Ignacio, Cayo
BELIZE
Phone: 501-9-22382

Colectividad Helenica
ECP
Carrera Septimo 2934
Bogota
COLUMBIA

Ss Constantine & Helena
ECP
Calle Loma & Colon y 39
Plaza de la Revolucion
Havana
CUBA
Phone: 53-7-99-36-21/3-7807

Nueva Concepcion OCC
Parcela #B105, Nueva
Concepcion
Escuintla
GUATEMALA
Phone: 5028847626
FAX: 5028847626

Holy Transfiguration AMC
Guatemala City
Guatemala

Holy Resurrection ECP
Metivier
Petion Ville
HAITI
Phone:

Maison Orthodoxe (Central Office)
Morne Calvaire ECP
Petion Ville
HAITI
Mailing: Box 407139
Ft. Lauderdale FL 33340
Phone: 509-57-48-05
FAX: 509-57-06-72

St George ECP
Coin Rue Metelleus et Oge
Petion Ville
HAITI
Phone: 509-57-4805

St Nectarios ECP
Morne Calvaire
Petion Ville
HAITI
Phone: 509-57-48-05

St John the Baptist OCC
Lamothe
Petion-Ville
HAITI
Phone:

Orthodox Mission AMC
San Pedro Sula
HONDURAS

St Nicholas OCC
2 Cherry Garden Ave
Kingston
JAMAICA
Phone: 809-924-2550

Ss. Cosmas & Damian
VAS
#36 Condado de Sayavedra
Atizapan de Zaragoza
MEXICO
Phone:

Orthodox Mission ECP
Chernavaca
MEXICO

Orthodox Mission AMC
Merida
MEXICO

St George Cathedral
AMC
Pirules 110 Jardinas del
Pedregal d
Mexico City 01900
MEXICO
Phone: 525-652-7772

Orthodox Church
AMC
c/o Pirules 110 Jardinas del
Pedreg
Mexico City 01900
MEXICO
Phone: 525-652-7772

St Innocent Orphanage
PAN
Calle Rocio, Lomas de San
Antonio
Rosarito
MEXICO
Phone: 714-559-5838

Project Mexico PAN
Tijuana
MEXICO
Phone: 714-559-5838

San German OCA
El Aguacate; Mazatlan Chi
MEXICO
Phone:

Heraldo de la Orthodoxia
OCA
Cancelleria de la Iglesia
Orthodoxa
Centro Mexico 06000 D.F
MEXICO
Phone:

Catedral de la Ascension del
Senor OCA
Penon de los Banos; Delg.
V.Carran
Mexico City 15520 D.F
MEXICO
Phone:

104

Santisimo Salvador y San
Nicolas
Mexico City DF OCA
MEXICO
Phone:

San German OCA
Guadalajara Jal
MEXICO
Phone:

Transfiguracion OCA
Chalco Mex
MEXICO
Phone:

Santisima Trinidad OCA
Ciudad Lago Mex
MEXICO
Phone:

Santa Cruz OCA
Colonia la Glorieta Mex
MEXICO
Phone:

Santa Sofia - Catedral de
ECP
Agua Caliente Esq. Saratoga
Col. Lo
Mexico City 11000 Mex
MEXICO
Phone: 525-589-6700

San Pedro y San Pablo
OCA
San Pablo Xalpa Mex
MEXICO
Phone:

Santa Maria OCA
Apipilhuasco Ver
MEXICO
Phone:

San Martin OCA
Poblado de San Martin Ver
MEXICO
Phone:

San Pedro OCA
Poblado de San Pedro Ver
MEXICO
Phone:

Santa Cruz OCA
Pisaflores Ver
MEXICO
Phone:

Catedral de la Anunciacion
ECP
Via Podras #32 Aptdo 7050,
Z-5
Panama City
PANAMA
Phone: 507-223-4572
FAX: 507-264-7185

St Elias OCC
c/o Elias Aboud; 25 Eagle
Crescent;
Maraval
TRINIDAD
Phone:

Capilla de San Jorge
ECP
Av. Libertador con Calle 51
Barquisimento
VENEZUELA
Phone: 5851-45-6846

San Antonio
AMC
Caracas
VENEZUELA

Capilla de San Antonio
ECP
Av. 16, #4450
San August, Estado Zulia
VENEZUELA
Phone: 5861-22-4920

Iglesia de la Asuncion
ECP
Avenida Valencia Parpacen
#71
La Florida, Caracas
VENEZUELA
Phone: 582-74-6375

Monastic Communities in North America

All Saints UCC
3733 Hawkins Rd
Sidney BC V0M 1H0
Phone: 604-826-9336
FAX:

All-Merciful Saviour Monastery
26621 99th Ave SW ROR
PO Box 2420
Vashon Island WA 98070-2420
Phone: 206-463-5918
FAX: 206-463-3461
asrom@earthlink.net

Annunciation of the Theotokos Florida GOA
Phone:

Burning Bush Palestinian Hermitage
3347 Augusta Rd ROR
Ellisville MS 39437-5667
Phone: 601-584-8128
FAX: 601-583-8621

Christ of the Hills Monastery
PO Box 1049 New Sarov   ROR
Blanco TX 78606-1049
Phone: 830-833-5363
FAX: 830-833-5813
newsarov@texanet.net

Christ the Savior Monastery ROR
27 Whitman St, Pawtucket RI
PO Box 6332
Providence RI 02940
Phone: 401-725-1692
FAX:

Community of Holy Myrrhbearers
144 Bert Washburn Rd OCA
Otego NY 13825-2265
Phone: 607-432-3179
FAX: 607-432-0794

Convent of Our Lady of Vladimir
3365 19th St.   ROR
San Francisco CA 94110-1816
Phone: 415-824-3475
FAX:

Convent of St Silouan   ROR
PO Box 25
Boscobel WI 53805-0025
Phone: 608-375-5500
FAX:

Convent of the Holy Myrrhbearers
3011 Roe Dr   HUS
Houston TX 77087-2409
Phone: 713-645-0843
FAX: 713-645-0104

Convent of Nativity of the Virgin
3774 Gravois Rd   ROR
PO Box 536
House Springs MO 63051-0536
Phone: 314-677-1131
FAX: 314-376-3223

Dormition ROR
RR 1 Box 192
Preston Hollow NY 12469-9620
Phone: 518-239-4650
FAX:

Dormition Skete   GOC
29020 C.R. 187, PO Box 3177
Buena Vista CO 81211
Phone: 719-395-6395
FAX: 719-395-9422

Dormition Skete   OCA
8113-111 Avenue
Edmonton AL T5H 1L3
CANADA
Phone/FAX: 403-428-3528

Emmaus House   OCA
PO Box 189
Cambridge NY 12816-0189
Phone: 518-677-8863
FAX:

Exaltation of the Cross Hermitage
Box 363-3790 Gravois Rd. ROR
House Springs MO 63051
Phone: 314-677-2345

Four Evangelists   HUS
3011 Roe Dr
Houston TX 77087-2409
Phone: 713-645-0843
FAX: 713-645-0104

Glorious Ascension Monastery
5052 S Dixie Rd SW ROR
P.O. Box 397
Resaca GA 30735-0397
Phone: 706-277-9442
FAX: 706-277-9443
mga@alltel.net

Greek Orthodox Convent   GMA
4211 Ditmars Blvd
Long Island City NY 11105-1433
Phone:
FAX:

Hermitage of St Mary Magdalene
4559 Dumfries Rd   AUX
Catlett VA 22019-1712
Phone: 703-788-3053
FAX:

Hermitage of the Holy Cross
3790 Gravois Rd   ROR
PO Box 717
House Springs MO 63051
Phone: 314-677-2345
FAX: 314-376-3223

Holy Annunciation Monastery
211 Bay State Rd   VAS
Melrose MA 02176-1442
Phone:
FAX:

Holy Apostles Convent   GOC
29001 C.R. 187, PO Box 3118
Buena Vista CO 81211
Phone: 719-395-8898
FAX: 719-395-9422
apostles@amigo.net

Holy Archangels
PO Box 422
Kendalia TX 78027
Phone: 210-833-2793
FAX: 210-833-2793

Holy Assumption Monastery
1519 Washington St.   OCA
Calistoga CA 94515-1501
Phone: 707-942-6244
FAX: 707-942-8076

Holy Cross Skete
184 Dent St   VAS
West Roxbury MA 02132-3242
Phone:
FAX:

Holy Dormition Monastery
3389 Rives Eaton Rd   OCA
Rives Junction MI 49277
Phone: 517-569-2873
FAX: 517-569-2873

Holy Monastery of the Theotokos
38526 Dunlap Rd   GOA
PO Box 549
Dunlap CA 93621-0549
Phone: 209-338-3110
FAX: 209-338-0832

Holy Nativity Convent
70 Codman Rd   AUX
Brookline MA 02146-7555
Phone: 617-566-0156
FAX:

Holy Nativity Convent
121 Saint Elias Ln   GOA
Saxonburg PA 16056-9615
Phone: 412-352-1533
FAX:

Holy Protection Monastery
Rt 1 Box 75
Geneva NE 68361
Phone: 402-759-4952
FAX: 402-759-3381
MonksIcons@AOL.COM

Holy Protection of the Theotokos
4600 93rd St
Pleasant Prarie WI 53158
Phone: 414-694-9850
FAX:

Holy Theotokos Monastery
111 Evergreen Rd   ECU
N Ft Myers FL 33903-3830
Phone: 941-997-2846
FAX: 941-997-2046

Holy Theotokos Skete   FOC
Box 188742
Sacramento CA 95818-8742
Phone: 916-455-9853
Kallistos@juno.com

Holy Transfiguration Monastery
278 Warren St   AUX
Brookline MA 02146-5927
Phone: 617-734-0608
FAX: 617-730-5783

Holy Transfiguration Monastery
83 Chermin du Monastere   ROR
Mansonville PQ J0E 1X0
CANADA
Phone: 514-292-3102

Holy Transfiguration
Guatemala   AMC

Holy Trinity Monastery
PO Box 36   ROR
Jordanville NY 13261
Phone: 315-858-0940
FAX: 315-858-0505
72204.1465@compuserve.com

Holy Trinity   gOA
Smithcreek MI

Holy Trinity Monastery
3790 Gravois Rd.   ROR
House Springs MO 63051
Phone: 314-677-2345

Kazan Skete of the Mother of God
2735 Victoria Dr   OCA
Santa Rosa CA 95407
Phone: 707-542-7798
FAX:

Kursk Mother of God Hermitage/ Nativity
ROR
Rt. 6 - Box 1050
Mahopac NY 10541-3403
Phone: 914-628-4975
FAX:

Mary/Martha Convent ANT
Box 70-65 Spinner Ln
Wagner SC 29164
Phone:

Mercy House   ROR
320 E 3rd St
New York NY 10009-7865
Phone: 212-533-5140
FAX:

Mother of God the Liberator
42-11 Ditmars Blvd. ECU
Astoria NY 11105-1433
Phone: 718-932-9292

Most Holy Mother of God   NGM
PO Box 496
Grayslake IL 60030-0496
Phone:
FAX:

Most Holy Mother of God   SOC
PO Box 247
Springboro PA 16435-0247
Phone: 814-587-6209
FAX:

Nativity of the Mother of God
32787 Early Rd   SOC
New Carlisle IN 46552-9675
Phone: 219-652-7994
FAX:

Nativity of the Virgin Mary
3774 Gravois Rd.   ROR
House Springs MO 63051
Phone: 314-677-1131

Nativity of St. John the Baptist
2805 S. Forest St.   GOA
Denver CO 80222
Phone: 303-691-9916

Nativity of the Theotokos
GOA
121 St. Elias Lane-Box 536
Saxonburg PA 16056
Phone: 412-352-3999

New Skete   OCA
New Skete Lane, PO Box 128
Cambridge NY 12816-2373
Phone: 518-677-3928
FAX: 518-677-2373

New Valaam Monastery
414 Maison Rd.   OCA
Kodiak AK 99615
Phone:
FAX:

New Valaam Monastery   VAS
Monk's Lagoon AK 99644
Phone: 907-248-9659

New Valaam Monastery - Monk's Lagoon
VAS
PO Box 90
Ouzinkie AK 99644
Phone: None
FAX: None

New Valaam Monastery - St Michael's Sket
VAS
PO Box 90
Ouzinkie AK 99644
Phone: None
FAX: None

Novo Diveevo Convent   ROR
100 Smith Rd.
Nanuet NY 10954-5200
Phone: 914-356-0425
FAX:

Oblates of St. Benedict ANT
3333Workman Mill Rd.
Whittier CA 90601
Phone: 562-692-6121

Our Lady of Kazan Monastery
2735 Victoria Drive OCA
Santa Rosa CA 95407
Phone: 707-542-7798

Our Lady of Kazan Monastery
324 Hazeldine Ave SW   VAS
Albuquerque NM 87102-4160
Phone: 505-242-6186
FAX:

Our Lady of the Sign Monastery
RR 1 Box 34   OCA
Cambridge NY 12816-9801
Phone: 518-677-3810
FAX:

Our Lady of Vladimir
3365 19th St. ROR
San Francisco CA 94110
Phone: 415-282-0985

Panagia Parigoritissa
827 Chemin de la Carriere GOA
Brownsburg (Chatham), PQ
J8G 1K7 CANADA
Phone: 514-533-4313

Panagia Vlahernon GOA
Florida
Phone:

Blessed Pasha and Pelagia
New Sarov   ROR
Blanco TX 78606
Phone: 210-833-5860

Paradise Palestinian Hermitage
3347 Augusta Rd.   ROR
Ellisville MS 39437
Phone: 601-584-8128

Priory St Augustine of Canterbury
PO Box 1016   AOM
Southwick MA 01077-1016
Phone: 860-741-0436
FAX:

Protecting Veil of the Theotokos
513 E 24th Ave Ste #5   OCA
Anchorage AK 99503
Phone: 907-279-0778
FAX:

Protection of the Holy Virgin
2343 County Rd 403   OCA
PO Box 416
Lake George CO 80827
Phone: 719-748-3999
FAX:

Protection of the Virgin Mary
RR #2   ROR
Bluffton AB T0C 0M0
CANADA
Phone: 403-843-6401

Resurrection Skete and Ministries
PO Box 1352   HEO
Indianapolis IN 46206-1352
Phone:
FAX:
lterry@iquest.net

Resurrection of Christ
1201 Hathaway Ln NE ROR
Minneapolis MN 55432-5714
Phone: 612-574-1001
FAX: 612-574-1001
Rusmnch@worldnet.att.net

Saint Barbara OCA
PO Box 91122
Santa Barbara CA 93190-1122
Phone: 805-963-1313
FAX:

St Andrew the Apostle CYP
18465 Chezik Rd
Blue River WI 53518-9425
Phone:
FAX:

St. Andrew's UIU
2237 Hunter Ave
Bronx NY 10475
Phone:

St Anna Convent CHR
7870 Birnam
Montreal PQ H3N 2T5
Phone: 514-276-8408
FAX:

St Anthony GOA
4784 St Joseph's Wy
Florence AZ 85232
Phone: 520-709-0366
FAX:

St Anthony Monastery
RR 2 Box 259 UOD
Knox IN 46534-9802
Phone: 219-772-7089
FAX:

St Barbara Monastery
PO Box 582 GOA ✓
New Monmouth NJ 07748-0582
Phone: 908-671-5932
FAX:

St Eliah UCU
3820 Moores Lake Rd
Dover FL 33527
Phone: 813-659-0123
FAX:

St Elizabeth ROR
1520 State Rt 167
Mohawk NY 13407-9802
Phone: 315-858-2208
FAX:

St Elizabeth the Grand Duchess
PO Box 398 CYP
Etna CA 96027-0398
Phone:
FAX:

St Gregory Palamas Monastery CYP
1307 Sawyers Bar Rd - PO BOX 398
Etna CA 96027-9401
Phone: (916) 467-3228
FAX:

St Gregory Palamas Monastery
2256 Ashland County Rd GOA
PO Box 206
Hayesville OH 44838
Phone: 419-368-5335
FAX:

St Gregory Palamas Monastery
2256 Ashland County Rd GOA
PO Box 206
Hayesville OH 44838-0206
Phone: 419-368-5335
FAX:

St Gregory of Sinai OCA
5717 Clinton Ave.
Richmond CA 94805
Phone: 510-215-0301
FAX:
sinai@sirius.com

St Herman Monastery UCU
4410 Franklin Blvd
Cleveland OH 44113-2846
Phone: 216-961-3806
FAX:

St Herman of Alaska Monastery VAS
PO Box 70 – 10 Beegum Gorge Rd.
Platina CA 96076
Phone: 916-352-4430
FAX: 916-352-4432
stherman@crl.com

St Hilarion Monastery
1905 S 3rd St WEA
Austin TX 78704
Phone: 512-442-2289
FAX: 512-416-6556
hilaroin2@juno.com

St Isaac of Syria Skete   ROR
Rt 1 - Box 168
Boscobel WI 53805-9619
Phone: 608-375-5500
FAX: 608-375-5555
stisaacske@aol.com

St. Irene Chrysovalantou
36-07 23rd Ave.   ECU
Astoria NY 11105

St. James JER
4400 Green River Rd.
Corona CA 91720
Phone: 909-736-7595

St James Hermitage RMA
505 One Half Ave
Prairie Farm WI 54762
Phone: 715-455-1553
FAX:

St John Chrysostomos GOA
4600 93rd St
Pleasant Prairie WI 53142
Phone: 414-694-9850

St John the Forerunner (Prodromos)
5 Timmer Ln   GOA
Goddendale WA 98620
Phone: 509-773-3667
FAX:

St John the Theologian
RR 8 Bethel St
Pickton ON K0K 2FO
Phone:
FAX:

St John the Theologian Monastery
5862 Allyn Rd   OCA
PO Box 1915
Hiram OH 44234
Phone: 216-274-2052
FAX: 216-274-0222

St John the Wonderworker
Denver CO HEO
Phone:
FAX:
russmonk@nilenet.com

St John's Prior   IND
3690 Hopkins Rd, Powder Spring
PO Box 350
Clark Dale GA 30111
Phone: 770-222-8506
FAX:
osj@earthlink.net

St John, Wonderworker   OCA
PO Box 563
Point Reyes Station CA 94956-0563
Phone: 415-663-1705
FAX:
frnikolai@worldnet.att.net

St Katherine Skete   DHE
1317 S 11th St
Lincoln NE 68502-1220
Phone: 402-476-2676
FAX:

St Kosmas of Aitolia GOA
14155 Caledon King Town
Line Road South-R.R. 1
Bolton ON 17E 5R7
CANADA
Phone: 905-859-2474
FAX: 905-859-2505

St Luke's Priory   ANT
PO Box 84
Stanton NJ 08885-0084
Phone: 908-236-7890
FAX:

St Mark Monastery NGM
PO Box 2093
Sheffield Lake OH 44054-0093
Phone:
FAX:

St Mark's Monastery   ROR
419 E 117th St
New York NY 10035
Phone: 212-289-3071

St. Markella   CHR
22-68 26th St.
Astoria NY 11105
Phone: 718-267-1764

St Mary of Egypt Skete   VAS
1901 N Pennsylvania St
Indianapolis IN 46202-1417
Phone:

/ ...nastery
...t GMA
...2632-2613
Phone:
FAX:

St Michael's Skete   VAS
Monk's Lagoon AK
Phone: 907-248-9659
FAX:

St Michael's Skete   VAS
PO Box 90
Ouzinkie AK 99644-0090
Phone: 907-248-9659
FAX:

St Michael's Skete   OCA
PO Box 38
Canones NM 87516
Phone: 505-638-5690
FAX:

St Neilos of Rossano   IGO
1101 Howard Ave.
Utica NY 13501
Phone: 315-798-4457

St Nicholas Monastery   ROR
PO Box 800
Glenham NY 12527-0800
Phone: 914-831-2164
FAX:

St Paisius Abbey   VAS
7777 Martinelli Rd
PO Box 130
Forestville CA 95436-9711
Phone: 707-887-9740
FAX: 707-887-9023

St Paisius Hermitage ROR
RD 2 Box 213-A
Troy PA 16947
Phone: 717-364-5243

St Panteleimon   GOA
7143 Cedar Rd
428 Calvin St
Grosse Pointe Farms MI 48236-3204
Phone: 313-884-0292
FAX:

St. Paul Skete   ANT
1627 Faxon Ave.
Memphis TN 38112
Phone:

St Sava Monastery   SOC
PO Box 519
Libertyville IL 60048-0519
Phone: 708-362-2440
FAX:

St Seraphim Skete & Chapel OCA
15th & Petrograd Aves   CP 1521
Rawdon PQ J0K 1S0
Phone: 514-834-8331
FAX:

St Seraphim of Sarov   ROR
515 Vermont Ave
PO Box 93
Moss Beach CA 94038
Phone: 650-728-3548
FAX:

St. Seraphim of Sarov   OCA
B.P. 1695
Rawdon, PQ J0K 1S0
CANADA
Phone: 514-834-2332

St Silouan Convent ROR
Box 25
Boscobel WI 53805-0025
Phone: 608-375-5500

St. Silouan Brotherhood   OCA
Box 179
Spencerville ON K0E 1X0
CANADA
Phone: 613-925-5226

St Syncletike Convent   CHR
55 Fairview
Farmingdale NY 11735
Phone: 516-293-2641
FAX:

St Tikhon of Zadonsk Monastery
St Tikhon's Road   OCA
PO Box 130
S Canaan PA 18459
Phone: 717-937-4067
FAX: 717-937-3100

St Tikhon's Monastery   OCA
St Tikhon's Rd
PO Box 130
S Canaan PA 18459-0121
Phone: 717-937-4067
FAX: 717-937-3100

St Xenia Skete   VAS
Wildwood Rural Branch
Redding CA 96001
Phone:
FAX:

St Xenia Skete Metochion   VAS
1901 N Pennsylvania St
Indianapolis IN 46202-1416
Phone: 317-925-3034
FAX:

Theophany Skete   VAS
824 Chestnut St
Chico CA 95928-5241
Phone: 916-893-1814
FAX:

Theotokos "Life-Giving Spring"
38526 Dunlap Rd   GOA
PO Box 549
Dunlap CA 93621
Phone: 209-338-3110
FAX:

Transfiguration   OCA
RD #1 Box 184X
Ellwood City PA 16117
Phone: 412-758-4002
FAX: 412-758-4002

Virgin Theotokos the Consoler
827 Chemin de la Carriere
Chatham, Brownsburg QB J8G 1K7
Phone:
FAX:

*Orthodox Monasteries in North America
(comprehensive web site)
http://www.nettinker.com/monasteries/

Other Orthodox Institutions

Education

A. Fantis Parochial School GOA
195 State St
Brooklyn NY 11201
Phone: 718-624-0501

ASC Byzantine Studies Program
11935 Abercorn ST
Savannah GA 31419
Phone: 912-356-3545

Annunciation Orthodox School
3600 Yoakum Blvd GOA
Houston TX 77006
Phone: 713-620-3600

Antiochian House of Studies, Theological
PO Box 638   ANT
Ligonier PA 15658-0638
Phone:

Archons of the Ecumenical Patriarchate
8 E 79th St   GOA
New York NY 10021
Phone: 212-570-3550
FAX: 212-861-2183

Cathedral School   GOA
319 E 74 St
New York NY 10021
Phone: 212-249-2840

D & G Kaloidis Parochial School
8502 Ridge Blvd   GOA
Brooklyn NY 11209
Phone: 718-836-8096

Eastern Orthodox School of
Religious Instruction   IND
4021 Elm St.
East Chicago IN 46312
Phone: 219-398-9823
FAX: 219-836-2909

Greek Ortho Parochial Sch of St Spyridon
GOA
120 Wadesworth Ave
New York NY 10033
Phone: 212-795-6870

Greek-American Institute   GOA
3573 Bruckner Blvd
Bronx NY 10461
Phone: 718-823-2393

Hellenic American School of Holy Trinity
GOA
41 Broadway
Lowell MA 01854
Phone: 508-453-5422

Hellenic American Academy
10701 S Glen Rd   GOA
Potomac MD 20854
Phone: 301-299-1566

Hellenic College/Holy Cross
50 Goddard Ave GOA
Brookline MA 02146-7415
Phone: 617-731-3500

Hellenic School of Holy Dormition
1910 Douglas Ave   CHR
Clearwater FL 34615-1411
Phone: 813-443-1411

Hellenic School of St Isisdore
910 Stewart Ave.   CHR
Bethpage NY 11714-3532
Phone: 516-933-1726

Hellenic School of St Nectarios 3044 N 27th
St.   CHR
Phoenix AZ 85016
Phone: 602-957-3054

Hellenic School of St Markella Cathedral
2268 26th St   CHR
Long Island City NY 11105-3152
Phone: 718-932-1592
FAX: 718-274-2875

Heritage and Learning Center
PO Box 638   ANT
Ligonier PA 15658-0638
Phone: 412-238-3677

Holy Cross Parochial School
8502 Ridge Blvd GOA
Brooklyn NY 11209-4308
Phone: 718-836-8096

Holy Trinity Orthodox Seminary
PO Box 36   ROR
Jordanville NY 13361
Phone: 315-855-0945
FAX: 315-855-0945
seminary@telenet.net

Holy Trinity Seminary
Box 1834 AOC
Glendora CA 91740-1834
Phone: 818-335-7369
FAX: 818-857-7642

Holy Virgin Protection Church School
ROR
Prospect St. & Cedar Hill Ave.
Nyack NY 10960
Phone: 914-358-4982

Iconography Institute & Center
Mt. Angel Abbey
St Benedict OR 97373

Institute for Eastern Orthodox Studies
3011 Rose Dr   HUS
Houston TX 77087-2409
Phone: 713-645-0843
FAX: 713-645-0104

Jamaica Day Sch of St Demetrios
84-35 152 St   GOA
Jamaica NY 11432
Phone: 718-526-2622

Justinian Centre   PAN
2001 N Andrews Ave
Ft. Lauderdale FL 33311
Phone:
Justiniancentr@geocities.com

Koraes Greek-American School
11025-45 S Roberts Rd   GOA
Palos Hills IL 60465
Phone: 708-974-3402

Mohyla Institute   UOC
1240 Temperance St
Saskatoon SK S7N 0P1
Phone: 306-653-1944
FAX: 306-652-7820

National Forum of Gr Orth Ch Musicians
1700 N Walnut St #302   GOA
Bloomington IN 47404
Phone: 812-855-6508
FAX: 812-855-9630

Nemanjic Institute for Serbo-Byzantine
37323 Hawkins Rd   PAN
Dewowey BC V0M 1H0
Phone: 604-826-9336
FAX: 604-820-9758

New Sarov Pastoral School
PO Box 1049   ROR
Blanco TX 78606-1049
Phone: 830-833-5363
FAX: 830-833-5813
Newsarov@texanet.net

OCAMPR Ethics Institute   PAN
105 Summit Ct
Westfield NJ 07090-2834
Phone: 908-233-5051
FAX: 908-232-5049
gmorelli@pilot.njin.net

OSJ Center for Applied Theology
PO Box 15783   OCA
Savannah GA 31405
Phone: 912-356-3545

Orthodox Christian Tutorial Program 3044
N. 27th St.   CHR
Phoenix AZ 85016-7926
Phone: 602-957-3054

Orthodox Pastoral Counseling Institute
PO Box 10354   PAN
Pittsburgh PA 15234-0354
Phone: 412-335-9988

Patriarch Athenagoras Orthodox Institute
2311 Hearst Ave   GOA
Berkeley CA 94709
Phone: 510-649-2450
FAX: 510-841-6605
PManolis@GTU.EDU

Plato Academy   GOA
601 S Central Ave
Chicago IL 60644
Phone: 312-626-1728

Registry   GOA
8 E 79th St
New York NY 10021
Phone: 212-570-3558
FAX: 212-570-2123

S Ellenas Parochial School
224 18th St   GOA
Brooklyn NY 11215
Phone: 718-499-5900

School of the Metamorphosis
98-07 38 Ave   GOA
Corona NY 11368
Phone: 718-478-8181

School of the Transfiguration
98-07 38th Ave.   GOA
Corona NY 11368
Phone: 718-478-8181

Serbian Seminary   NGM
Grayslake IL 60030-0496
Phone: 708-223-4305

Society for the Study of Eastern Orthodoxy

2619 Northfield #F
Waukegan IL 60085
Phone: 708-249-8350

Socrates Greek-American School
6041 W Diversey Ave   GOA
Chicago IL 60639
Phone: 312-622-6323

Socrates Greek-American School
6041 W Diversey Ave   GOA
Chicago IL 60639-1139
Phone: 312-622-5979

Soterios Ellenas Parochial School
224 18th St   GOA
Brooklyn NY 11215-5303
Phone: 718-499-5900

St Andrew's College UOC
475 Dysart Rd
Winnipeg MB R3T 2M7
Phone: 204-474-8901
FAX: 204-275-0803

St Anthony the Great Orthodox College   CHR
Alamagordo NM 88311-1432
Phone: 718-932-1592

St Athanasius Academy   ANT
120519 E Stockton Blvd, Ste 170
Elk Grove CA 95624
Phone: 916-686-6230
FAX: 916-686-6233
frjack@saaot.edu

St Athanasius Academy   ANT
6778 Pasado Rd.
Goleta CA 93117-4908
Phone: 805-685-3111

St Athanasius Catechetical School
5621 Zanola Dr.
Mableton GA 30126-3040
Phone: 770-3095123

St Basil Academy   GOA
Rt 9
RT 2 Box 8A
Garrison NY 10524
Phone: 914-424-3500
FAX: 914-424-4172

St. Columcille of Iona House of   AOC
Orthodox Chrstian Studies
Box 674
Anaconda MT 59711-0674
Phone/FAX. 406-563-5426

Ss Cyril & Methodius High School
6200 Geary Blvd.   ROR
San Francisco CA 94121-1822
Phone: 415-752-5122

St Demetrios Greek-American School
30-03 30 Dr   GOA
Astoria NY 11102
Phone: 718-728-1754

St Demetrios-St Catherine Annex
22-30 33 St   GOA
Astoria NY 11105
Phone: 718-728-1100

St Elias School of Orthodox Theology
740 s 11th St Ste 9 FOC
PO Box 22237
Lincoln NE 68508
Phone: 402-475-6492
FAX: 402-488-2587
eliastheol@aol.com

St Fanourios Cathedral School
44-02 48th Ave   VAS
Woodside NY 11377
Phone:

St Herman's Orthodox Theo. Seminary
414 Mission Rd   OCA
Kodiak AK 99615-6386
Phone: 907-486-3524
FAX: 907-486-5935

St Isaac School   ROR
Rt 1 Box 168
Boscobel WI 53805-9619
Phone: 608-375-5500
FAX: 608-375-5555
stisaac@aol.com
St. Chrysostom Institute of
Orthodox Christian Studies
Regis University
3333 Regis Blvd.
Denver CO 80221
Phone. 303-458-3513
Lbundy@regis.edu

St John of Damascus Art Academy
RR1 Box 307, Bolivar PA 15923
PO Box 638   ANT
Ligonier PA 15658
Phone: 412-238-3268
FAX: 412-238-2102

St John's College Residence Hall Program

PO Box 15783
Savannah GA 31405
Phone: 912-356-3545
FAX:

St John's Institute   UOC
11024-82nd Ave
Edmonston AB T6G 0T2
Phone: 403-439-5788
FAX: 403-439-0989

St Macarius the Roman Orthodox Referenc
ROR
1180 Orthodox Way
Liberty TN 37095-9801
Phone:

St Nicholas Day School
9501 Balboa Blvd   GOA
Northridge CA 91325-1901
Phone: 818-886-6751

St Nicholas Ranch & Retreat Center
38526 Dunlap Rd   PO Box 400
Dunlap CA 93621-0400   GOA
Phone: 209-338-2103

St Paisius Missionary School VAS
7777 Martinelli Rd
Forestville CA 95436
Phone: 707-887-9740
FAX: 887-9023

St Romanus Chanters Training Program
ANT
9980 Hwy 9
Ben Lomond CA 95005
Phone: 408-336-2228

St Sophia Ukrainian Orthodox Seminary
UCU
PO Box 240
South Bound Brook NJ 08880-0240
Phone: 908-469-7555

St Stephen's Course of Studies in Orthodoxy ANT
358 Mountain Rd
Englewood NJ 07631-3727
Phone: 201-871-1355
FAX: 201-871-7954

St Tikhon's Orthodox Theo. Seminary
S Canaan PA 18459   OCA
Phone: 717-937-4411
FAX: 717-937-4939

St Vincent College Program for Orthodox
ANT
Latrobe PA 15650
Phone:

St Vladimir's Institute
620 Spadina Ave   UOC
Toronto ON M5S 2H4
Phone: 416-923-3318
FAX: 416-964-6085

St Vladimir's Orthodox OCA
Theological Seminary
575 Scarsdale Rd
Crestwood NY 10707
Phone: 914-961-8313
FAX: 914-961-4507

Three Hierarchs Parochial School
1724 Ave P   GOA
Brooklyn NY 11229
Phone: 718-375-1885

Universal Accrediting Service
PO Box 22537   FOC
Lincoln NE 68542-2237
Phone:

Valaam Academy VAS
7777 Martinelli Rd
Forestville CA 95436-9711
Phone: 707-887-9740

Wm Spyropoulos Greek American Day
School   GOA
43-15 196th St
Flushing NY 11358-3520
Phone: 718-357-5583
FAX:

Orthodox Publications and Publishers

AARDM Press
32317 32nd Ave., N.E.
Minneapolis MN 55418

A M S Press
56 E 13th St
New York NY 10003
Phone: 212-777-4700

Again Magazine   ANT
10090 Hwy 9 #A
Ben Lomond CA 95005-9217
Phone: 408-336-5118
FAX: 408-336-8882

Alexandre-Alexander Publishers & Dist.
2875 Douglas Ave
Montreal QE H3R 2C7
Phone: 514-738-5517
FAX: 514-738-4718
john@top.ca

Alive in Christ   OCA
Diocesan Center
S Canaan PA 18459
Phone: 717-876-1241

All Saints of Russia Press
3274 E Iliff Ave
Denver CO 80209
Phone: 303-757-3533

Alleluia Press
Box 103
Allendale NJ 07401
Phone:

Amnos Publications GOA
2501 S Wolf Rd
Westchester IL 60154
Phone: 708-562-2744
FAX: 708-562-2752
a45pappas@aol.com

BAOC Consistory   BAJ
PO Box 5982
Somerset NJ 08875-5982
Phone: 732-873-8026
blautoc@ix.netcom.com

Bee   CHR
St. Anthony Orthodox Publications,
Phoenix AZ 85016-7926
Phone: 602-957-3054

Burning Bush Monastic Journal

OCA
3389 Rives Eaton Rd.
Rives Junction MI 49277
Phone. 517-569-2873

Center for Traditional Orthodox Studies
PO Box 398
Etna CA 96027
Phone: 916-467-3228

Christ the Saviour Publishing
Box 63377
St Louis MO 63163
Phone: 314-664-4560

Christian Activist
PO Box 740
Mt Hermon CA 95041
Phone: 408-353-3240
tca1@tca1.org

Chronicle ROR
PO Box 1049
Blanco TX 78606-1049
Phone: 830-833-5363
FAX: 830-833-5813

Chrysostom Press
PO Box 536
House Spring MO 63051
Phone: 314-677-4333

Church Messenger CRC
312 Garfield St
Johnstown PA 15906
Phone: 814-539-9143
FAX: 814-536-4699

Church Messenger (Carkouny Paslaniec)
401 Atlantic Ave   BAJ
Brooklyn NY 11217-1702
Phone: 718-875-0595
belautoc@ix.netcom.com

Church Messenger (editorial office) 280
Clinton St CRC
Binghamton NY 13905-2018
Phone: 814-539-9143
FAX: 814-536-4699

Conciliar Press   ANT
10090 Hwy 9
PO Box 76
Ben Lomond CA 95005
Phone: 800-967-7377
FAX: 408-336-8882
shouston@gov.net

Credinta   RMA
19959 Riopelle St
Detroit MI 48203
Phone: 313-893-8390

Credo   ANT
PO Box 84
Stanton NJ 08885-0084
Phone:

Diocesan Voice   GOA
372 Santa Clara Ave.
San Francisco CA 94127

DOXA   OCA
PO Box 38
Canones NM 87516-0038
Phone:

Dawn   OCA
PO Box 191109
Dallas TX 75219-8109
Phone: 214-522-4149
FAX: 214-526-7170

Desert Voice   CHR
St. Anthony Orthodox Publications,
Phoenix AZ 85016-7926
Phone: 602-957-3054

Diocesan Voice   GOA
372 Santa Clara Ave
San Francisco CA 94127
Phone: 415-753-3075
FAX: 415-753-1165

Dormition/Apostles Publishing
Box 3118
Buena Vista CO 81211
Phone: 719-395-8898
FAX: 719-395-9422

Dumbarton Oaks
1703 32nd St NW
Washington DC 20007
Phone: 202-342-3259

Dynamis Bible Readings
7515 E 13th St N
Wichita KS 67206-1223
Phone: 316-636-4676

Eastern Orthodox Books
PO Box 302
Willits CA 95490
Phone:

Eastern Orthodox Foundation
PO Box 432
Indiana PA 15701
Phone: 412-349-4821
FAX: 412-349-7357
ghnatko@twd.net

Edwin Mellen Press
PO Box 450
Lewiston NY 14092
Phone: 716-754-2788

EIKONA Recordings
Box 4674
Englewood CO 80155
Phone: 303-221-1355
www.eikona.com

Enlightener   VAS
1827 S 11th St.
Lincoln NE 68508
Phone:

Epiphany Journal   VAS
16 Channel Rd
PO Box 2250
South Portland ME 04106-5107
Phone: 207-767-1889

Essays and Notes Newsletters OCA
144 Bert Washburn Rd.
Otego NY 13825-2265

Eye on the Commonwealth
2001 N. Andrews Ave
Ft Lauderdale FL 33311

Faber & Faber, Inc.
705 Cascadilla St
Ithica NY 14851
Phone: 800-666-2211

Firebird
PO Box 303
Belleville MI 48112-0303
Phone: 313-699-0870

First Hour   PAN
206 Sarles Ln
Pleasantville NY 10570
Phone:

Go Forth (Church Newsletter/Bulletins)
2 Lakeshore Blvd., Box 35
Grand Isle VT 05458

Greek Orthodox Theological Review
GOA
50 Goddard Ave
Brookline MA 02146
Phone: 617-731-3500
FAX: 617-566-9075

Harvard Ukrainian Research Institute
1583 Massachusetts Ave
Cambridge MA 02138
Phone: 617-495-3692

Harvest   OCA
PO Box 397
Resaca GA 30735-0397
Phone: 706-277-9442

Hellenic College Press
50 Goddard Ave
Brookline MA 02146
Phone: 617-731-3500

Herald   UOC
9 St Johns Ave
Winnipeg MB R2W 1G8
Phone: 204-586-3093
FAX: 204-582-5241

Holy Cross Press   GOA
50 Goddard Ave
Brookline MA 02146
Phone: 617-731-3500

Holy Trinity Monastery Pub. ROR
Jordanville NY 13361
Phone: 315-858-0940

Iconography.com Internet Services
Phone: 510-229-8137
Info@iconography.com
www.iconography.com

Illuminator   GOA
5201 Ellsworth Ave
Pittsburgh PA 15232-1421
Phone: 412-621-5529
FAX: 412-621-1522

In Communion
1811 GJ Alkmaar
Kanisstraat 5
Phone: 3172511-2545
FAX: 3172515-4180
101363.304@compuserve.com

Institute of Byzantine & Mod Grk Studies
115 Gilbert Rd
Belmont MA 02178
Phone: 617-484-6595

Jacob's Well   OCA
24 Colmar Rd
Cherry Hill NJ 08002-1206
Phone:

Joyous Light   OCA
PO Box 185
Grass Lake MI 49240-0185
Phone: 517-522-3656
FAX: 517-522-5907

Kathedra OCA
825 Harrington Rd
Rockville MD 20852-1030
Phone:

Life Transfigured Journal OCA
RD 1 Box 184x
Ellwood City PA 16117

Light & Life Publishing Cmpany
4818 Park Glen Rd
Minneapolis MN 55416
Phone: 612-925-3888

Limestone Press
University of Alaska, History Dept
Fairbanks AK 99775
Phone: 907-474-6997

Little Falcons Booklets
PO Box 371
Grayslake IL 60030
Phone: 847-223-4300

Life Transfigured Journal   OCA
R.D. 1, Box 184-X
Ellwood City PA 16117
Phone. 724-758-4002

Light of Christ   PAN
3027 Foxhall Rd NW
Washington DC 20016-3430
Phone:

Living Orthodoxy   ROR
1180 Orthodox Way
Liberty TN 37095-9801
Phone: 615-536-5239

Lumina Lina   OCA
PO Box 185
Grass Lake MI 49240-0185
Phone: 517-522-3656
FAX: 517-522-5907

Macrina Publications
1200 Madison Box 525
Denver CO 80206
Phone: 303-316-8027

National Herald
41-17 Crescent St
Long Island City NY 11201
Phone: 718-784-5255
FAX: 718-729-2569

News & Needs (IOCC Newsletter)
711 w. 40TH St., Suite 306
Baltimore MD
Iocc@igc.apc.org

Nikodemos Orthodox Publication Society
PO Box 383   ROR
Richfield Springs NY 13439-0383
Phone:

ONE - Orthodox New England OCA
95 Butterworth Ln.
Southington CT 06489
Phone:

One Thing Needful Journal
65 Spinner Lane   OCA
Box 70
Wagener SC 29164

Oakwood Publicastions
3827 Bluff St.
Torrance CA 90505
Phone: 310-378-9245
FAX. 310-378-6782
www.oakwoodpub.com

One Church   PER
158 Stiles St
Elizabeth NJ 07208-1811
Phone: 216-788-0151

One Church   PER
727 Miller St
Youngstown OH 44502-2326
Phone: 216-788-0151

Orchid Land Publications
Keaʻau HI 96749
Phone: 808-966-8923
FAX: 808-982-5603
Orlapubs@ilhawaii.net

Orthodox America   ROR
PO Box 383
Richfield Springs NY 13439-0383
Phone:

Orthodox Apologist DHE
HC 65 Box 146A
Riverside WA 98849-9613
Phone:

Orthodox Beacon   ROR
Box 1047
Vashon Island WA 98070
Phone: 206-463-5918

Orthodox Brotherhood of the
Virgin Mary
5220 Front St.
Jenners PA 15546-9603
Phone: 814-629-9177

Orthodox Christan Cassettes
2919 N 56th St
Springdale AR 72762
Phone: 501-750-3808
FAX: 501-927-2867
occassette@aol.com

Orthodox Christian Communications
Network
Box 35
Grand Isle VT 05458
Phone. 802-372-4361

Orthodox Christian Education Commission
PO Box 69 Colvin Station
Syracuse NY 13205
Phone:

Orthodox Christian Educational Society
PO Box 287
W Brookfield MA 01585
Phone: 508-867-7039

Orthodox Christian Prison Ministry PO Box 1949   ANT
Hollywood CA 90078-1949
Phone: 213-467-2720
FAX: 213-467-5079
ocpm@juno.com

Orthodox Christian Mission Center Newesletter
Box 4319
St. Augustine FL 32085-4319
Phone. 904-829-5132
Fax. 904-829-5132
Ocmc@aug.com

Orthodox Christian Publications Center
PO Box 588   OCA
Wayne NJ 07474
Phone: 201-694-5782
FAX: 201-305-1478

Orthodox Christian Recorded Books
33 Mt Vernon St
Gardiner ME 04345
Phone: 888-480-8656

Orthodox Christian Witness AUX
10300 Ashworth Ave. N.
Seattle WA 98133-9410
Phone: 206-522-4471
FAX: 206-523-0550

Orthodox Family   ROR
PO Box 45
Beltsville MD 20704-0045
Phone: 301-890-3552

Orthodox Family Life
2507 Nedra Ave
Akron OH 44305
Phone:
pmonest@aol.com

Orthodox Herald
PO Box 9
Hunlock Creek PA 18621
Phone: 717-256-7232

Orthodox Life (English)   ROR
PO Box 36
Jordanville NY 13361-0036
Phone: 315-858-0940
FAX: 315-858-0505

Orthodox Messenger   ROR
75 E 93rd St
New York NY 10128-1331
Phone: 212-410-4258

Orthodox Mission Newsletter
Box 90
San Ignacio, Cayo
BELIZE

Orthodox Observer GOA
8 E 79th St
New York NY 10021
Phone: 212-628-2590
FAX: 212-570-4005

Orthodox Path
PO Box 2833
Garden Grove CA 92642-2833
Phone:

Orthodox Reader Reviews   PAN
3225 W Minarets
Fresno CA 93711
Phone: 209-431-4817
sntgeorge@pacbell.net

Orthodox Russia   ROR
PO Box 36
Jordanville NY 13361-0036
Phone: 315-858-0940
FAX: 315-858-0505

Orthodox Septuagint
Rt 23, Box 1450
Lake City FL 32025-8110
Phone:

Orthodox Tradition CYP
Box 398
Etna CA 96027-0398
Phone:

Orthodox Voice   DHR
PO Box 34362
Omaha NE 68134-0362
Phone:

Orthodox Voices   ROR
PO Box 23644
Lexington KY 40523-3644
Phone: 606-271-3877

Orthodox West   OCA
141 E Foster Rd
Santa Maria CA 93455-3122
Phone:

Orthodox Word   VAS
PO Box 70
Platina CA 96076-0070
Phone:

Path of Orthodox   SOC
PO Box 36
Leetsdale PA 15056
Phone: 412-741-8660
FAX: 412-741-9235

Pilgrim   FOCI
PO Box 22237
Lincoln NE 69542-2237
Phone:
eparchy@usa.net

Pravoslavnaya Put   ROR
PO Box 36
Jordanville NY 13361-0036
Phone: 315-858-0940
FAX: 315-858-0505

Pravoslavnaya Zhizn   ROR
PO Box 36
Jordanville NY 13361-0036
Phone: 315-858-0940
FAX: 315-858-0505

Praxis Institute Press
2931 W. Belmont Ave.
Chicago IL 60618
Phone. 312-598-6294
FAX. 312-588-3366
Preservation Press
Box 612
Swedesboro NJ 08085

Proini
25-50 Crescent St
Long Island City NY 11102
Phone: 718-626-7676
FAX: 718-267-1112

Ragusan Press
2527 San Carlos Ave
San Carlos CA 94070
Phone: 415-592-1190

Riverside Book Company
250 W. 57th St.
New York NY 10107
Phone. 212-765-2680

Reaching Out Newsletter (Carribean)
C/o Box 407139   ECU
Ft. Lauderdale FL 33340
Phone. 509-57-4805
FAX. 509-57-0672

Regina Orthodox Press
PO Box 5288
Salisbury MA 01952
Phone: 800-636-2470
FAX: 978-462-5079

Russian Orthodox Journal   OCA
10 Downs Dr
Wilkes-Barre PA 18705
Phone: 717-825-3158
FAX: 717-825-3158

Russian Orthodox Youth Committee 32-05
31st Ave   ROR
Astoria NY 11106
Phone: 718-721-9390
IDutikow@aol.com
Russky Palomnyk / Russian Pilgrim PO Box
70 VAS
Platina CA 96076-0070
Phone:

Sacred Art Journal   PAN
Box 206
Hayesvo;;e OH 44838-0206
Phone: 419-368-5335

Samaritan Newsletter
422 East-Penn Run, Box 432
Indiana PA 15701

Solia - The Herald   OCA
Box 185
Grass Lake MI 49240-5907
Phone: 517-522-3656
FAX: 517-522-5907
Roeasolia@aol.com

St Anthony Orthodox Publications
3044 N 27th St
Phoenix AZ 85016
Phone: 602-957-3054

St Athanasius Academy Publications
10519 E Stockton Blvd Ste 170 ANT
Elk Grove CA 95624
Phone: 916-686-5230
FAX: 916-686-6232

St George Publishing House
2930 31 Ave
Rock Island IL 61201
Phone: 309-786-8163
FAX: 309-786-8188

St Gregory's Press   IND
100 ABBEY LN
Milford NJ 07480-3909
Phone: 201-838-8795
FAX: 201-838-8795

St Herman Seminary Star   OCA
414 Mission Rd - Pouch 1
Kodiak AK 99615
Phone:

St Herman of Alaska Brotherhood
PO Box 70
Platina CA 96076
Phone: 916-343-2859

St Hilarion Press   IND
1905 S 3rd ST
Austin TX 78704-4122
Phone: 512-442-2289
FAX: 512-416-6556
hilarion@prismnet.com

St Nectarios Press
10300 Ashworth Ave N
Seattle WA 98133-9410
Phone: 206-522-4471
FAX: 206-523-0550
snpress@orthodoxpress.org

St Nikodemos the Hagiorite Pub Society
2101 Ritchie St
Aliquippa PA 15001
Phone: 412-375-7867

St Stephen's Press
Box 467

Mt Tabor NJ 07878
Phone: 973-627-0234

St Tikhon's Seminary Press
PO Box B
S Canaan PA 18459
Phone: 717-937-4390

St Vladimir's Seminary Press
575 Scarsdale Rd
Crestwood NY 10707
Phone: 800-204-BOOK
FAX: 914-961-5456

St Vlaimir's Theological Quarterly
575 Scarsdale Rd   OCA
Crestwood NY 10707
Phone:

Source Books
Box 794
Trabuco Canyon CA 92678
Phone. 800-695-4237

Southern Orthodox Radio Comms.
Enterprises
Box 1776
Tarpon Springs FL 34688-1776

Struggler AUX
8111 Vaden Dr.
Brentwood TN 37027-7306
Phone: 615-377-6477

The Struggler
2512 E Forgeus Pl
Tuscon AZ 85716
Phone: 520-327-8981
Vbockman@aol.com

Synaxis Press
PO Box 689
Lynden WA 98264
Phone:

The Annunciation Press
Phone: 800-975-ICON
FAX: 781-255-1871
TAPIcons@aol.com

The Church Messenger   (CRC)
312 Garfield St
Johnstown PA 15906
Phone: 607-797-4471
FAX: 607-797-1090

The Epistle   GOA
573 N Highland St
Memphis TN 38122
Phone: 901-323-9530
FAX: 910-327-4440

The Greek American
25-50 Crescent St
Long Island City NY 11102
Phone: 718-626-7676
FAX: 718-626-7830

The Greek Star
4710 N Lincoln Ave
Chicago IL
Phone:

The Illuminator   GOA
5201 Ellworth Ave
Pittsburgh PA 15232
Phone: 412-621-5529
FAX: 412-621-1522

The Newsletter   ECU
Orthodox Ch. Of the Carribean
Box 407139
Ft. Lauderdale FL 33340

The Orthodox Church   OCA
PO Box 675
Syosset NY 11791
Phone: 516-922-0550
FAX: 516-922-0954

The Orthodox Vision   OCA
14 Shadow Pl
Billings MT 59102
Phone: 406-254-1194

The St Nina Quarterly
PO Box 397252
Cambridge MA 02139-7252
Phone:

The Struggle
1829 S 580 W
Woods Cross UT 84087
Phone: 801-299-8622
 HYPERLINK mailto:Vbockman@aol.com
Vbockman@aol.com

Syndesmos News
7900 W. 120th St.
Palos Park IL
Phone. 708-361-1684

The Veil   OCA
2343 County Rd 403
PO Box 416
Lake George CO 80827
Phone: 719-748-3999

The Word ANT
358 Mountain Rd
Englewood NH 07631
Phone: 201-871-1355
FAX: 201-871-7954

Theosis Publishing Co.
CS Box A0082
Oklahoma City OK 73162
Phone:

Third Millenium Publications
P.O. Box 40-1111 N Coteau St
Gary SD 57237
Phone: 605-272-5305
FAX: 605-272-5306
TMB@TMBible.com

Torch of Orthodoxy CHR
St Anthony Orthodox Publications,
Phoenix AZ 85016-7926
Phone: 602-957-3054

Tree of Life   VAS
543 Cherokee Ave
Atlanta GA 30312
Phone: 404-577-6330

True Vine   AUX
Box 129
Roseland FL 32957-0129
Phone:

Truth
225 Hause Ave
Pottstown PA 19464-2647
Phone:

Ukrainian Orthodox Herald
9034 139th St   UOA
Jamaica NY 11435-4214
Phone:

Vestal Publishing Company Inc.
280 Cliffwood Ave

Cliffwood NJ 07721
Phone: 732-583-3232
FAX: 732-583-5207

Vigil　　OCA
605 Iowa St
Oak Park IL 60302-1649
Phone: 708-361-1684
FAX: 708-923-1706

Vineyard OCA
523 E Broadway
Boston MA 02127-4415
Phone:

Voice of Orthodoxy in America
PO Box 3177　　AUX
Buena Vista CO 81211
Phone: 7199-395-889
FAX: 8719-395-942

Way　　GOA
601 S Central Ave
Chicago IL 60644-5059
Phone: 312-626-5400
FAX: 312-626-4814

Word Magazine (Subscription Office) 358 Mountain Rd　　　　ANT
Englewood NJ 07631-3727
Phone: 718-748-7940
FAX: 718-855-3608

Social Services/Pan-Orthodox Groups

American Orthodox Mission to Russia
1065 Sutter St　　PAN
San Francisco CA 94109-5817
Phone: 415-931-0866

American Society of Medical Missionaries
AOC
PO Box 1360
Priest River ID 83856
Phone: 208-448-2504

Ana's Home Care for Elderly　BAM
906 N Euclid
Upland CA 91786
Phone: 909-981-2882
KPatter306@aol.com

Apostolic Orthodox Catholic Church Miss.
AOC
1200 N Diamond Ave, Lo 1327
Anchorage AK 99515
Phone: 907-344-0192

Archangel Raphael Orphanage Guatemala
AMC

Books for Life　　ANT
Prison Library Project
Box 1949
Hollywood CA 90078-1949
Phone: 323-467-2720

Brotherhood of St. Moses the Black
4000 Cleveland Ave
St Louis MO 63110
Phone: 314-773-6609

Clarendon Manor BAM
906 N Euclid Ave
Upland CA 91786
Phone: 909-981-2882
KPatter306@aol.com

Chivalric Order of St. Michael Arch. 353 S 46th St.　　FOC
Lincoln NE 68510
Phone:

Convocation of Orthodox Christian Prison ANT
PO Box 1949
Hollywood CA 90078-1949
Phone: 213-467-2720
FAX: 213-467-5079
ocpm@juno.com

Council of Eastern Orthodox Churches
PAN
300 Barber Ave
Worcester MA 01606-2476
Phone: 508-854-0620

Daughters in God's Service
PO Box 1477　　AOC
Wildomar CA 92595
Phone: 909-674-1377

Department of Youth　　ANT
18 Crystal Hill Ter
Westwood MA 02090-2710
Phone: 781-551-3372
FAX: 781-551-3478

joseph@purpura.net

Eastern Orthodox Committee on Scouting
862 Guy Lombasrdo　　　PAN
Freeport NY 11520
Phone: 516-868-4050
FAX: 516-868-4052

Friends of Mt. Athos
Prof. R.W. Allison
Bates College
Dept. of Religion
Lewiston ME 04240

FROC Mission Hotline Project
6610 Cypress Point Rd　　　OCA
Alexandria VA 22312-3126
Phone: 703-354-3242
slanta@erols.com

Fund for Assistance to the Russian Orthodox
75 E 93rd St　　　ROR
New York NY 10128-1331
Phone: 212-534-1601

Fund of St John of Kronstadt, Inc.
PO Box 56　　　ROR
Utica NY 13503-0056
Phone: 315-724-2093

Greek Orthodox Counseling and Social Ser
GOA
24 W Preston St
Baltimore MD 21201-5700
Phone: 410-727-1831

Guadalupe Homes for Children
1460 Cooley Dr
PO Box 848
Colton CA 92324
Phone: 909-825-5588
FAX: 909-825-8004

Hellenic Foundation GOA
5700 N Sheridan Rd
Chicago IL 60660
Phone: 312-728-2603

Holy Angels Flying Orthodox Mission
824 Chestnut St.
Chico CA 95928
Phone: 530-893-1814
FAX: 530-343-2859

VALAAM@aol.com

Holy Cross Center for Counseling
ANT
105 Summit Ct
Westfield NJ 07090-2834
Phone: 908-233-5051
FAX: 908-232-5049
gmorelli@pilot.njin.net

Holy Cross Prion Ministry
PO Box 4681
Danbury CT 06613-4681
Phone: 203-426-1298

Holy Mother of God Orthodox Jail Minist.
AOC
37 Shippee School House Rd
Foster RI 02825
Phone: 401-647-2867

Holy Trinity Nursing & Rehabilitation Ct
300 Barber Ave　　　PAN
Worcester MA 01606-2476
Phone: 508-852-1000
FAX: 508-852-1622

House of Mercy　　　PAN
812 N Alvarado St
Los Angeles CA 90026-3103
Phone: 213-483-6952

Immigrant & Needy Legal Aid Ministry
AOC
620 W alosta Ave, Ste 212
Glendora CA 91746
Phone: 818-857-7640
FAX: 818-857-7642

International Orthodox Christian Chariti
711 W 40th St Ste 306　　　PAN
Baltimore MD 21211-2109
Phone: 410-243-9820
FAX: 410-243-9824
iocc@igc.apc.org

Marriage Enrichment/Retrouvaille Minis.
8728 Bluff Ln　　　AOC
Fair Oaks CA 95628
Phone: 916-966-1361

Mercy House　　　ROR
320 E 3rd St
New York NY 1009-7865

Phone: 212-533-5140

Moscow Patriarchate Social Sevices 8630
Fenton St Ste 910   PER
Silver Spring MD 20910-3803
Phone:

Mother of Mercy   OCA
310 13th Ave NE
St Petersburg FL 33701
Phone: 813-823-2145

National Sisterhood of Presbyteres
93 Tall Oaks Dr. GOA
Wayne NJ 07470
Phone: 201-696-7097

NY State Orthodox Prison Ministry
NY DOC, 1220 Washington Ave
Albany NY 12226-2050
Phone: 518-457-8106

Orthodox Benevolent Fund & Society PO
Box 743   ROR
Rye NH 03870-0743
Phone: 603-964-5114
FAX: 603-964-5472

Orthodox Charities Department
PO Box 1100
Youngstown FL 32466-1100
Phone: 216-750-0505

Orthodox Christian Adoption Referaal Svc
OCA
PO Box 675
Syosset NY 11791-0675
Phone: 516-922-0550
FAX: 516-922-0954
arlene@oca.org

Orthodox Christian Center & Mission
280 New Braintree Rd   PAN
West Brookfield MA 01585-3218
Phone: 508-867-7039

Orthodox Christian Education Commission
PAN
PO Box 174, Cantuck Station
Yonkers NY 10710
Phone: 201-768-8422
FAX: 201-768-3146
w2bjb@aol.com

Orthodox Christian Library Outreach
285 Alden Ave   PAN
New Haven CT 06515-2113
Phone: 203-387-3882

Orthodox Christian Mission Center
PO Box 4319
St Augustine FL 32085
Phone: 904-824-1727
FAX: 904-829-1635

Orthodox Christian Schools, Inc.
Dr Mary Ford, St Tikhon's Seminary
S Canaan PA 18459
Phone: 717-937-4309

Orthodox Community Outreach Center
574 Pennsylvania St
Denver CO 80203-3616
Phone: 303-871-8060

Orthodox Community Services
217 S Maple St   DHE
Centralia IL 62801-3527
Phone: 618-532-4456

Orthodox Counselling Center
PO Box 1100
Youngstown FL 32466-1100
Phone: 216-750-0505

Orthodox Christian Prison
Ministry   ANT
Box 1949
Hollywood CA 90078-1949
Phone: 323-467-2720
FAX: 323-467-5079

Orthodox Food Center
102 Russell St
300 Barber Ave
Worcester MA 01610-2476
Phone: 508-799-0040

Orthodox Pastoral Counseling Institute
PO Box 10354
Pittsburgh PA 15234-0354
Phone: 412-335-9988

Orthodox People in America Inc.
9861 Baptist Church Rd.   HOJ
Affton MO 63123

Phone: 314-752-5515

Orthodox People in America Orphans Benev
6018 Southern Avenue
Affton MO 63123
Phone: 314-752-5515

Orthodox People Together
Box 1128
Torrance CA 90505
Phone: 310-378-9245
Fax: 310-378-6782

Orthodox Social Services
3044 N 27th St   CHR
Phoenix AZ 85016
Phone: 602-957-3054

Paper Icon Project
Box 1128
Torrance CA 90505
Phone: 310-378-9245

Pastoral Counseling Associates
1805 S Bellaire St Ste 109
Denver CO 80222-4309
Phone: 303-692-8006

Philoxenia House   GOA
162 Goddard Ave
Brookline MA
Phone: 617-277-4342

Prisoner's Fund - St. Athanasius Academy
ANT
PO Box 606
Ben Lomond CA 95005-0606
Phone:

Project Mexico
4949 Alton Pky
Irvine CA 92714-7559
Phone: 714-559-5838

Project Mexico & St Innocent Orphanage
PO Box 713033
Santee CA 92070-3033
Phone: 619-448-1368
FAX: 619-448-0169

Rachel's Children
PO Box 805
Melville NY 11747

Phone: 516-271-4408

Raphael House Family Shelter
1065 Sutter St   VAS
San Francisco CA 94109-5817
Phone: 415-474-4621
FAX: 415-771-4251

Religious Books for Russia, Inc.
PO Box 522
Glen Cove NY 11542-0522
Phone: 516-671-7716
FAX: 516-671-1012

Religious Books for Russia, Inc.
Wentways, Littleworth Ln.
Sea Cliff NY 11579
Phone: 516-671-7716
FAX: 516-671-1012

Resurrection Orthodox Counseling Center
GOA
20104 Center St.
Castro Valley CA 94546-4712
Phone: 510-653-8220

Russian Womens Home of Mercy of the Holy   OCA
1232 15th Ave.
San Francisco CA 94122-2006
Phone: 415-664-5551

Spiritual Famine Relief Fund
PO Box 992132   ROR
Redding CA 96099-2132
Phone:

Ss Cosmas & Damian Adult Home
2099 Forest Ave   OCA
Staten Island NY 10303
Phone: 718-720-8800
FAX: 718-447-8095

St Basil Workers Hospital/Food Program
255 Poland Ave
Struthers OH 44471-1651
Phone: 216-755-6959

St Bridget Youth House & Mission
20 Steiner St   VAS
San Francisco CA 94117-3325
Phone:

St. Dismas the Penitent Prison

Ministry   VAS
543 Cherokee Ave SE
Atlanta GA 30312-3248
Phone:

St Elias Retreat Center   GOA
121 Saint Elias Ln
Saxonburg PA 16056-9615
Phone: 412-352-1533

St Herman's House of Hospitality
4410 Franklin Blvd   UOA
Cleveland OH 44113-2846
Phone: 216-961-3806

St Innocent Orphanage
4949 Alton Pky
Irvine CA 92714-7559
Phone: 714-559-5838

St John Kronstadt Convalescent Center
4432 James Ave
Castro Valley CA 94546
Phone: 510-889-7000
FAX: 510-889-7622
stjohns510@aol.com

St Michael's Home for the Aged
3 Lehman Ter   GOA
Yonkers NY 10705
Phone: 914-476-3374
FAX: 914-476-1744

St Philip's Prayer Discipline ANT
1970 Clearview Rd- Box 565
Souderton PA 18964

St Raphael Healing Ministry
84 Liberty St, W.H.   FOC
Newburgh NY 12550
Phone:

Teleios Ministries   ANT
2815 S Bay St, Eustis FL 32726
PO Box 1267
Tavares FL 32778-1267
Phone: 352-357-1549

Tolstoy Foundation ROR
200 Park Ave S
New York NY 10003-1503
Phone: 212-677-7770

Tolstoy Foundation Nursing Home

Valley Cottage NY 10989-0599 ROR
Phone: 914-268-6551

W.O.M.E.N.
5045 Eldridge St
Golden CO 80403
Phone: 310-316-8027
WOMENUSA@aol.com

Women's Orthodox Ministries & Education
PAN
1805 S Bellaire St Ste 109
Denver CO 80222-4309
Phone: 303-692-8006

Campus Fellowships

Orthodox Campus Fellowship
University of Berkeley
Berkeley CA 94720
Phone: 510-649-2450

Orthodox Campus Fellowship
Yale University
New Haven CT 06520-2113
Phone: 203-387-3882

Orthodox Campus Fellowship
University of Iowa
Iowa City IA 52242-1652
Phone: 319-363-1559

Orthodox Campus Fellowship
Idaho State University
Pocatello ID 83209-6206
Phone: 208-232-5519

Orthodox Campus Fellowship
University of Chicago
Chicago IL 60637
Phone: 708-974-3400

Orthodox Campus Fellowship
Bradley University
Peoria IL 61625-3329
Phone: 309-682-5824

Orthodox Campus Fellowship
1318 Louisiana
Lawrence KS 66044-3491
Phone: 913-271-6411

Orthodox Campus Fellowship

1133 Village Dr
Manhattan KS 66502-2566
Phone: 913-776-6797

Orthodox Campus Fellowship Washburn University
Topeka KS 66621
Phone: 913-271-6441

Fellowship of Orthodox Christian Univers

Boston MA 02139
Phone: 617-547-1234

Orthodox Campus Fellowship
Northeastern University
Boston MA
Phone: 617-277-4742

Orthodox Campus Fellowship
Boston University
Boston MA 02115
Phone: 617-277-4742

Orthodox Campus Fellowship
Harvard University
Cambridge MA
Phone: 617-547-1234

Orthodox Campus Fellowship
Massachusetts Institute of Technolo
Cambridge MA 02138
Phone: 617-547-1234

Orthodox Campus Fellowship
Boston College
Chestnut Hill MA 02167
Phone: 617-277-4742

Orthodox Campus Fellowship
Tufts University
Medford MA 02155
Phone: 617-277-4742

SYNDESMOS Youth Group - North American R
5 Alandale Pky
Norwood MA 02062-4001
Phone: 617-769-2443

Camus Ministry News   ANT
PO Box 164
W Roxbury MA 02132
Phone:

Orthodox Campus Fellow
University of Maryland
College Park MD 20742
Phone: 410-263-2550

Orthodox Campus Fellowship
University of Michigan
Ann Arbor MI 48109
Phone: 313-459-8473

Orthodox Campus Fellowship
University of Minnesota - Duluth
Duluth MN 55812
Phone:

Orthodox Campus Fellowship
University of Minnesota
Minneapolis MN 55455
Phone: 612-781-7667

Orthodox Campus Fellowship
Duke University
Durham NC 27706
Phone: 919-682-1414

Orthodox Campus Fellowship / Transfigur

Murray Dodge Hall, Princeton U
109 Rollingmead
Princeton NJ 08540
Phone: 609-924-7368
tdskvir@aol.com

Princeton University Press
41 William St
Princeton NJ 08540
Phone: 800-777-4726

Orthodox Campus Fellowship
Columbia University
New York NY 10027
Phone: 212-927-0596

Orthodox Campus Fellowship
Ohio State University
Columbus OH 43210
Phone: 614-224-9020

Orthodox Campus Fellowship
Kent State University
Kent OH 44242
Phone: 216-434-4521

Orthodox Campus Fellowship
University of Oklahoma
Norman OK 73019
Phone: 918-584-7300

Orthodox Campus Fellowship
University of Oregon
Eugene OR 97403
Phone: 503-683-3519

Orthodox Campus Fellowship
University of Wisconsin - Madison
Madison OR 53706
Phone: 414-544-6661

Orthodox Campus Fellowship
Indiana University of Pennsylvania
Indiana PA 15705
Phone:

Antiochian Village   ANT
PO Box 638
Ligonier PA 15658
Phone: 412-238-3677
FAX: 412-238-2102

Orthodox Campus Fellowship
Slippery Rock University
Slippery Rock PA 16057
Phone: 412-282-6868

Orthodox Campus Fellowship
Pennsylvania State University
State College PA 16802
Phone:

Orthodox Campus Fellowship
Washington & Jefferson College
Washington PA 15301
Phone: 412-745-5205

Orthodox Campus Fellowship
Texas A & M
College Station TX 77843
Phone: 713-526-5377

Orthodox Campus Fellowship
Southern Methodist University
Dallas TX 75275
Phone: 214-991-1166

Orthodox Campus Fellowship
North Texas State University
Denten TX
Phone: 214-991-1166

Orthodox Campus Fellowship
Virginia Tech
Blacksburg VA 24061
Phone: 703-362-3601

Orthodox Peace Fellowship
1811 GJ Alkamaar
Kanisstraat 5
Phone: 3172-5112545
FAX: 3172-5154180
101363.304@compuserve.com

Youth Camps and Shrines

St Vladimir Chapel & Youth Camp PO Box 70   OCA
Ohagamuit AK 99657
Phone: 987-584-5134

Burial Site of St. Herman of Alaska Spruce Island AK OCA
Phone:

St Herman's Camp OCA
Woody Island AK
Phone: 907-486-3524

Archangels Pan-Orthodox Camp
Prescott AZ 863XX-5211   GOA
Phone: 602-991-3009

St Sophia Camp   GOA
1324 S Normandie Ave
Los Angeles CA 90006
Phone: 213-737-2424

Ascension Cathedral Camp
4700 Lincoln Ave GOA
Oakland CA 94602
Phone: 510-531-3400

Ascension Cathedral Camp
Ravencliff CA   GOA
Phone: 510-531-0057

Annunciation Cathedral Camp
245 Valencia St   GOA
San Francisco CA 94103
Phone: 415-864-8000

Annunciation Cathedral Camp GOA
Yosemite CA 95389
Phone: 415-861-1296

Camp St. Nicholas
HC 2 Box 9994   ANT
Frazier Park CA 93225-9712
Phone: 805-245-3571
FAX: 805-245-0710

Orthodox Christian Youth Camp
4610 E Alameda Ave Ste D1 GOA
Denver CO 80222-1301
Phone: 303-333-7794
FAX: 303-333-7796

Holy Trinity Camp
808 N Broom St   GOA
Wilmington DE 19806
Phone: 302-654-4446

Holy Trinity R.O. Retreat Cr.
29110 Holy Trinity Rd.   ROR
Round Mountain CA 94117-2146
Phone:

Shrine of Our Lady of Regla
1920 SW 6th St   ANT
PO Box 351233
Miama FL 33135-1233
Phone: 305-642-7878

St George Summar Camp
95 Elm St.   ROR
Elmwood Park NJ 07407-1610
Phone: 518-883-8585

St Mary Camp   GOA
McGregor MN 55760
Phone: 612-825-9595

St Photios National Shrine   41 St
George St   GOA
PO Box 1960
St Augustine FL 32085
Phone: 904-829-8205
FAX: 904-829-8707

St Stephen Summer Camp   GOA
2480 Chairmont Rd NE
Atlanta GA 30329
Phone: 404-634-9347

St Sava Monastery Camp   SOC

32400 N Milwaukee Ave
Libertyville IL 60048-9709
Phone: 708-362-1760

Camp Fanari   GOA
2501 S Wolf Rd
Westchester IL 60154
Phone: 708-562-2744

Camp Fenari   GOA
2501 S Wolf Rd
Westchester IL 60154-4948
Phone: 708-562-2744

Diocese of Boston Summer Camp
162 Goddard Ave   GOA
Brookline MA 02146
Phone: 617-277-4742

Diocese of Boston Summer Camp
162 Goddard Ave   GOA
Brookline MA 02146-7414
Phone: 617-277-4742

CYC Summer Camp   GOA
24 W Preston St
Baltimore MD 21201
Phone: 410-727-1831
FAX: 410-727-7602

Chesapeake Youth Camp   GOA
Glyndon MD 21071
Phone: 410-995-0353

Diocese of Detroit Summer Camp
17400 2nd Ave   GOA
Detroit MI 48203-1809
Phone: 313-868-1844

Camp Vatra   OCA
Jackson MI
Phone: 313-562-1521

Diocese of Detroit Summer Camp
Rose City MI 48654 GOA
Phone:

Diocese of Detroit Summer Camp
760 W Wattles Rd   GOA
Troy MI 48098
Phone: 810-362-9575

Minnesota Eastern Orthodox Camp Finland
MN 55603   GOA

Phone: 612-825-9595

Minnesota Eastern Orthodox Camp 3450
Irving Ave S   GOA
Minneapolis MN 55408-3334
Phone: 612-825-9595

St Mary's Greek Orthodox
Church Camp GOA
3450 Irving Ave S
Minneapolis MN 55408
Phone: 612-825-9595

Eastern Orthodox Youth Camp
12001 Womail Rd GOA
Kansas City MO 64145
Phone: 816-942-9100

Orthodox Catholic University
PO Box 2334
St Louis MO 63114
Phone: (314) 995-93
FAX: (314) 432-83
OrthUniv@AOL.COM

St Mary Madgalene Retreat House
125 Hartsie - 150 Angell Ln OCC
Waveland MS 39576
Phone: 228-466-4508
FAX: 228-466-4508
fr.paul@reu.org & fr.paul&juno.com

St Andrew Memorial   UCU
PO Box 495
South Bound Brook NJ 08880-0495
Phone: 732-764-9706

St Andrew's Camp   OCA
1280 State Rd 49
Cleveland NY 13042
Phone: 315-675-8409

St Vladimir's Orthodox Theological Sem.
575 Scarsdale Rd   PAN
Crestwood NY 10707-1699
Phone: 914-961-8313
FAX: 914-961-4507
info@svots.edu

Good Shepherd Camp   GOA
St. Basil Academy
Garrison NY 10524
Phone: 908-233-8533

St Basil Camp   GOA
Rt 9D
Garrison NY 10524
Phone: 212-570-3534

St George Great Martyr (summer camp)
New Pavlovsk NY   ROR
Phone: 518-883-8585

Camp Angelos Youth Camp   GOA
3131 NE Gilsan St
Portland OR 97232
Phone: 503-234-0468

All Saints Camp   UCU
Rd 3 Goshen Rd
Emlenton PA 16373
Phone: 412-867-5811
FAX: 412-867-9911

Antiochan Village   ANT
PO Box 638
Ligonier PA 15658
Phone:
FAX: 412-238-3677

Antiochian Village   ANT
PO Box 638
Ligonier PA 15658
Phone: 412-238-3677
FAX: 412-238-2102

Camp Nazareth   CRC
339 Pew Rd
RD 2 Box 2616
Mercer PA 16137
Phone: 412-662-4840
FAX: 412-662-4840

Camp Nazareth   GOA
5201 Ellsworth Ave
Pittsburgh PA 15232
Phone: 412-621-8543

Diocese of Pittsburg Summer Camp 5201
Ellsworth Ave GOA
Pittsburgh PA 15232-1421
Phone: 412-621-5529

St Tikhon's Camp   OCA
S Canaan PA 18459
Phone: 717-937-4411

St Sava Children's Camp   SOC

RR 1 Box 247
Springboro PA 16435-9650
Phone: 814-587-2627

St Stephen Camp   GOA
Aiken SC
Phone: 404-633-5870

Agape Community Orthodox School 1180
Orthodox Way ROR
Liberty TN 37095-9801
Phone: 615-536-5239

Orthodox Campus Fellowship
Vanderbilt University
Nashville TN 37240
Phone: 615-333-1047

Orthodox Christian Summer Camp
GOA
Yorktown TX 78164
Phone: 713-526-5377

St Silas Camp   GOA
7220 Granby St
Norfolk VA 23505-4002
Phone: 804-355-3687

All Saints Center   GOA
2100 Boyer Ave E
Seattle WA 98112
Phone: 206-325-4347

Icons and Iconographers

Tom Doolan
Box 11672
Berkeley CA 94701
Phone: 510-215-0301

Luke Dingman
Box 226
Brookdale CA 95007
Phone: 408-336-2114

Angel Shore
710 Hill St
Capitola CA 95010-2115
Phone: 408-462-5553

Carol Roach
224 Lolita St
Encinitas CA 92024-3236

Phone: 619-753-1703

Jan Isham
6778 Pasado Rd
Goleta CA 93117
Phone:

Vladimir Krassovsky
900 Monte Verde Dr
Pacific CA 94044
Phone: 415-359-0901

St Catherine Iconography School
VAS
1901 N Pennsylvania St
Indianapolis IN 46202-1417
Phone: 317-925-3034

Icons by the Hand of Carolyn
1148 Linden Ave
Baltimore MD 21227
Phone: 410-747-5502

Michael Piechocinski
9504 Whetstone Dr
Gaithersburg MD 20879
piec@erols.com

Rade Vilotijevic
730 Fort Washington Ave #6A
New York NY 10040
Phone:

Vladislav Andrejev
2332 W Main St
Whitney Pt NY 13862
Phone: 607-692-2696

Dennis Bell
1157 Crescent Pl
Painesville OH 44077
Phone: 216-352-0194

St John of Damascus Association of Iconographers, Iconologists & Architects
Box 206
Hayesville OH 44838-0206
Phone: 419-368-5335

Adrian Avram
239 NW 8th #4
Corvallis OR 97330
Phone:

Fr. Alexis Duncan

2810 Napa Valley
Cumming GA 30041
Phone: 770-888-2270

Fr Theodore Jurewicz
925 W 9th St
Erie PA 16502
Phone: 814-459-2107

Holy Trinity Icon Studio
Box 36
Jordanville NY 13361
Phone: 315-858-0940

Hieromonk Hariton
RR 2 Box 213a
Troy PA 16947-9541

Ioana Taurand
1180 Orthodox Way
Liberty TN 37095-4266
Phone: 615-536-5239

Sister Cecilia
Theotokos of the Sign Monastery
RR1 Box 134
Cambridge NY 12816-9704

Mat. Darya Carney
2015 Argyle Ave. #4
Hollywood CA 90068-3336
Phone: 213-455-7641

Xenia Pokrovsky
84 Oxford St. #3
Sommerville MA 02143
Phone: 617-793-0387

Luke Gehring
122 German St.
Erie PA 16507-1613

Gregory Melnick
404 Tennyson Ave.
Syracuse NY 13204
Phone: 315-475-2827

Archbishop ALYPY
1800 Lee St.
Des Plaines IL 60018-2024
Phone: 845-824-6531

Philip Zimmerman, Director

St. John Sacred Arts Academy
Rt 711N Box 638
Ligonier PA 15658
Phone: 412-238-3677

John Barns
1204 Penn St
Harrisburg PA 17102
Phone: 717-233-8105

Erin Kimmett
Phone: 800-975-ICON
FAX: 781-255-1871

Pavel N. Tikhomirov
Box 5266
San Mateo CA 94403
Phone: 408-662-3272
FAX: 408-662-8337

Archangel Studio
86 S 26th St
Pittsburgh PA 15203
Phone:

Michael Kapeluck
131 S 23rd St
Pittsburgh PA 15203

Vladimir Blagonadezhdin
104-310 East 14th Ave.
Vancouver BC'
CANADA V5T 2M8
Phone/FAX. 604-874-1764

Cal Hellas Icons
10177 Byerly Ct.
Cupertino CA 95014
Phone: 408-255-5868

St. Tikhon the Tree Dweller
Icons
11 Winthrop Dr
Aiken SC 29802
Phone: 603-641-1191

Dormition/Holy Apostles Icons
Box 3118
Buena Vista CO 81211
Phone: 719-395-8898
FAX: 719-395-9422

St. Isaac Skete Icons
Rt. 1 Box 368

Boscobel WI 53805-9619
Phone: 608-375-5500
FAX: 608-375-5555

Monastery Icons
1482 Rango Way
Borrego Springs CA 92004
Phone: 760-767-0044
FAX: 760-767-0049

Holy Transfiguration Icons
278 Warren St.
Brookline MA 02146-5997
Phone: 617-734-0608
FAX: 617-730-5783

Dormition Skete Icons
29020 County Rd. 187
Box 3118
Buena Vista CO 81211
Phone: 719-395-6395

Theotokos Community Icons
Rt. 1 Box 115A
Rochelle TX 76872
Phone: 915-463-5538
FAX: 915-463-5612

VF Murals & Icons
25 St Dennis Dr #816
Don Mills ON M3C 1E6
CANADA
Phone: 416-421-6775

Elias Damianakis
6646 Waldorf Ct
New Port Richey FL 34655
Phone: 813-372-0711

Byzantine Art Studio
5517 Lincoln Blvd.
Hudson OH 44236
Phone: 330-656-5866

Tatiana Grant
Box 210194
San Francisco CA 94121
Phone: 408-458-2231

Military Chaplains

U. S. Air Force

*Rev. Henry Steven Close
Ch.Capt, USAF
37 TRW/HCFB
Lackland, AFB, TX 78236

Phone: 210-671-2491

VRev Frank Mayernick
Ch, Lt Col, USAF
86 AW.HC
PSA 2 Box 9269
APO AE 09012

VRev Gregory H. Pelesh
Ch, Col, USAF
Director's Staff
National Security Agency
9800 Savage Rd.
Ft.Meade, MD 20755-6600
Phone 301-688-4314
FAX: 301-497-2888
FAX: 301-497-2888

*Rev. Mark Sahady
Ch, Capt. USAF
55 WG/HC
301 Lincoln Hwy.

Offutt AFB, NE 68113
Phone: 402-294-6244, 6051

VRev Ken James Stavrevsky
Ch, Maj, USAF
10 ABW/HC
5134 Cathedral Dr.
USAF Academy CO 80840-2700

Phone: 719-333-3300

VRev John W. Stefero
Ch, Col, USAF
AWC/XOC
325 Chennault Cir
MacDill AFB
Tampa FL
Phone: 334-279-1589

U. S. Air Force Reserve

VRev Gregory Havniak
CH, MAJ, USAFR
PO Box 675
Syosset, NY 11791
Phone: 516-922-0550

VRev James Jadick
Ch, Maj, USAFR
RD1 Box 259
Herkimer, NY 13350
Phone: 315-866-3272

VRev John Tkachuk
CH, Maj, USAFR
4381 Harvard Ave
Montreal, QC H4A 2W9
Phone: 514-481-5093

*Rev Adam Yonitch
CH Maj, USAFR
377 CSW/HC

U. S. Army

Rev John Edwards Anderson
CH (CAPT) USA
7th SFG
Ft Bragg, NC 28303
Phone: 910-432-5340

Rev Paul Schelbach
CH (CAPT) USA
HHC 2-8 Inf Bat (Mech)
Fort Hood, TX 76544
Phone: 817-288-6327

Rev Peter Baktis
CH (CAPT) USA
HHC 3/58 AVN
CMR 430 Box 241
APO< AE 09096
Phone:

Rev Edward Macura
CH (MAJ) USA
HHb 1-30 FA Rgmt
Ft. Sill, OK 73503
Phone: 405-442-4838

Rev Peter Tenencio
CH (CAPT) USA
Director of Combat Development
Chaplains Center and School
Ft Jackson, SC 29207
Phone: 803-751-8196, 8738

Rev Peter Dubinin
CH (CAPT) USA
Installation Staff Chaplain
Fort Campbell, KY 42223
Phone: 502-798-6124

U. A. Army National Guard

Rev Alexander Webster
CH (MAJ)
HHC 2nd Brgd, 29 ID(L)
Bolling Green, VA
Phone: 703-280-0770
Seminary: 908-469-7555

U. S. Navy

*Rev William Bartz
CDR,CHC, USN
MARCORCOMDEVCOM
(Code 053) CHAP
3098 Range Rd.
Quantico, VA 22134-5126
Phone: 703-784-2131

*Rev John Constantine
LT, CHC, USNR
Naval Air Station North Island
Box 25 (Code 17)
San Diego, CA 92135-5004
Phone: 619-546-8213

Rev Jerome Cwiklinski
LCDR, CHC, USN
PO Box 25517
Juneau, AK 99802
Phone: 907-463-2131

Rev Mark Koczak
LCDR, CHC, USN
Commanding General-Marine
Corp Base
PSC 20004
Camp Lejeune, NC 28542-0004
Phone: 910-451-3210, 0692

*Rev Karl Kish
LT, CHC, USNR
Naval Air Station
Box 6 (Code 800)
Jacksonville, FL 32212-5000
Phone: 912-772-3051

Rev Andrew Nelko
LT, CHC, USNR
2nd Marine Air Wing
Marine Corp Air Station
Cherry Point, NC 28533-0050
Phone: 919-466-2141

*Rev Theophanis Degaitas
LCDR, CHC, USN
1st Marine Air Wing Unit 37101
FPO AP 96603-710
Phone: 645-7539

Rev David Pratt
LT, CHC, USNR
Bldg 1, (C105)
2701 Sheridan Road
Great Lakes, IL 60088-5001
Phone: 847-688-7046

*Rev Milton Gianullis
LCDR CHC, USNR
USS Harry S. Truman
Newport News, VA

*Rev Milan Sturgis
LCDR, CHC, USNR
Military Sealift Command
1966 Morris Street
Norfolk, VA 23511-3496
Phone: 757-444-4506

U. S. Naval Reserve - Active or Inactive Reserves

Rev Peter Carmichael
LT, CHC, USNR-R
18 Hunter Drive
Perry, NH 03038

*Rev James Moulketis
CDR, CJC, USNR-R
360 Williams Way
Wykoff, NJ 07481-2109

*Rev Samuel Kalamaras
CDR, CHC, USNR-R
2301 San Jose Circle
Tampa, FL 33629-0439

*Rev John Shallhoub
LCDR, CHC, USNR-R
727 Barn Street
Jacksonville, NC 28540-3755

Hospital Chaplains

Arizona

Tucson
*Rev Anthony Moschonas
1145 E. Port Lowell Rd
Tucson, AZ 85719

California

Long Beach
*Rev Michael Kouremetis
11252 Wembley Rd
Los Alamitos, CA 90720

Arkansas

Little Rick
*Rev Andrew E. Clarke
1100 N. Napa Valley Dr
Little Rick, AK 72211

Connecticut

Newington
VRev Sergie Bouteneff
5490 Main St
Trumbull, CT 06611

New Haven
VRev Michael Westerberg
34 Burton St
New Haven, CT 06515

Massachusetts

Watertown
*Rev Peter B. Koskores
182 Belmont Ct. Apt 3
Brockton, MA 02401

Florida

Bay Pines
*Rev John Liadis
12763 112th St N
Largo, FL 34648

Miami
*Rev Demosthenes Mekras
244 SW 24 Rd
Miami, FL 33129

Georgia

Decatur
*Rev Homer Goumenis
2500 Clairmont Rd NE
Atlanta, GA 30329

Illinois

North Chicago Medical Center
*Rev George E. Phillipas
13631 Brainard Ave
Hegewisch, IL 60633

Oak Forest
VRev Sergei Garklavs
1121 N. Leavitt St
Chicago, IL 60622

New York

Albany
VRev Igor Burdikoff
22 Fairlawn Dr
Latham NY 12110

Brentwood, LI
*Rev Paul Apostolakos
157-15 24th Rd
Whitestone, NY 11357

Bronx/Manhattan, NY
VRev Gregory Havrilak
PO Box 675
Syosset, NY 11791

Canandalgua
VRev Cyril Stavrevsky
185 Benton St
Rochester, NY 14620

Michigan

Kalamazoo
*Rev Basis Stamus
3506 W. Michigan Ave
Kalamazoo, MI 49007

Minnesota

St. Cloud
*Rev Anthony M. Coniaris
3450 Irving Ave S.y
Minneapolis, MN 55408

New Hampshire

Manchester
*Rev James Christon
Medford Farms 129
RFD 4, Box 353
Goffston, NY 03045

New Jersey

Lyons
*Rev. Anthony Pappas
1101 River Rd
Piscataway, NJ 08854

Pennsylvania

Altoona
VRev Andrew Matychak
2029 13th Ave
Altoona, PA 16601

Danville
VRev Andrew Shuga
1228 Second Ave
Berwick, PA 18603

Lebanon
VRev Daniel Ressetar
5501 Locust Ln
Harrisburg, PA 17109

Philadelphia
VRev John Udics
26-A Kimberly Mews
Folcroft, PA 19032

Montrose
*Rev Constantine Eliades
24-03 Murray St
Whitestone, NY 11357

Ohio

Wade Park-Brecksville
VRev John Klembara
16029 Maple Park Dr
Maple Heights, OH 44137

Massillon
Rev Basil Slimak
5125 12th St NW
Canton, OH 44708

Wilkes Barre
VRev Claude Vinyard
PO Box 62
Moscow, PA 18444

VRev Joseph Martin
591 N. Main St
Wilkes Barre, PA 18705

Rhode Island

Providence
*Rev Peter B. Koskores
182 Belmont Ct. Apt 3
Brockton, MA 02401

Virginia

Roanoke
*Rev Nicholas Bacalis
PO Box 5055
Roanoke, VA 24012

Hampton
Rev Peter Makris
60 Traverse Rd
Newport News, VA 23606

Pittsburgh
VRev Paul Suda
1600 Guyton Rd
Allison Park, PA 15101

VRev Paul Zlatyk
150 Elmtree Rd
New Kensington, PA 15068

Waymart
VRev John Kowalczyk
305 Walnut St
Jermyn, PA 18433

Washington, DC
*Rev Nicholas T. Stavrakis
13924 Marianna Dr
Rockville, MD 20853

Wisconsin
*Rev Milan Markovina

South Carolina

Charleston
*Rev Nicholas C Trivelas
115 Congress St
Charleston, SC 29403

Fr. Michael Pollitts
Chaplain/Addiction Therapist
Detroit VA Medical Center
4646 John R St
Detroit MI 48201
Phone: 313-576-1000 x4989

Note: Material in this section taken primarily from 1998 OCA Yearbook.

Prison Ministries
(see also Social Services)

Orthodox Christian Prison Min.
*Fr. Duane Pederson
Box 1949
Hollywood CA 90078-1949
Phone: 323-467-2720
FAX: 323-467-5079

Rev. Emmanuel Manzouris
NY St. Correctional Services
909 River St.
Troy NY 12180

Rev. Peter Karloutsos
30 Clapboard Ridge Rd.
Danbury, CT 06811

Rev. Nicholas Lassios
Tunnel Rd.
Newton CT 06470

Rev. James Tsoules
893 Church Rd.
Elmhurst, IL 60126

*Contact for pan-Orthodox programs, conferences under jurisdiction of SCOBA.

ADDENDUM

Holy Ascension Parish UAO
1671 Golden Gate #2
San Francisco CA 94115
415-563-8514

Holy Spirit Skete/Parish UAO
380 Oak Springs Rd.
Paradise CA 95967

St. John's Skete UAO
1435 Fairfax
Denver CO 80220

Descent of the Holy Spirit UOP
San Luis Obispo CA
Miling: 1245 Green Oaks Dr
Los Osos CA 93402
Phone/Fax: 805-528-6863

St. Paul ANT (New Mission)
Naples FL

Holy Cross Mission ANT
Daytona Beach FL

St Mary ANT of
St Paul MN merged with
St George ANT of
St Paul MN

Appendix

OTHER DIRECTORIES OF EASTERN AND ORIENTAL ORTHODOX COMMUNITIES

COPTIC ORTHODOX CHURCHES IN NORTH AMERICA – Archdiocese of North America (Bishop SURIEL), Box 373, Cedar Grove NJ 07009. Phone: 973-857-0078; FAX: 973-857-1315

ARMENIAN CHURCH OF NORTH AMERICA – Contact Eastern Diocese. Phone: 212-686-0710; FAX: 779-3558

DIRECTORY OF ORIENTAL ORTHODOX CHURCHES IN NORTH AMERICA – Subdeacon Vladimir Raasch, Editor, Minnesota

GREAT BRITAIN: Directory of Orthodox Parishes and Clergy in the British Isles (1998) – Orthodox Fellowship of St John the Baptist, 26 Denton Close, Botley, Oxford OX2 9BW, ENGLAND

BELGIUM (AND LUXEMBOURG): L'Eglise Orthodoxe en Belgique – Bernard Peckstadt, de Vrierestraat 19 – B 8301 Knokke-Heist, BELGIUM

SWITZERLAND: Calendrier – Ed. De l'Archeveche de Suisse, 282 route de Lausanne, CH 1292 Chambesy, SWITZERLAND

ORTHODOXIA (1998-99) – Directory of Orthodox (Eastern and Oriental) Bishops of the World. Edited and Compiled by Dr. Nikolaus Wyrwoll. Available through OCCNET, Box 1128, Torrance CA 90505 USA. Phone: 800-747-9245; FAX: 800-903-ICON (4266)

Advertisers and Supporters

Alexandre-Alexander
All Saints of America Orthodox Christian Church
All Saints of Russia Press
Alleluia Press
Cal-Hellas Icons
Conciliar Press
Dormition Skete & Holy Apostles Convent
Doxa Magazine
Dr. Dale E. Heath
Dynamis
Eastern Christian Supply Company
Eastern Orthodox Books
Ecclesiastical Goods, Inc.
Eighth Day Books
Gibson Travel
Gloria Incense
Hanna Trade International
Heavenly Realm Tapes & CDs
Holy Cross Bookstore
Holy Myrrhbearers Monastery
Holy Nativity Convent
Holy Transfiguration Monastery
Holy Trinity Orthodox Church
House of Mercy
Icon & Book Service
Iconography.com
International Orthodox Christian Charities
Light & Life Publishing Company
Little Falcons Publications
Macrina Publications
Miloje Milinkovic, Fresco & Icon
Mission HOTLINE, FROC
Monastery Icons
National Shrine Church Supplies
NDC, Inc.
Nikodemos Orthodox Society
Oakwood Publications
Oblates of St. Benedict
Orchid Land Publications
Orthodox Christian Book Service
Orthodox Christian Communications Network
Orthodox Christian Mission Center
Orthodox Christian Prison Ministry
Orthodox Christian Recorded Books
Orthodox Family Life
Orthodox Information Data Associates
Orthodox Publications
Patriarchate of Jerusalem
Pavel N. Tikhomirov, Iconographer
Russos Imports
Sourozh
St. Archangel Michael Serbian Orthodox Church
St. Athanasius Academy
St. George Orthodox Church
St. George Publishing House
St. Herman of Alaska Christian School
St. Mark's Orthodox Monastery
St. Nectarios Press & Bookstore
St. Nina Quarterly
St. Stephen's Course of Studies
St. Stephen's Press
SVS/St. Vladimir's Seminary Bookstore
Tabitha of Joppa
The Annunciation Press
The Brotherhood of St. Moses the Black
The Orthodox Christian Education Commission
The Russian Orthodox Youth Committee
Theotokos Community
Third Millennium Publications
Vestal Publishing Company, Inc.
VF Studio Murals & Icons
Video Icon Workshop
Vladimir Blagonadezhdin
W.O.M.E.N.

ICON AND BOOK SERVICE

of the
MONASTERY OF THE HOLY CROSS
1217 QUINCY ST., NE.
WASHINGTON, D.C. 20017
TEL: (202) 526-6061 FAX: (202) 526-3316

LARGE SELECTION OF BOOKS ON:

Eastern Christian History, Theology, Spirituality, Iconography, Lives of the Saints, Writings of the Fathers, General Introductory Texts for those wishing to learn more about the **Eastern Orthodox Church,** its life and practice.

ALSO AVAILABLE:

Hand-painted Icons, Icon Reproductions (Paper Prints and Prints mounted on wood), in a wide selection of sizes (from Holy Card to Poster Size) and Country of Origin (Russia, Greece, Bulgaria, the Sinai)

WE ALSO CARRY AN INVENTORY OF:

EASTERN LITURGICAL MUSIC ON CASSETTES AND CD'S,
RELIGIOUS ARTICLES AND BYZANTINE CHURCH SUPPLIES
(Chalice Sets, Gospel Covers, etc., can be special-ordered from Greece and Russia)
INCENSE IN A WIDE RANGE OF FRAGRANCES (Imported & Domestic)
ICON GREETING CARDS (Christmas/Easter-General & Blank Note Cards)

HOURS
Mondays - CLOSED
Tuesday-Friday: 10 am to 6 pm
(closed for prayers and lunch Noon -1pm)
Saturday: 9 am to 4 pm

LEARN THE ANCIENT ART OF ICONOGRAPHY

> We have found Mr. Blagonadezhdin to be extremely knowledgeable in his field of expertise. Mr. Blagonadezhdin is not only familiar with history and contemporary trends in Russia but is also developing a good appreciation of Canadian phenomena insofar as these relate to his area of specialized training and productivity.
>
> Canadian Museum of Civilization.

VIDEO ICON WORKSHOP
WITH A RUSSIAN MASTER VLADIMIR BLAGONADEZHDIN

Mr. Blagonadezhdin is an iconographer of the highest level, who has been painting icons and teaching iconography for the past 25 years. His work is in public and private collections in the US, Europe and Canada, including the Museum of Civilization in Ottawa. Now Mr. Blagonadezhdin is successfully teaching the art of iconography in Vancouver Academy of Art.

BYZANTINE STYLE EGG TEMPERA TECHNIQUE

You will save money and time. You can have a workshop in your studio at any day, any time! You will be taught: Composition, How to transfer the drawing, Gold Leaf application, How to make egg emulsion, How to mix pigments with emulsion, How to paint with egg tempera, Detailing & varnishing. You will learn every step and every line to create a masterpiece. **You can also use this unique and beautiful technique in contemporary art.**

1. Introduction Level - 1 cassette (2 Hours) — -$75
2. Student Level -2 cassettes (4 Hours) — -$135
3. Professional Level - 3 cassettes (6 Hours) — -$195
4. Icons, Flowers and Music - 1 cassette (2 Hours) — -$45
5. Icons, Prayers, Flowers and Music - 1 cassette (2 Hours) — -$45

Please add G.S.T / P.S.T where appropriate and shipping & handling $5
Please allow two to four weeks for delivery

For inquires please call or fax (604) 874-1764.
E-mail: blagonadezhdin@bc.sympatico.ca
To order cassette please make cheque or money order payable to:
Vladimir Blagonadezhdin
#104-310 East 14th Avenue
Vancouver, BC, Canada
V5T 2M8

Web site: **www.iconsart.com**

ART-TO-GO-FORTH

For a price list of Orthodox Chip Art on Disk, call or write

Οιδα
Post Office Box 35
2 Lakeshore Boulevard
Grand Isle, VT 05458-0035
(802) 372-4361

Orthodox Church Bulletins

Weekly - Monthly

Black & White Masters in popular sizes

GoForth...

"an outstanding resource which can be used as a bulletin for each Sunday of the year"

as quoted in UPDATE (Official Publication for the USAF Chaplain Service)

Οιδα

2 Lakeshore Blvd, PO Box 35
Grand Isle, VT 05458-0035
(802) 372-4361

FONTS-TO-GO-FORTH

✠

+ Fonts designed from traditional sources that will make your church publishing look its best.
+ Fonts for Cyrillic and Greek languages.
+ Headline fonts based on Russian or Greek letterforms.
+ Substantial discounts for church use.
+ Available for both Macintosh and PC platforms, both in Postscript and TrueType formats.

✠

Carter & Cone Type

SOPHIA

ABCDEF 12345 !×#$&

Based on text styles from sixth-century Constantinople. Includes 10 joining characters to create ligatures.

✠

Linotype-Hell

CYRILLIC FONTS

Ђ ѣ À à Ѐ è Ѣ ѳ Ѳ 12345 !C&

GREEK FONTS

Over 15 high quality fonts (and keyboard drivers for the Macintosh). Also available are other Latin and Non-Latin faces at competitive discounts for Church use.

✠

OIDA

ANGLIISKI

Based on Old Slavonic with abbreviations & symbols for the order of services

IkonWrite

Based on letter forms in Russian & Byzantine Iconography, with 57 ligatures and 7 crosses.

✠

For current prices and to order, call or write:

Οιδα
2 Lakeshore Boulevard
Post Office Box 35
Grand Isle, VT 05458-0035
(802) 372-4361

Give your parish and home the beauty and dignity of Orthodox iconography

with "Windows Into Heaven" mounted icon reproductions

OPEN a "Window Into Heaven" in your cathedral or chapel, in religious school classrooms, at home and in the office, with these exquisite mounted icons. They offer you a unique combination of the old and the new: the grace and beauty of the most ancient tradition of Orthodox sacred art, brought faithfully to life by a contemporary iconographer–with deep, rich colors and all text in English.

- **Over 120 icons** of Christ, the Theotokos, the Great Feasts, and the Saints and Angels
- All subjects in sizes from **4 inches to 8 feet tall!**
- Iconographic crucifixes, diptychs, triptychs, & unique icon specialties…**all at affordable prices!**
- Greeting cards, note cards, and holy cards
- Car shrines, icon magnets, icon paperweights, religious jewelry…and much, much more!
- **FREE GIFTS OF YOUR CHOICE** with orders over $200

Order your FREE catalog today!

- Call toll-free 1-800-729-4952
- Fax (760) 767-0049
- E-Mail MonksIcons@AOL.com

MONASTERY ICONS
Visit us at www.monasteryicons.com

"Monastery Incense burns very evenly, is not irritating at any stage of burning, and the fragrances are great!"
writes, Fr. Pavel S. of Florida.
Try all 12 exquisite fragrances, available through our FREE catalog.

Orthodox Publications

Internet publications (in Russian, English, and Spanish) on Christian faith and life, on Holy Scriptures, on prayer and sacraments, on life of saints, and selected writings from the holy fathers are available at:

http://www.fatheralexander.org

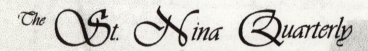

The St. Nina Quarterly

Editorial Board
Nancy Holloway, D.Min.
Demetra Velisarios Jaquet, M.Div.
Valerie Karras, Th.D.
Karen Rae Keck
Bonnie A. Michal
Despina Demise Prassas, M.Div.
Teva Regule
Christina Shaheen Reimann, M.A.
Helen Creticos Theodoropoulos, Ph.D.

Honorary Board
His Grace Bishop Kallistos (Ware)
Rev. Fr. Stanley S. Harakas, Ph.D.
Rev. Fr. Nicholas Apostola, M.A., M.Div.
Kyriaki FitzGerald, Ph.D.
Susan Ashbrook Harvey, Ph.D.
Elisabeth Behr-Sigel, Lu.D.

For more information contact
The St. Nina Quarterly
P.O. Box 397252
Cambridge, MA
02139-7252

Mission Statement

The St. Nina Quarterly is a publication dedicated to exploring the ministry of women in the Orthodox Church and to cultivating a deeper understanding of ministry in the lives of all Orthodox Christian women and men. We profess firm faith in our Church's teaching that each of us is created in the image of God and called to grow into His likeness. We believe that all persons are endowed with gifts of the Holy Spirit in ways that uniquely express the fullness of their humanity and contribute to the fullness of the entire community of believers.

Our mission is the discovery and cultivation of these gifts for the nurturance of the entire Body of Christ. To this end, we will strive to educate, inform, and provide space for an ongoing, creative dialogue aimed at reaching across all boundaries to support and encourage the growth and vitality of the God-given ministries of all of our sisters and brothers in Christ.

To each one is given the manifestation of the Spirit for the common good. I Corinthians 12:7

Pavel N. Tikhomirov
Orthodox Iconographer

All major schools of iconography. Expert restoration.

P.O. Box 5266 San Mateo, CA 94403
Fax (415) 372-9833

P.O. Box 2134 Aptos, CA 95001
Tel (408) 662-3272 Fax (408) 662-8337

The Sounds of Mystical Christianity
ANCIENT AND CONTEMPORARY

Ask for our growing catalogue of Orthodox chants from around the world, books-on-tape, tapes for children, lectures by Fr. Seraphim Rose, and tapes of the "O Gentle Light" radio show, which is aired weekly in Chico, California.

Heavenly Realm Tapes and CDs
252 East 4th St., Chico, CA 95928
Telephone: (530) 343-2859

DYNAMIS

Meditations on the Daily Bible Readings Of the Orthodox Lectionary

Subscriptions: $2.00/Month (1st Class Mail)
ST GEORGE CATHEDRAL
7515 E 13TH ST N
WICHITA KS 67206-1223

Free Daily by Email: A3dynamis@aol.com

WebSite: Free Daily, Weekly, or Monthly
http://orthodoxdynamis.home.ml.org
Information: 316/636-4676 or 316/685-7365

LITTLE FALCONS

theme booklets on
Candles
Incense
Cross
Bells
Oil
Water
Bread
Wine

36 pgs, 4-c cover
7 x 9 format
all ages, plays
articles, stories,
puzzles, saints,
songs, icons

New Gracanica Metropolitanate
Fr. Thomas Kazich, Editor of Publications

Write for further information:
Little Falcons Publications,
P.O. Box 371, Grayslake, IL 60030

At Last—
a Bible for all of Christendom

The
Third Millennium Bible
(TMB®)

- Complete Authorized Version of 1611 including its deuterocanonical books carefully updated
- Reverent, historic Biblical English
- Contains no feminist language or contemporary emendations
- Modern, easy-to-read size and format

"This updating of one of our language's greatest and most basic classics is a Godsend for those who delight in and cherish the traditional devotional language of English-speaking people..."
FatherAndrew, St. Michael's Skete, Cañones New Mexico

"The preservation of the integrity of our language and of traditional texts, especially those that are part of the bedrock of our civilization and way of life, are cardinal requisites if we are to survive as a free, God-fearing people."
Father James Thornton, Garden Grove, California

The *Third Millennium Bible*® is simply the most beautifully worded, the most traditional, and the most complete modern Bible available in the English language.

- Available November 1998 -

For more information, or to place orders, contact:
Third Millennium Publications®
PO Box 40, Gary, SD 57237 USA

http://www.tmbible.com
E-mail: tmb@tmbible.com
Business Phone: 1-605-272-5305

Toll-free: 1-877-TMBible
(1-877-862-4253)
Fax: 1-605-272-5306

ECCLESIASTICAL GOODS, INC.
Post Office Box 742
Long Beach, Mississippi 39560

Eastern and Western Rite Vestments

Tel: (601) = 864 – 1568

Call or write to us today for more information.

OCCN

IC XC / NI KA

ORTHODOX CHRISTIAN RECORDED BOOKS
Audio Publisher of Books, Lectures and Prayers

"....my mother and my brethren are these that hear the word of God, and do it.". Luke 8:21

Call toll free
1-888-480-8656
or write for our expanding list of available recordings

Orthodox Christian Recorded Books (OCRB)
33 Mt VERNON STREET
GARDINER, MAINE 04345

OCCN

IC XC / NI KA

2 Lakeshore Boulevard, POB 35, Grand Isle VT 05458

Voice: (802) 372-4361, Fax: (802) 372-5986, E-mail: OCCN@aol.com

Russian Gift & Jewelry Center

800/787-7442 * Fax 800/787-7427 (Russia-7) * E-Mail: info@russiangift.com

Your source for:

* Imported Icons
* Gold & Silver Crosses
* Enamel Crosses
* Enamel Faberge Style Eggs from - The Jeweler to the Czars, St. Petersburg
* Icons, Books & Famous Russian Handcraft, the Largest Selection
* Traditional Wooden Ornament, Toys, Figurines, Nested Dolls, Easter Eggs, Famous Gzhel Porcelain & More

Visit our Wholesale Showroom at: www.russiangift.com

18025 Sky Park Circle, Suite G * Irvine, CA 92614

HOLY TRINITY ORTHODOX CHURCH

"Serving the Orthodox Community Since 1979"

(352) 686-6050

11200 Elgin Blvd. • Spring Hill, FL 34608-2110

---

419 EAST 117TH STREET
NEW YORK, NY 10035

RUSSIAN ORTHODOX CHURCH
OUTSIDE RUSSIA

St. Mark's Orthodox Monastery

ORTHODOX COMMUNITY OF ST. JOHN THE BAPTIST

(212) 289-3071

ALL SAINTS OF AMERICA
ORTHODOX CHRISTIAN CHURCH

Rev. Fr. John J. Kreta
Priest-in-charge

Box 45 • 313 Twin Lakes Rd • Salisbury, CT. 06068 • (203) 824-1340

VF STUDIO
murals & icons

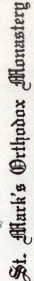

Vladislav Fedorov
25 St. Dennis Dr. # 816
Don Mills, ON
M3C 1E6

Tel: (416) 421 6775
E-mail: vladislav@myna.com

Rev. Father George (Khuri) Jweinat

ST. GEORGE ORTHODOX CHURCH
Of the Jerusalem Patriarchate
Serving the Greater San Francisco Community

399 San Fernando Way
San Francisco, Ca. 94127
Residence: 650-692-4519

Office: 415-334-2234
Pager: 202-6336
FAX: 334-2275

The Brotherhood of St. Moses the Black

This is an appeal to all Orthodox Churches and persons in America for donations of icons. All sizes and iconostasis icons to be sent to the Orthodox Churches in Kenya, Africa.

Fr. Moses Berry
4000 Cleveland, Ave.
St. Louis, MO 63110
314-773-6609

Thank You

Federated Russian Orthodox Clubs

Betty Yanowsky Slanta
Chairman, Mission HOTLINE

703-354-3242

6610 Cypress Point Road
Alexandria, VA 22312

REV. JUAN CORREA, OSJ   213-483-6952
FOUNDED IN 1986   FAX: 213-483-2561

HOUSE OF MERCY
Community Social Service Center

812 NORTH ALVARADO STREET
LOS ANGELES, CALIFORNIA, 90026

Send for our
CATALOG OF ORTHODOX GREETING CARDS, PRAYER BOOKS AND CHURCH SUPPLIES
($2.00 refundable with order)

Holy Myrrhbearers Monastery
144 Bert Washburn Road
Otego, NY 13825-9650
(607) 432-3179

A women's monastery of the Orthodox Church in America

St. Herman of Alaska Christian School
Established 1991

Providing a classical education
in a contemporary world
to children K1 - 8.

- *Academic Excellence*
- *Comprehensive Art & Music Curriculum*
- *Small, Multi-aged Classes*

Ongoing enrollment.

64 Harvard Ave.
Allston, MA 02134
(617) 782-0878

From this day, from this hour, from this minute, let us strive to love God above all, and fulfill His holy will.
-St. Herman of Alaska

DORMITION SKETE & HOLY APOSTLES CONVENT

Write for our Catalogues on:
Orthodox Books on the Lives of the Saints and Orthodoxy, Hand-painted Icons or a selection of over 300 Mounted or Unmounted Icons Prints, All-natural Incense, and our bimonthly publication,
The Voice of Orthodoxy in America.

MAIL REQUEST TO: POB 3118
Buena Vista, CO 81211
CALL: 719-395-8898
FAX: 719-395-9422
E-MAIL: apostles@amigo.net
or visit our WEBSITE:
BuenaVistaCO.com\GOC

THREE TRACTS
1. What is a religion? 2. Forms and motifs of Christianity
3. Orthodox Christian Beliefs
+ Questions to put to other-believing Proselytizers

A pan-Orthodox booklet that is different: the same traditional beliefs presented *after* a thematic portrayal of their development—for the faithful and interested other-believers

$4.50 + postage
(no credit cards please)

(ask for special rates for orders of 12+ by ecclesiastical establishments)

ORCHID LAND PUBLICATIONS
Kea'au, HI 96749-1416
☎ *vox* 808+966-8923
☎ *fax* 808+982-5603
email orlapubs@ilhawaii.net
www.ilhawaii.net/~orlapubs

Ω
OAKWOOD PUBLICATIONS
PHILIP TAMOUSH, PUBLISHER

3827 Bluff Street, Torrance, California 90505-6359
(310) 378-9245 (Office & Fax) • 1-800 747-9245 (Phone/Fax Orders)
E-Mail: oakwoodpub@juno.com • Web Site: http/www.nettinker.oakwood.com

Publishers of Fine Books on Icons, Iconography, Icon Theology; Enamel Icon Pins; Note & Greeting Cards

Bold Type: New Items

Illuminated Gospel of St. Matthew	$39.95	Icon Painter's Notebook	$22.95
Iconographers Sketchbooks (V. 1&2)	19.95	Psalms in the Divine Liturgy	19.95
Heroes of the Icon	10.95	Icons in Early Christianity	10.95
Iconographer's Pattern Book	29.95	Art of the Icon: Theology of Beauty	18.95
Painter's Manual of Dionysius of Fourna	12.95	Dynamic Symmetry in Icons	7.95
Image God the Father & Other Readings	9.95	Icon Collections in the U.S	3.95
Icons & Icon Painting Video w/transcript	16.95	Ministry of Women in the Church	8.95
Place of the Heart: Orthodox Spirituality	8.95	Contemplations of Judas Iscariot	10.95
Orthodox Fathers, Orthodox Faith	10.95	Of Preaching in America	10.95
Directory of Orthodox Parishes, 1998 Millennium Edition	8.95	**ORTHODOXIA** (Directory of Bishops of the World)	20.00
A New Era Begins (SCOBA Bps. Meet)	7.95	A New Era Begins (Video)	7.95
Biography of Alexander Men	14.95	Awake to Life: Sermons of Fr. Men	4.95
About Christ & The Church (Men)	6.95		
Enamel Icon Pins/Pendants & Silver/Gold Plated Crosses – All Styles	0.75-2.50		
Standing Gold/Silver Plate Crosses/Icon Key Chains/Auto Visor Clip	4.00-20.00		
Contemporary Greeting & Note Cards (Alaska & Byzantine Scenes)	5.95/dz.		

Son of Man: A definitive biography of Christ written by the martyred priest Fr. Alexander Men over a 30-years. Part of a multi-volume History of Religion written by him. $24.95

Architecture of the Orthodox Church: Canons and A Manual: A series of readings and instructions about the design and construction of Orthodox Churches in North America. Interior and Exterior canons, plans, designs, iconographic schemes. Edited by Sevasti Bergstrom. Featuring articles by noted American theologians, architects and designers.

Books on Tape and Audio Tape Lectures

All tape sets beautifully packaged. Listen in your car, at home, or with study groups.

Way of the Pilgrim & A Pilgrim Continues His Way. The complete texts from the R. M. French edition read by Sue Talley (5 tapes, over 7 hours). A classic of Russian spirituality. $17.95

The Invocation of the Holy Name: A Prayer for All Seasons Delivered by Bp. KALLISTOS (Ware). (4 tapes, 6 hours). New lectures by the preeminent Orthodox scholar concerning prayer, the invocation of His Name, and other topics. $13.95

Discovering the Inner Kingdom: The Prayer of the Heart Bp. KALLISTOS (Ware) (2 tapes, almost 3 hours). New lectures emphasizing the Jesus Prayer and its use in practice, saying the Jesus Prayer, prayer in practice. $8.95

Living Orthodoxy in the Modern World: The Meaning of Great Lent Bp. KALLISTOS (Ware) (1 tape, 1½ hours). The challenges of Great Lent and its application to Orthodox Christians in the modern world. $4.50

Orthodox Music on Synthesizer

A unique new series Orthodox classics (of the Eastern and Western Church) performed by Sue Talley, composer/arranger. Listen in home, at receptions, in the car, while praying. Also suitable for pre-reception/banquets, and even pre-Sacramental music, where permitted, e.g., before weddings & baptisms. Classic Orthodox hymns, including both Byzantine and Slavic melodies.
Audio Cassette ($7.95) and Compact Disc ($12.95).

We Magnify Thee: Hymns of the Church: East and West: Rejoice, O Virgin; Let My Prayer Arise; Russian Hymn to the Tsar; Pascha; Sunset to Sunrise; Great Creator; Amazing Grace; Holy, Holy, Holy and more.

Interior Castles (Hymns of the Western Church): Jacob's Ladder; Pachelbel Canon; Let All Mortal Flesh; Ave Maria; God the Omnipotent and others.

At Light & Life Publishing Company we carry Orthodox Christian books for all jurisdictions. In addition, we offer:

- Bibles
- Prayer Books
- Church Music
- Religious Education Materials
- Icons, Posters and Note Cards
- Video Cassettes for all ages
- Audio Cassette Tapes
- Compact Discs
- Software for Orthodoxy
- Jewelry
- etc.

LIGHT & LIFE PUBLISHING · 4818 Park Glen Road · Minneapolis, MN 55416
TELEPHONE 612-925-3888 • FAX 612-925-3918
http://www.light-n-life.com

CONCILIAR PRESS
A Ministry of the Antiochian Orthodox Archdiocese

PUBLISHERS OF FINE EASTERN ORTHODOX LITERATURE

Orthodox Study Bible
—exclusive distributors of the NEW revised paperback *Orthodox Study Bible*
AGAIN Magazine
—a quarterly publication of contemporary Orthodox thought
The Handmaiden
—a journal for women serving God within the Orthodox Tradition
Brochures
—brief introductions to Orthodoxy, designed for evangelism and outreach
Topical Booklets
—concise explanations of basic Orthodox doctrines or topics of spirituality
Books
—a growing number of titles focusing on introduction to Orthodoxy, spirituality, history, and Orthodox world view
Icon Cards
—full color icon Christmas cards, greeting cards, and blank note cards
Catalog Items
—icons, home altars, music, and other gift items

WRITE OR CALL FOR A FREE CATALOG
P.O. Box 76, Ben Lomond, CA 95005 • Tel 800 967-7377 or 408 336-5118 • Fax 408 336-8882

Nikodemos Orthodox Publication Society
P. O. Box 383-F, Richfield Springs, NY 13439-0383

NEW!

Letters to Spiritual Children by Abbot Nikon. Written in Russia in the 50s and 60s, these letters of spiritual direction provide a contemporary distillation of the age-old wisdom of the Church. Here is a volume of enduring value to anyone seriously and sincerely desiring to attain, as Fr. Nikon surely did, the Kingdom of Heaven. 132 pp., pbk.—$8.50.

Rush to Embrace by Rev. Alexey Young. The author, a former Roman Catholic, explains why today's "union fever" places Orthodoxy at great risk, and urges his fellow Orthodox Christians to consider the consequences of uniting with the Roman Church so radically different in dogma and in spirit. 96 pp., illus., pbk.—$6.50.

Also publishers of **Man of God: Saint John of Shanghai & San Francisco**, and **Grand Duchess Elizabeth**. Send SASE for complete list.

Book orders, please add 10% p&h; $2.50 minimum

ORTHODOX AMERICA   A newspaper-format journal

Features: *Spiritual Heroes of the 20th century, Orthodox missions, Lives of Saints, ancient and contemporary texts on spiritual life, contemporary issues, scriptural commentary, book reviews, and more!*

Subscriptions: $10/yr (8 issues); churches, clergy, students, libraries: $8; 30% discount on 5 or more copies to one address. *Outside US, please inquire.*

Send for FREE sample copy, or subscribe today —for yourself or your church.

Eastern Orthodox Books

Spiritual Writings
Lives of Saints
Fathers of the Church
Prayer & Doctrine

Economically priced printings of theologically sound works that have guided Orthodox Christians throughout the centuries.

Catalog Available Upon Request

EASTERN ORTHODOX BOOKS
P.O. Box 302
Willits, CA 95490

Orthodox Family Life

Reach out to your parish families!
Give them the tools they need every season to learn and live the Orthodox Christian Faith!

Orthodox Family Life is a quarterly journal filled with fast-day and feast-day resources, ethnic traditions, family activities, and articles on Christian parenting, teaching your children the Faith, and living in today's secular world as an Orthodox Christian! Insert a page of your own Church School News, then copy and distribute the journal to every family in your Church School or parish!

Laser copy-master subscriptions are **$40** per year and include unlimited reproduction rights within your parish.

For a subscription, sample copy, or back issue orders contact:
Orthodox Family Life, Phyllis Meshel Onest, M.Div., Editor, 2507 Nedra Ave., Akron, OH 44305 or e-mail **pmonest@aol.com**

Visit us on the World Wide Web at **http://www.theologic.com**

Gloria Incense

225 Chandler Avenue
Johnstown, PA 15906

FAX: (814) 536-4699

Quality Incense since 1955

ORTHODOX PUBLICATIONS FROM EUROPE

Catalog includes titles on:
* Writings from the Holy Mountain, Greece and Russia
* The Celtic and Anglo-Saxon Church
* English, Greek, Russian & Spanish Languages

Interested? Contact:
ORTHODOX CHRISTIAN BOOK SERVICE
STUDIO 7, TOWNHOUSE FARM
ALSAGER ROAD, AUDLEY, STAFFORDSHIRE
ENGLAND, ST7 8JQ

TEL: **+44 -7000-790330**
FAX: +44 -1782-723930
email: 101600.262@compuserve.com

RUSSOS IMPORTS

Literature • Artifacts • Icons

Theofilos & Hope Russos

at OLD WORLD
7561 Center Ave., Suite 50-A • Huntington Beach, CA 92647
Bus (714) 901-9778 • Res (714) 638-0128 • Fax (714) 534-1622
www.russosimports.com

Free Illustrated Catalogue

Twenty-eight titles including:

EVANGELION and APOSTOLOS Lectionaries
  BYZANTINE DAILY WORSHIP, 1250 pp. 3d printing $48.75
  OUR FAITH (Byzantine Catechism for Adults) $18.75

Historical Books
  SEPTUAGINT PSALMS IN ENGLISH $18.75

Poetry • Marriage Counseling • Inspirational

ALLELUIA PRESS books are being used by every branch of the Oriental Church.
Over one thousand churches use our lectionaries
Over thirty-five years of service to the Byzantine Rite.

To order above books or to receive a free catalogue write to:
Alleluia Press, Box 103 Allendale, NJ 07401

Same day shipment. Satisfaction guaranteed. Minimum mailing & handling $3.00. New Jersey residents add 6% sales tax if applicable.

The Russian Orthodox Youth Committee

under the patronage of
His Eminence,
Metropolitan Vitaly

1998 Icon Calendar
$12 Postpaid
(US & Canada)

Mrs Irene Dutikow
Office Manager/Secretary

32-05 31st Avenue
Astoria, NY 11106

718-721-9390 • 718-726-7870

Martianoff's Calendar

1998 edition
$12/copy

32-05 31st Avenue
Astoria, NY 11106

718-721-9390
718-726-7870

SOUROZH

A Journal of Orthodox Life and Thought

Number 62   November 1995

CONTENTS

Metropolitan Theodosius	*The Path to Autocephaly and Beyond*
Father Matta el-Meskeen	*The Birth of Christ and the Birth of Man*
Patriarch Bartholomew of Constantinople	*The Orthodox Faith and the Environment*
Archbishop Anatoly of Kerch	*Ecumenism, Evangelization and Religious Freedom*
J. Stephen Muse	*Mental Health in the Life of Orthodox Clergy*

Published by the Russian Patriarchal Diocese of Sourozh in Great Britain.

Articles - sermons - news items - book reviews.

A window on the Orthodox Church worldwide: its theology, art, spiritual life, place in the ecumenical movement and situation in the modern world.

Subscription for 1998: U.S. $25 for four issues.
(For airmail, please add $8)
Index to numbers 1-70 included FREE with new subscriptions on request.

To: The Subscriptions Secretary, Sourozh,
13 Carver Road, Herne Hill, London SE24 9LS, U.K.

Name: ....

Address: ....

....

....

I enclose my subscription of U.S. $25 for 1998

I do / do not want the index to numbers 1-70.

St Stephen's Press
U.S. Distribution: P.O. Box 467, Mount Tabor, NJ 07878, Tel. (973) 627-0234

Fr Sergei Hackel, *The Orthodox Church* (revised edition 1994) $9.50
An illustrated introduction, for teenagers or adults.
Particularly useful for initial enquirers.

An invaluable addition to any parish library!

Other titles include:

Bishop Basil of Sergievo, *The Light of Christ: Sermons for the Great Fast* $9.50
Bishop Kallistos of Diokleia, *The Seed of the Church: The Universal Vocation of Martyrdom* $4.95

Prices include postage within the USA. Trade and parish discounts available.

St. George Publishing House

Phone: 309-786-8188
Fax: 309-786-8188

PENTIKOSTARION IN GREEK
From Byzantine to Western Notation.
Vespers and Matins for Sunday of Thomas through All Saints. Includes Ascension Thursday.
$100.00

ΠΕΝΤΗΚΟΣΤΑΡΙΟ, ΣΤΗΝ ΕΛΛΗΝΙΚΗ

Από Κυριακή του Θωμά μέχρι των Αγίων Πάντων (και Πέμπτη της Αναλήψεως), όλα μεταγραμμένα από Βυζαντινά στην Ευρωπαϊκή.
Τιμή: $100.00

St. George Greek Orthodox Church
The Rev. Basil Papanikolaou
Attn: John C. Velon
2930 31st. Ave.
Rock Island, IL 61201

HOLY WEEK IN GREEK
From Byzantine to Western Notation.
Every service starting Palm Sunday Evening through Agape.
$100.00

ΜΕΓΑΛΗ ΕΒΔΟΜΑΔΑ-ΠΑΣΧΑ

Από το βράδυ Κυριακής Βαΐων μέχρι την Αγάπη του Πάσχα, όλα μεταγραμμένα από τη Βυζαντινή στην Ευρωπαϊκή Μουσική.
Τιμή: $100.00

TRIODION IN GREEK
From Byzantine to Western Notation.
Vespers and Matins for every Sunday including Palm Sunday and Saturday of Lazarus Matins.
$75.00

ΤΡΙΩΔΙΟ, ΣΤΗΝ ΕΛΛΗΝΙΚΗ

Όλες οι Κυριακές του Τριωδίου (Εσπερινός, Όρθρος) μέχρι την Κυριακή των Βαΐων, μεταγραμμένο από τη Βυζαντινή σε Ευρωπαϊκή.
Τιμή: $75.00

ANASTASIMATARION IN GREEK
From Byzantine To Western Notation.
All 8 tones plus Vespers in all 8 tones.
$100.00

ΑΝΑΣΤΑΣΙΜΑΤΑΡΙΟ, ΣΤΗΝ ΕΛΛΗΝΙΚΗ

Μεταγραμμένο από τη Βυζαντινή στην Ευρωπαϊκή Μουσική.
Τιμή: $100.00

Postage additional for orders outside USA

Please write for catalog

Iconography.com

All about Icons on the Internet

FREE • FREE • FREE
- Non-Commercial Hosting
- Orthodox Link Exchange
- Site Promotion
- Discussion Groups
- Chat Server

Commercial Offering
- Full Shopping Cart/Catalog System
- Web-based Fulfillment System
- High Performance Unix Servers
- Full CGI Scripting Capabilities
- FAST SQL Database Engine
- Secure Apache Web Server
- CyberCash Interface
- Quick-Start Program

Proud to Host:

Oakwood Publications - www.oakwoodpub.com
Irina & Sons Icon Gallery - www.nettinker.com/icongal
Conciliar Press - www.conciliarpress.com
Orthodox Monasteries of North America - www.nettinker.com/monasteries/

http://www.iconography.com/
Telephone (510)229-8137 - e-mail info@iconography.com

Come Pray With Us!

The Oblates of St. Benedict is a gathering of lay women and men who wish to dedicate their lives to God and the Orthodox Church by following the prayer rule of St. Benedict (AD 480-550) toward a richer and fuller spiritual life.

There are many men and women throughout the United States, England, and Europe that have chosen this discipline of life.

At this time we are in the process of establishing an Orthodox community of Benedictine monks.

For more information, please write to:

Brother Paschal Cano, O.S.B.
Community of the Resurrection
C/O St. Michael Orthodox Church
3333 Workman Mill Road
Whittier CA 90601-1615
(562)692-6121

Interested in studying Orthodox theology and history?
Unable to attend a seminary or theological school?

ST. STEPHEN'S COURSE OF STUDIES IN ORTHODOX THEOLOGY
is your answer.

St. Stephen's Course, sponsored by the Antiochian Orthodox Christian Archdiocese, offers several correspondence programs of one to three years duration, depending on the needs of the student.

Send for a descriptive catalog by writing to:

ST. STEPHEN'S COURSE OF STUDIES
ANTIOCHIAN ORTHODOX CHRISTIAN ARCHDIOCESE
358 MOUNTAIN ROAD
ENGLEWOOD, NJ 07631

Please send me a catalog with application for **ST. STEPHEN'S COURSE OF STUDIES IN ORTHODOX THEOLOGY.**

Name: _____
　　　　　　　Please Print

Address: _____

City _____ State _____ Zip Code _____

BOOKS
that nourish
the heart
the soul
and the intellect

CLASSICS
of theology and history
patristics and liturgy
philosophy and literature
biblical studies
and spirituality

Eighth Day Books offers an extraordinary selection of
the Classics of the Orthodox Christian Tradition--- as
well as a multitude of other books rooted in and
nourished by the Tradition.

We're a different sort of bookstore. Call us
for a free catalog and see for yourself.
You'll be delighted by
the company we keep.

EIGHTH DAY BOOKS
3700 E. Douglas
Wichita, KA 67208   Phone: 800-841-2541

MILOJE MILINKOVIC
Fresco and Icon Artist

907 E. Joliet St.
Schererville, IN. 46375

Phone: 219-864-9708
Fax: 219-322-9702

800th Anniversary of the Monastery Chelandari (1298-1998) St. Sava & St. Simeon, founders of Monastery. Byzantine Frescoes (St. George Serbian Orthodox Church in Schererville, IN). By Artist Miloje Milinkovic.

The Annunciation Press

The Annunciation Press is pleased to offer you a wide array of Orthodox products. We specialize in Byzantine Iconography and related products by the hand of Erin Kimmett.

- Greeting Cards • Icon Coloring Books
- Infant Communion Bibs • Christmas Cards
- Mounted Icons • Orthodox Appointment Calendars
- Holy Cards • Bookmarks
- Wedding Programs and Announcements
- Original Byzantine Iconography

Church Bookstore and Retail Discounts Available.

Contact us for a free catalog and price list.
Toll-free: 1-800-975-ICON • Fax: 781-255-1871
E-mail: TAPIcons@AOL.com • Web: http://www.APIcons.com

St. Archangel Michael
Serbian Orthodox Church

9805 Commercial Ave. * Chicago, Illinois 60617
(773) 375-3848 church office (708) 895-8998 cultural center
(773) 375-3586 fax (708) 895-6958 fax

Rev. Fr. Milos M. Vesin, Pastor

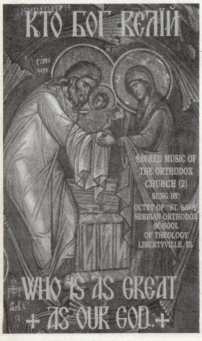

Located in Lansing, a southeast suburb of Chicago, **"Narrow Path" Bookstore St. Archangel Michael Serbian Orthodox Cultural Center** welcomes all!
18550 Stony Island Avenue
Lansing, IL 60438
(708) 474-8417 bookstore
(800) 513-8447 orders only
e-mail: nena@netnitco.net

Publisher and Producer of the New Release - **"Who is as Great as our God!"** Cassette Tapes and Compact Discs Available Now (Church Slavonic)!

Sacred Music of the Orthodox Church performed by the **"St. Sava"** Octet of St. Sava Orthodox School of Theology - Libertyville, Illinois - directed by **Rev. Fr. Milos M. Vesin, Professor of Music**.

"Narrow Path" Bookstore specializes in **books** about **Orthodoxy, Serbian history and culture.** We also feature a large assortment of exquisite **icons**, in all sizes, a wide selection of 14k yellow gold & sterling silver **crosses** and **medallions**, and many souvenirs. All proceeds from "Narrow Path" Bookstore will be directed toward the **new church project.** Call to order a **catalog** of our products or to make an appointment to visit our showroom at our cultural center. **CALL FOR FREE CATALOG (800) 513-8447**

Total Parish Education

The Orthodox Christian Education Commission (OCEC)

"Serving all of your educational needs"

The only educational agency under the direct jurisdiction of Standing Conference of Orthodox Bishops (SCOBA)

For more information and a catalog of materials and workshops, contact:

OCEC
PO Box 174
Centuk Station
Yonkers, NY 10710

Phone: 201-768-7966
e-mail: w2bjb@aol.com
www.orthodoxed.com

Cal-Hellas_{sm}

"Your Source For Icons and Church Supplies"

- **Imported Icons**
- **Crosses**
- **Vigil Lamps**
- **Altar Items**
- *Incense & Incense Burners*

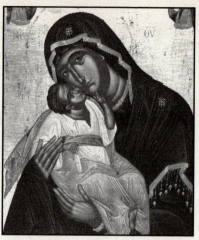

DEALER INQUIRES WELCOME • CALL FOR COLOR BROCHURE

E-Mail: calhellas@pacbell.net
Web Site: http://www.gpg.com/calhellas/
1-800-428-ICON (4266) • Fax: 408-253-7368
10177 Byerly Court, Cupertino, CA 95014

Theotokos Community
Icons and Bookstore

also

Custom Icon Mounting

at a reasonable cost.
Let us mount your prints.

For Information:

Phone 915-463-5538
Fax 915-463-5612
E-Mail: hubbard@centex.net
WebSite: www.mercuryTX.net
Rt. 1 Box 115A
Rochelle, TX 76872

Tabitha of Joppa

custom made

Vestments

Altar Linens

Dalmatics

Cassocks

for fabric and galloon samples contact:

Emily Sarisky
610-861-2731

2043 W. Broad St.
Bethlehem, Pa. 18018

EASTERN CHRISTIAN SUPPLY CO.

Personal Devotional Items
Books
Church Furnishings and Supplies
Beeswax Candles and Tapers
Hand Woven Icon Scarves
Hand Woven Scarves

606 White Fir Lane
P.O. Box 677
Etna, CA 96027

PHONE (530) 467-5620
FAX (530) 467-3996
Internet Store http://www.easternchristian.com
E-Mail http://www.eastchr@telis.org

We sell the finest Liturgical items and Church furnishings at very reasonable prices. Church furnishings are imported directly from our own suppliers in Greece.
For further information, request our Liturgical Items Catalog, Fabric Catalog, Pectoral Cross Catalog, or Book and Personal Items Catalog.
Please call, write, FAX, or shop our internet store.
We look forward to serving you.

Father Jerome Zubricky and staff

HOLY TRANSFIGURATION MONASTERY
278 WARREN STREET, BROOKLINE, MA 02146

CATALOG NUMBER SIX

Three-Ring Binder • 28 pages full color and 75 pages black and white, illustrating and listing hundreds of icons, crosses, books, incense, tapes, CDs, icon lamps, and other articles of Orthodox worship, with complete price list.

$8.00 with no additional charge for shipping

THE GREAT HOROLOGION

908 PAGES, HARD BOUND • 2 COLOR • LARGE FORMAT, 8˝ x 11½˝

The Daily Cycle of Services • More than 500 concise accounts of Feasts and Saints' Lives, with their Troparia • The Katavasiae and the *Eclogarion* for Vigils • 9 Akathists and Supplicatory Canons Index of Saints and Feasts with over 4,500 entries

$120.00. Please inquire about shipping charge

Toll-free: (800) 227-1629 • (617) 734-0608 • Fax: (617) 730-5783

"In the Bible it is said that Moses heard the voice of the Lord saying to him, 'Moses, Moses. Tell thy brother Aaron to light a lamp before Me day and night. For this is pleasing in My sight and is an acceptable sacrifice to Me.' That is why the Holy Church of God has adopted the custom of lighting lamps and candles before the holy icons of the Lord, of the Mother of God, and of the holy Angels and holy men who pleased God." —Saint Seraphim of Sarov

The Holy Nativity Convent makes hand-dipped pure beeswax candles in a varied assortment of sizes. In addition, we sew Orthodox vestments, cassocks, and covers for the Communion vessels. We also have a large assortment of icon reproductions in single or double solid brass frames, and icon buttons. For a complete brochure write to the

Holy Nativity Convent
70 Codman Road, Brookline, MA 02146-7555
or call 1-617-566-0156

DOXA

A Quarterly Review
Serving the Orthodox Church

DOXA is the official publication of St. Michael's Skete, a small Orthodox monastery in a remote canyon in northern New Mexico.

DOXA strives to be both traditional and timely. We also try very hard to be charitable as well as forthright. DOXA is challenging to write; few would deny that the magazine is an interesting and sometimes controversial read!

DOXA is entirely supported by its readers' contributions. Please contact us for your free subscription:

DOXA Magazine
P. O. Box 38
Cañones, NM 87516
(505) 638-5690

A UNIQUE SERVICE...
PRESENTING THE GREEK HERITAGE

Founded in 1987 by Dr. John Hadjinicolaou, Director of the *Montreal Centre for Greek Studies*, ALEXANDRE-ALEXANDER brings to New World audiences, works on Orthodoxy and Greek culture from many exceptional Greek publishers:

- EKDOTIKI ATHENON
- AGRA
- AKRITAS
- DENISE HARVEY
- DOMOS
- PROHOROS
- MALLIARIS
- PERIVOLI TIS PANAGIAS
- ASTIR
- ARMOS
- TERTIOS
- ESTIA
- TROHALIA
- POURNARAS
- MELISSA
- ALEXANDER PRESS

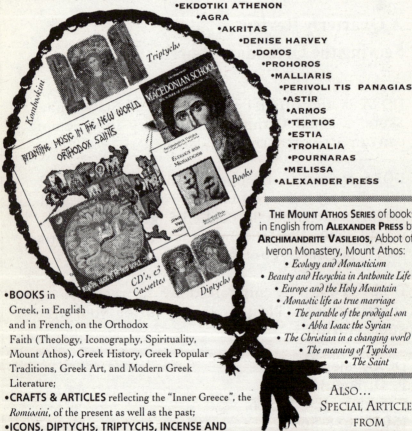

THE MOUNT ATHOS SERIES of books in English from **ALEXANDER PRESS** by **ARCHIMANDRITE VASILEIOS**, Abbot of Iveron Monastery, Mount Athos:
- Ecology and Monasticism
- Beauty and Hesychia in Anthonite Life
- Europe and the Holy Mountain
- Monastic life as true marriage
- The parable of the prodigal son
- Abba Isaac the Syrian
- The Christian in a changing world
- The meaning of Typikon
- The Saint

- **BOOKS** in Greek, in English and in French, on the Orthodox Faith (Theology, Iconography, Spirituality, Mount Athos), Greek History, Greek Popular Traditions, Greek Art, and Modern Greek Literature;
- **CRAFTS & ARTICLES** reflecting the "Inner Greece", the *Romiosini*, of the present as well as the past;
- **ICONS, DIPTYCHS, TRIPTYCHS, INCENSE AND KOMBOSKINI;**
- **VIDEOS, CASSETTES, RECORDS, CDs.**

CATALOGS AVAILABLE

ALSO... SPECIAL ARTICLES FROM **MOUNT ATHOS**

ALEXANDRE-ALEXANDER
2875 DOUGLAS AVE., MONTREAL, QC, CANADA H3R 2C7
CALL: (514) 738-5517, 738-4018 TOLL FREE: 1-888-257-5517 FAX: (514) 738-4718
E-MAIL: johnh@top.ca

VESTAL PUBLISHING COMPANY, INC.

WALL CALENDARS
(New & Old Style)

Greek
Russian
Serbian
Ukrainian
OCA

Your <u>ONE</u> source for all your religious printed needs!

Serving Churches throughout U.S. & Canada for over half a century!

-:- Publishers of "The Orthodox Weekly Bulletin" -:-

NEW PRODUCTS!
(All Full Color)

← POST CARDS

NOTE CARDS →

(with matching envelopes)

Byzantine Prayer Cards *(Regular & Microperf)*
Icon Plaques *(Full Color)*
Easter & Christmas Bulletins *(Full Color)*
Offering Envelopes • Icon Note Paper

280 Cliffwood Avenue, Cliffwood, NJ 07721
Phone: (732) 583-3232 - Fax: (732) 583-5207

Orthodox Books on Scripture

Orthodoxy's traditional claim of divine inspiration for its Greek Old Testament, the Septuagint, has waited 2000 years for readable *Introductions* to that sacred Scripture of the Apostles and Church Fathers. With comparative analyses of many Greek and Hebrew texts Professor Heath validates the Septuagint as Scripture in the Orthodox Tradition.

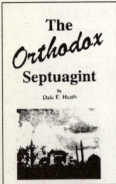

Giving heed to the homiletical exhortations of St. Chrysostom and the Capadocians, and not less to the monumental Septuagint studies of Cambridge and Oxford Universities, Dr. Heath offers the literary and religious history of the Septuagint in readable, preachable language for thoughtful laymen or busy parish priests.

The books are available from the author at $15.00 each, postpaid:
Dr. Dale E. Heath
Eastside Village
Rt. 23, Box 1450
Lake City, FL 32025

The Scripture of St. Paul
The Orthodox Septuagint
The Inherent Nature of Scripture

PATRIARCHATE OF JERUSALEM

His Beatitude Patriarch Theodoros I

Representatives Of His Beatitude In North America

The Very Rev. Fr. George Jweinat
St. George Orthodox Church
399 San Fernando Way
San Francisco, Ca 94127
Tel: (415) 334-2234 Fax:(415) 334-2275
Pager # (415) 202-6336

St. George Orthodox Church
Rev. Fr. Moueen Hanna
4687 Snyder Lane, Rohnert Park
P.O.Box. 5695
Santa Rosa, Ca 95402
Tel: (408) 629-4040

St. James Orthodox Church
Rev. Fr. Giris Hanna
65 W. Rincon Ave.
Campbell, Ca 95008
(408) 281-2080

* *

* Want to study the Orthodox Christian faith?
* Can't go away to school?
* Have time to study at home?

Here's your chance!!

St. Athanasius Academy of Orthodox Theology has a true Correspondence Study Program:

* one designed with you in mind.
* one you can count on to provide you with courses that truly teach
* one you can study in your own good time, without deadlines

*But that is not all, for we will be here for you,
to answer your questions and help you along the way.*

For information, just call or write:

**ST. ATHANASIUS ACADEMY OF ORTHODOX THEOLOGY
CORRESPONDENCE STUDY DIVISION
10519 E. STOCKTON BLVD., SUITE 170
ELK GROVE, CA 95624
(916) 686-6230 [PHONE]   (916) 686-6232 [FAX]**

 Internet Site: www.saaot.edu   e-mail: corr-stud@saaot.edu

**AN ACADEMIC COMMUNITY OF THE
ANTIOCHIAN ORTHODOX CHRISTIAN ARCHDIOCESE OF AMERICA**

Check out our

TIMELY TOPICS BOOKLETS and **BOOKLETS FOR THE YOUNGER SET**

PLUS LEARN ABOUT!

THE ORTHODOX STUDY BIBLE PROJECT: OLD TESTAMENT

St. Athanasius Academy, which brought you *THE ORTHODOX STUDY BIBLE: NEW TESTAMENT AND PSALMS* now sets forth on a new project -- to add the whole of the Old Testament, as found in the *SEPTUAGINT*.

St. Athanasius Academy, 10519 E. Stockton Blvd., Suite 170, Elk Grove, CA 95624
or Internet: www.saaot.edu

W.O.M.E.N.
WOMEN'S ORTHODOX MINISTRIES AND EDUCATION NETWORK

Supporting Orthodox women's loving service to Christ through their Church, community, and educational work.

- Promote understanding of our Faith through books, tapes, and study group materials

- Catalog and distribute educational materials, form a speakers bureau, and coordinate seminars

- Help and support existing and developing Church ministries of Orthodox women worldwide

- Develop educational materials that address women's concerns

- Introduce women in similar areas of service to the Orthodox Church, and foster sisterhood

- Share the news of Orthodox women, their resources, and their service to the Church

- Publish a book and tapes titled "Orthodox Women Today" about inspirational Orthodox women

- Publish a newsletter for members

"The role of women in the life of the Orthodox Church has been the subject of numerous conferences and seminars held throughout Europe and the United States during the past 25 years. The Women's Orthodox Ministries and Education Network is the newest attempt by and for Orthodox Christians to examine the ways that women in the Church may participate more fully in proclaiming and living the saving message of Christ our Lord." **Bishop Isaiah, Greek Orthodox Diocese of Denver**

TO JOIN WOMEN, OR FOR MORE INFORMATION, CONTACT
WOMEN
3440 Youngfield #272
Wheat Ridge, CO 80033 USA
Phone: 303 316-8027   E-mail: WOMENUSA@aol.com

No other source offers you this wide selection of *Quality* church products... at the most competitive prices!...

...and <u>all</u> for a worthy cause.*

NATIONAL SHRINE CHURCH SUPPLIES

- Custom or Stock Icons
- Candles
- Imported Incense
- Charcoal
- Censers
- Chalices
- Wax Remover
- Sanctuary Lamps
- Sacred Altar Items
- Communion Kits
- Holy Water Bottles
- Candle Safety Cups
- Sacramental Wine

We have many additional items available.
Please contact us with your specific needs.

NATIONAL SHRINE CHURCH SUPPLIES
P.O. BOX 1960
ST. AUGUSTINE, FL 32085

1-800-222-6727 • Fax 1-904-829-8707

*National Shrine Church Supplies is operated by the St. Photios Foundation, Inc. Proceeds from sales are used to support the St. Photios Greek Orthodox National Shrine in St. Augustine, Florida.

Macrina Publications

QUALITY PUBLICATIONS BY, FOR, AND ABOUT ORTHODOX CHRISTIAN WOMEN

Macrina Publications gives a portion of its proceeds to support the Women's Orthodox Ministries and Education Network (WOMEN), an international network of Orthodox Christians whose goal is to support Orthodox women's loving service to Christ through their Church, community and educational work.

For catalogs and ordering information,
Call (303) 316-8027;
Fax (303) 321-3702

Macrina Publications
1200 Madison, Box 525
Denver, CO 80206 USA

HOLY CROSS BOOKSTORE
HOLY CROSS ORTHODOX PRESS
HELLENIC COLLEGE PRESS

Specializing in
- Orthodox Theology
- Church History
- Bibles and Commentaries
- Liturgical Texts in Greek and English
- Liturgical and Sacramental Theology
- Byzantine History
- Lives of Saints
- Spirituality
- Iconography
- Reference Books
- Children's Books
- Hellenism
- Cook Books
- Icons
- Byzantine Music CDs and Cassettes
- and much more!

Call for a Catalog

50 Goddard Avenue • Brookline, MA 02146
(617) 731-3500   (617) 232-4544
FAX 617-566-9075   800-245-0599
HCBKS@omaccess.com
Visit our Web Site http://www.goarch.org/access/hcbks

Introducing the Children's Orthodox Prayer Book

The Children's Orthodox Prayer Book is designed especially for pre-school to teenage children. The prayers are set in large, easy-to-read type, especially helpful for those just beginning to read. The prayers are accompanied by instructions and explanations by Priest Steven Allen and illustrations by Magdalena Friedman. The prayers cover all aspects of daily prayer life and are organized in sections such as "Prayers During the Day" and "Pre-Communion Prayers." It is hoped that the book will help children to become familiar with the daily prayers at an early age, to encourage a love for prayer and the consistent practice of it. The book is published with the blessing of Bishop Kyrill of Seattle.

The books are hardbound with gold-stamped cover and are available in blue and red. The 64-page book is specially sized for smaller hands. Books may be ordered for $12 each plus $2 for shipping and handling (plus $1 for each additional book). Order 3 copies or more and pay only $10 each. Trade discounts will be given to bookstores. Please send your check or money order to:

ALL SAINTS OF RUSSIA PRESS
Fr. Steven Allen / All Saints of Russia Orthodox Church
3274 East Iliff Ave. / Denver, CO 80209
Telephone: (303) 757-3533

P.O. Box 4319 • St. Augustine, Florida • 32085-4319

A dozen ways to become involved in the worldwide outreach of the OCMC:

1. Become a full time missionary;
2. Join a short-term Mission Team;
3. Participate in the annual OCMC Retreat;
4. Organize a Pentecost Mission Walk;
5. Sign-up to be an Agape Canister partner;
6. Recruit members for the Mission 1000 Endowment Fund;
7. Support the Ss. Cyril & Methodios Orthodox Mission Society to receive the OCMC newsletter;
8. Pray daily for Orthodox missions and missionaries;
9. Help find sponsors to provide monthly support for indigenous Orthodox priests in Africa and Asia;
10. Include the OCMC in your Will;
11. Help evangelize America by making your daily life a dynamic witness to our Orthodox Faith;
12. Pray some more.

For more information on any, or all of the above, contact the OCMC at:
Phone: 904/829-5132 • Fax: 904/829-1635
E-mail: ocmc@aug.com • Website: http://www.goarch.org/access/ocmc

Religious Jewelry
by Nena
in devotion to St. Marina

Wholesale supplier to churches, monasteries, and bookstores... wide variety of Orthodox crosses and medallions available in 14k gold and sterling silver.

Style: ORC

NDC, Inc.
P.O. Box 3114 * 562 Cedar Ct.
Munster, Indiana 46321
(219) 836-2737   (219) 836-9937 fax
e-mail: nena@netnitco.net
(888) 265-4287

Gibson Travel

Call on us for all your travel needs

310-337-0537

Darlene Smay   CSTP# 1017101-40

Orthodox Christian Prison Ministry

Under the Blessing of Metropolitan PHILIP
Antiochian Orthodox Christian Archdiocese of North America

Through the generosity of our donors, quality Orthodox Christian materials are provided to prisoners in over 600 local, state and federal prisons in North America.

These high-quality materials are also available for parish and/or individual use. For a catalog display sheet of icons, prison ministry training materials and other quality items, please write:

Orthodox Christian
Prison Ministry
P O Box 1949
Hollywood, CA 90078-1949

Phone 213-467-2720
FAX 213-467-5079
E-mail ocpm@juno.com

Holy Apostle Silas is Patron Saint for Orthodox Christian Prison Ministry

Pray for prisoners and for their Salvation!

Hanna Trade International

**Custom Design and Precision Wood Craft
of Church Furnishings**

Icon Holder + Icon Stand + Icons + Icon Plaque
Altar + Gospel Stand + Holy Mystery Table + Crosses + Wall Shrines
Laser engraving and Stain Glass

CNC MACHINERY FOR WOOD CARVING AND WOOD TURNING

We are Domestic Manufacturer and Import/Export Coptic Orthodox group,
small but proud, growing in the Lord.
Dedicated to loving and serving Christ and one another.
No matter how big or small your project,
please give us a call. We are willing to help.

Refaat Hanna   Tel: (909) 781-2147
President   Fax: (909) 781-2148

<u>P.O. Box 5616 Riverside, CA 92517-5616</u>

ST. NECTARIOS PRESS AND BOOK CENTER

Publishers and distributors of traditional Orthodox materials

A WIDE VARIETY OF BOOKS FOR ALL AGES
also BAPTISMAL CROSSES AND GREETING CARDS.
Wholesale and retail   Prompt efficient service

OUR OVER 600-ITEM CATALOG INCLUDES

ORTHODOX BOOKS, CD'S, TAPES, CROSSES, AND OTHER RELIGIOUS ITEMS

SOME RECENT PUBLICATIONS ARE:

- *A LENTEN COOKBOOK FOR ORTHODOX CHRISTIANS*
- *SAINTS OF ANGLO-SAXON ENGLAND, Vol. 3*
- *A PILGRIM'S GUIDE TO THE HOLY LANDS FOR ORTHODOX CHRISTIANS*
  - by the Holy Nativity Convent, Brookline, MA
- *THE RIVER OF FIRE.* Dr. Alexandre Kalomiros
- COMING SOON, A NEW CHILDREN'S BOOK:
  - *KATIE VISITS A MONASTERY*

VISA, MASTERCARD, AMERICAN EXPRESS AND DISCOVER CARDS

For free catalog contact:
ST. NECTARIOS PRESS
10300 ASHWORTH AVENUE N.
SEATTLE, WASHINGTON 98133-9410

Toll-free U.S. and CANADA: 1-800-643-4233
1-206-522-4471   FAX 1-206-523-0550

Web site: www.orthodoxpress.org
E-mail: snpress@orthodoxpress.org

Sometimes The Best Medicine Someone Can Have Is A Healthy Pig.

In the midst of war and unrest, a family, or an entire community, can lose everything, including its will to survive. When refugees from Bosnia found themselves struggling to build a new life in the Federal Republic of Yugoslavia, International Orthodox Christian Charities gave them a loan so they could purchase pigs and farming equipment. This simple gesture gave their lives meaning and provided them the ability to earn an income, feed their families, and realize that their lives were not useless but, in fact, quite meaningful. This is just one of many ways IOCC is responding to people in need. And with your continued support we can help other communities rebuild from the ground up.

711 West 40th Street
P.O. Box 630225
Baltimore, MD 21263-0225

Tel: (410) 243-9820
Fax: (410) 243-9824
E-mail: iocc@igc.apc.org

International Orthodox Christian Charities